Edmund Spenser

THE FAERIE QUEENE

Book Five

Edmund Spenser

THE FAERIE QUEENE

Book Five

Edited, with Introduction, by
Abraham Stoll

Hackett Publishing Company, Inc.
Indianapolis/Cambridge

Copyright © 2006 by Hackett Publishing Company, Inc.

06 07 08 09   1 2 3 4 5 6 7

For further information, please address
   Hackett Publishing Company, Inc.
   P.O. Box 44937
   Indianapolis, IN 46244-0937

   www.hackettpublishing.com

Cover art: Walter Crane illustration and ornament for Book Five, *The Faerie Queene*, ca. 1890.

Cover design by Abigail Coyle
Interior design by Elizabeth Wilson
Composition by Professional Book Compositors
Printed at Edwards Brothers, Inc.

Library of Congress Cataloging-in-Publication Data

Spenser, Edmund, 1552?–1599.
   The faerie queene / Edmund Spenser.
      v. cm.
   Contents: Book one / edited, with introduction, by Carol Kaske —
Book five / edited, with introduction, by Abraham Stoll
   Includes bibliographical references and indexes.
      ISBN 0-87220-808-7 (bk. 1) — ISBN 0-87220-807-9 (pbk. : bk. 1) —
   ISBN 0-87220-802-8 (bk. 5) — ISBN 0-87220-801-X (pbk. : bk. 5)
      1. Knights and knighthood—Poetry. 2. Epic poetry, English. 3. Virtues
—Poetry. I. Kaske, Carol V., 1933– II. Stoll, Abraham Dylan, 1969–
III. Title.
PR2358.A3K37 2006
821'.3—dc22

                                                          2005026668

Contents

ABBREVIATIONS

Citations from other books of *The Faerie Queene* are documented in this volume in the conventional format, listing book, canto, stanza, and line number. For example, I.i.37.2 refers to Book One, Canto One, stanza 37, line 2. Citations from Book Five do not list the book number: ix.25 refers to Book Five, Canto Nine, stanza 25.

A View	Spenser, Edmund. *A View of the State of Ireland.*
Gough	Spenser, Edmund. *The Faerie Queene, Book V,* ed. Alfred B. Gough.
Hamilton	Spenser, Edmund. *The Faerie Queene,* ed. A. C. Hamilton.
Metamorphoses	Ovid. *Metamorphoses.*
Orlando	Ariosto, Ludovico. *Orlando Furioso.*
SE	Hamilton, A. C., et al. *The Spenser Encyclopedia.*
Variorum	Greenlaw, Edwin, et al. *The Works of Edmund Spenser: A Variorum Edition: Faerie Queene Book Five.*

INTRODUCTION

Book Five of *The Faerie Queene* is structured around Sir Artegall's quest to liberate Irena, whose kingdom has been usurped by a tyrant. Many side plots spring up along the way, including Artegall's defeat at the hands of an Amazon and rescue from the shame of cross-dressing by Britomart—herself a female knight and Artegall's betrothed. And many controversies have sprung up in the course of the poem's reception—Spenser's apparent celebration of political violence and the aims of English empire have made Book Five one of the centers of debate in *The Faerie Queene*. Although these debates and stories are implicated in the rest of the poem, Book Five can be studied coherently on its own. Standing alone, it emerges as one of the most challenging meditations on justice in English literature.

The title to Book Five, "The Legend of Artegall, or of Justice," can be read in two ways. As Artegall pursues his quest, he often seems wise and brave, and a model of justice. In this way he represents what is just, and is truly the knight of justice—so that, in one reading of the title, the word "or" tells us that Artegall is equivalent to Justice. But he also often seems foolish and violent. Readers cannot help but doubt whether many of his actions and decisions are truly just, especially when his sidekick Talus so often erupts, meting out drastic levels of corporal punishment. Each episode of violence pushes us to disagree with Artegall's version of justice, and so demands a thoughtful evaluation of the entire situation. It becomes not merely Artegall himself who figures forth justice, but the combination of all the figures and all the events of Book Five—it is the entire narrative, so that an alternative reading of "The Legend of Artegall, or of Justice" says that the legend as a whole, rather than Artegall, is equivalent to Justice. At stake in these two readings are a number of discriminations: whether Artegall is a hero or antihero of justice; whether Faerie Land, as an embodiment of Elizabethan justice, fosters hope or despair; and whether our reading of Spenser's allegory centers on individual personifications or on the dynamics of the story world as a whole.

On his journey through the landscape of Faerie, Artegall meets so many examples of injustice, so many giants and tyrants, because, as Canto One explains, the world has fallen from perfection. No longer in the Golden Age, when Justice ruled, the land is now corrupt with injustice. In this it mirrors Spenser's own age, when, as he says in the Proem, "the world is runne quite out of square" (1.7). Spenser's involvement in the politics of Elizabeth's court, particularly in the English colonization of Ireland, colors the whole of Book Five, making it the part of *The Faerie Queene* most replete with history. It is a document that captures key political concerns of Elizabethan England, bringing the history alive through allegory. But it also frames politics in ways that have remained pertinent throughout the ages. An earlier editor of Book Five, Alfred Gough, found it descriptive of his own period, World War I. And it seems equally relevant today. Spenser's personal experiences in Ireland clearly made him sensitive to the difficulty of applying idealized notions of justice to practical situations. Trained in the most idealized terms by Astraea (who leaves the wicked earth in disgust), Artegall must find a way to make justice thrive in the messy circumstances of actual events. This task of moving from justice in the ideal to justice on the ground was an essential political project in Spenser's time, and it is still so in the twenty-first century, when ideals of democratic and religious justice are so often reshaped by the pressures of the real world. To read Book Five is to enter into a remarkably experienced vision of the politics of justice.

There are six books in *The Faerie Queene,* each pairing a knight with a virtue—such as Book One, matching the Redcrosse Knight with Holinesse, or Book Three, with Britomart and Chastity. There is also a fragment of a seventh book, called the *Mutabilitie Cantos,* which represents all that we have of the second half of *The Faerie Queene.* In the "Letter to Raleigh," reproduced at the end of this volume, Spenser reveals that he planned twelve books, although six books already places *The Faerie Queene* among the longest poems in the English language. Even though incomplete, Spenser's poem has established itself as one of the most influential, one of the most strange and beautiful, in English literature. *The Faerie Queene* derives much of its fantastic mood, with its knights, giants, fairies, pagans, and enchanters, and much of its style, with its sprawling and interlaced narratives, from the romance tradition, especially from the great Italian poet Ariosto. But while composing it, Spenser seems to have admitted the desire, according to his friend Gabriel Harvey, "to emulate, and hope to overgo" Ariosto's *Orlando Furioso.* What Spenser adds to Ariosto is his experiment in sustained allegory. Shaping the poem around the signifying practices of allegory, Spenser creates a more serious and more religious romance than Ariosto's, but also a more baffling one.

1. Spenserian Allegory

Allegory literally means, "speaking otherwise," implying that the text has a secondary meaning beyond what it literally says. In a plain reading of the plot of Book Five, Irena is merely a damsel in distress, with the particular qualities described in the narrative. But allegorically she can also

be read as Ireland, and so signifies an extensive field of historical and po-
litical meanings. Although for most readers Book Five is very much
about England's domination of Ireland, the word "Ireland" itself never
appears: it cannot be assumed that anything in the poem means only what
it says. Allegory multiplies and undermines signification. And with inter-
pretation, therefore, less directly tied to the plainest meanings of the text,
allegory has allowed readers enormous latitude. One prominent case is
the long tradition of reading classical authors as purveyors of Christian
truths. John Harrington, in a translation of Ariosto published a year after
The Faerie Queene was first printed, reads the pagan myth of Perseus slay-
ing Gorgon as an allegory for a clearly Christian world view. The mon-
ster Gorgon allegorizes, according to Harrington, "all bodily substance,"
which is overcome by "the angellical nature" on its way to heaven (4v).

In these Christian interpretations of classical myth, allegory is brought
to the text by the reader. There is no guarantee, in fact no necessity, that
the author intended to write allegorically—in such cases allegory is a way
of reading. But in other cases allegory is intended by the author, making
it a way of writing or a genre. Dante wrote allegory, and so did Spenser:
as the "Letter to Raleigh" makes clear, Spenser's poem is written as "a
continued Allegory, or darke conceit." In its simplest form, Spenser's alle-
gory makes abstract ideas material: by personifying the idea of envy in a
figure called Envie, or by embodying Justice in Artegall. But in its self-
consciousness, Spenserian allegory becomes far more complicated.
Spenser is alive to the complexities of allegorical interpretation, and intent
on making the reader equally aware. For example, in the episode of the
Egalitarian Giant in Canto Two, Spenser queries the very grounds of
allegory by parodying its tendency to make abstractions material. The
Giant, an expression of an early-modern radicalism akin to communism,
has a pair of scales and wants to weigh the entire world in order to redis-
tribute the wealth. Absurdly, this includes trying to weigh air and fire
(ii.31), and eventually even words. But what is insubstantial, obviously,
cannot be put into an actual scale, and "streight the winged words out of
his ballaunce flew" (ii.44.9). The ridiculousness of throwing words onto
a scale (which the Giant does), and of their flying out of it (which
Spenser's ironic narrative makes happen), lays bare the absurdity of a
language that puts abstract ideas into concrete entities and personifica-
tions. Spenser is challenging allegory, and, to make it even further self-
consuming, the challenge is advanced by Artegall, who is himself an
embodiment of abstract Justice. The scene becomes an ironic allegory
about allegory's deficiencies, or as Annabel Patterson says, it is about "the
way allegory, by setting static emblems in narrative motion, is bound to
reveal their inherent failures of logic or truthfulness" (112). That the

center of the parody, moreover, is a pair of scales, which appears in Canto One as the chief allegorical emblem of the goddess of justice Astraea (i.11.9), projects the episode over the whole of Book Five—highlighting the difficulties of allegorizing Justice.

Spenserian allegory has often suffered under the assumption that it works neatly and can be paraphrased coherently, so that the Egalitarian Giant might be categorized as an allegory of the injustice of communism. But such readings, which have been present throughout the centuries, reduce *The Faerie Queene* to mere platitudes. They led Coleridge to declare, "The dullest and most defective parts of Spenser are those in which we are compelled to think of his agents as allegories" (103). While there is a long roster of famous complaints about Spenserian allegory, modern critics have succeeded in showing it to be not a storehouse of dusty morals, but a startling source of beauty and poetic complexity. Some important modern treatments are: Fletcher 1964, Gross, Lewis 1936 and 1967, Quilligan 1979, Roche, Teskey, Treip, and Tuve. Also see *SE*: "allegory."

2. Justice

In the "Letter to Raleigh," Spenser names Aristotle as the primary source for his moral virtues, and *The Nicomachean Ethics,* particularly its fifth book, introduces a number of ideas that are key to Spenser's treatment of justice. Aristotle asserts that justice depends upon the golden mean, so that "the unjust is that which violates proportion" (V.iii.14). He identifies two types of justice: distributive, which deals with the honor and wealth due to members of a society; and corrective, which operates to make sure that, in exchanges such as business transactions and theft, each individual gets a fair share. The episodes involving Munera and Pollente in Canto Two and Braggadochio in Canto Three are among the many instances in which Artegall is faced with the task of corrective justice. The Egalitarian Giant of Canto Two and Radigund of Cantos Four and Five can be understood in terms of Aristotle's distributive justice. In these last two cases, however, a modern reader may have doubts about Aristotelian justice. When the Egalitarian Giant asks, "Were it not good that wrong were then surceast, / And from the most, that some were given to the least?" (ii.37.8–9), our impulses might say yes, the rich should share with the poor, even though Artegall rejects the argument. And when Radigund's female rule is ended and Britomart "The liberty of women did repeale, / Which they had long usurpt; and them restoring / To men's subjection, did true Justice deale" (vii.42.5–7), our sense of fairness might disagree with "true Justice." But both Artegall and Britomart are acting justly according to Aristotle's notion of distributive justice, which, he stresses, does not imply that each member of society deserves equal wealth and honor, but rather that each gets wealth and honor in proportion to his or her position. The lower classes and women quite justly get less, as they did in the hierarchical Elizabethan society. The modern reader must consider in what ways Spenser's narrative approvingly conveys this (to us) outmoded form of justice, and in what ways it is uneasy with it.

Another important concept from Aristotle, and one that allows significant freedom to critique authoritarian codes of justice, is that of equity. Aristotle describes equity as "a rectification of law where law is defective because of its generality" (V.x.6)—it is a move to the spirit rather than the letter of the law, because written laws cannot always be justly applied to specific circumstances. Equity was an important legal concept in the Renaissance and received practical application in the courts of Chancery, where Spenser held office for several years. It is a flexible and challenging concept because it allows us to set aside written law in order to seek justice in particular cases and according to the workings of individual conscience. Although Artegall is taught equity by Astraea (i.7), he seems to pay too little attention, so that Guyon has to remind him of it (iii.36). And it is left to Britomart to explicitly embody equity. In Isis Church we are told that Isis represents equity (vii.3), and in her dream Britomart clearly becomes associated with Isis. Soon after, she does what Artegall had never done: she becomes so dismayed by Talus' violence that she calls him off from one of his slaughters (vii.36). In the last cantos of Book Five, Artegall also calls Talus off (xi.65 and xii.8), which gives hope that Artegall has learned equity from Britomart (but cf. xii.25). Equity is related to mercy, which has a complex presence in Book Five. In his deployment of Talus, Artegall may or may not learn to be merciful. Elsewhere, not all mercy serves justice: Artegall is captured by Radigund precisely because he so pities her that he throws away his sword (v.13). The difficulty of knowing when to show mercy, and when to carry out justice despite the shadow of cruelty, is a crucial problem in any age. In Spenser's age it was especially germane to Elizabeth's judgment of Mary, Queen of Scots. Having delayed taking decisive action for years, Elizabeth finally executed her in 1587. When Spenser allegorizes the trial and execution in Canto Nine, his figure for Elizabeth at this moment of capital punishment is named Mercilla.

In addition to Aristotle, Plato's *Republic* and Cicero's *De Officiis* are likely influences on Spenser's ideas of justice. Relevant Renaissance texts include Thomas Elyot's *The Boke Named the Governor* (1531) and Jean Bodin's *Six Books of the Republic* (1576). For further reading on Spenser and justice, see Aptekar, Dunseath, Phillips, and *SE*: "justice and equity."

3. Ireland

According to Angus Fletcher, in Book Five "Justice expands in its implications into empire" (1971, 204). Ironically, the Legend of Justice has left many readers convinced of the injustice of Spenser's politics, because of his deep involvement in England's bloody colonization of Ireland. Artegall's quest to save Irena is clearly an extended allegory for the Elizabethan relationship to Ireland: Irena, at times spelled "Eirena," refers to the Gaelic name for Ireland, Éire; her kingdom is on "the salvage island" (xi.39.3), a single day's sail from Faerie Land/England (xii.4); and the villain Grantorto is clearly dressed as an Irish soldier (xii.14). Further allusions to the events and people of the conflict are scattered throughout Book Five. *The Faerie Queene,* moreover, was largely written in Ireland, with Book Five likely composed at Spenser's plantation in Munster, Kilcolman. This makes the poem a product of the material conditions of colonialism, since the Kilcolman estate came into the hands of New English settlers, and eventually into Spenser's possession, as a result of the seizure and division of the lands of the rebel Earl of Desmond. The Desmond revolt was quashed in the early 1580s by shockingly violent tactics—a strategy of destruction and starvation that Willy Maley calls "genocidal" (1997, 61). Spenser owned Kilcolman from 1588 until 1598, when, during an uprising in Munster, the estate was sacked.

Spenser's role in the colonization of Ireland was extensive and culpable, as a landowner and, earlier, as secretary to Lord Grey, Elizabeth's deputy in Ireland from 1580 to 1582. Grey was notorious for brutality, and Spenser almost certainly witnessed his infamous massacre of prisoners at Smerwick, as well as many other instances of Grey's slash-and-burn policies. Talus recreates these slaughters in Book Five, and Spenser may well want them to feel excessively violent. On the other hand, in his political treatise *A View of the Present State of Ireland,* Spenser appears to recommend Grey's strategy of violence and starvation as a way to subdue and reform Ireland. In one famous passage, the character Irenus describes the starvation in Munster in chilling detail:

> . . . they were brought to such wretchednesse, as that any stony heart would have rued the same. Out of every corner of the woods and glynnes they came creeping forth upon their hands, for their legges could not beare them; they looked like anatomies of death, they spake like ghosts crying out of their graves; they did eate the dead carrions, happy where they could finde them, yea, and one another soone after, insomuch as the very carcasses they spared not to scrape out of their graves; and, if they found a plot of watercresses or shamrocks, there they flocked as to a feast for the time, yet not able long to continue therewithall; that in short space there were none

almost left, and a most populous and plentifull countrey suddainely left voyde of man and beast; yet sure in all that warre, there perished not many by the sword, but all by the extremitie of famine, which they themselves had wrought (101–2).

Irenus, who largely functions as Spenser's alter ego, pities the starving people of Munster—but brings them up while advocating that similar measures be used against the people of Ulster. Several other passages make it undeniable that, in *A View,* Spenser recommends a cruel suppression of the Irish and of Irish culture—reformation "by the sword" (93). It should be kept in mind, however, that there is more subtlety to *A View* than the often-quoted negative passages suggest. It is written not as expository prose, but as a dialogue, which makes it hard to say precisely that Spenser himself thinks one thing or another. And its detailed use of Irish history, mythology, ethnography, social custom, and language combine to make a nuanced, humanist engagement with the Irish and the problems of the emerging British empire. Spenser may have been an agent of English colonial violence, but he evidently loved Ireland, as is clear when he sets the divine council of the *Mutabilitie Cantos* on Mount Arlo, the peak visible from his castle at Kilcolman. C. S. Lewis said, "Spenser was the instrument of a detestable policy in Ireland, and in his fifth book the wickedness he had shared begins to corrupt his imagination" (1953, 349). But Lewis also said, "*The Faerie Queene* should perhaps be regarded as the work of one who is turning into an Irishman" (1966, 126). For further reading, see Brady, Coughlan, Hadfield 1997, Maley 1997, and *SE*: "Ireland, the cultural context" and "Ireland the historical context."

4. Artegall

Artegall's name suggests several possible meanings: "(thou) art egalitarian"; "(the) art of equality"; and, when spelled alternately as Arthegall in the 1590 and 1609 editions, "equal to Arthur." The name has also been considered of Irish origin, and, in ironic contrast, Artegall has been read as echoing Arthur Grey, Spenser's patron (*Variorum,* 160–61). Artegall clearly becomes a figure for Lord Grey in Canto Twelve when he returns home dogged by Envie, Detraction, and the Blatant Beast. But it would be reductive to see Grey as a primary allegory throughout. Artegall has a history and a career before Book Five that have little to do with Ireland, nor, at least on the surface, with justice. In Book Three we learn from Merlin's prophecy that Artegall was a changeling, half brother to Arthur but stolen by fairies, and that he and Britomart will give descent to the line of British kings (III.iii.23–29). In Book Four he appears at a tournament in disguise, on his shield the motto "Salvagesse sans finesse"—savagery without refinement or art. Britomart defeats him as the Savage Knight (IV.iv.39–44). Artegall then seeks revenge, but their second fight ends in reconciliation, the revelation of Artegall's true identity, love, and the promise to marry at some future time (IV.vi.3–44).

Artegall next appears in Book Five, now as the titular knight of Justice. In Canto One we learn how he was trained by Astraea and how she left him on earth to carry out justice. But Artegall's subsequent adventures raise detailed doubts as to whether he is fit for such a task. In Canto One he demonstrates the wisdom of Solomon in revealing Sir Sanglier's guilt, but imposes an eclectic and far too light punishment on that murderer. In Canto Two he displays wonderful athleticism in his battle with Pollente, and great rhetorical skill in his debate with the Egalitarian Giant. But both episodes end in egregious violence—the mutilation of Munera and the summary execution of the Giant. In Canto Five Artegall blunders his way into captivity and the humiliation of his masculinity at the hands of Radigund, so that he must be rescued by Britomart in Canto Seven. Artegall does free Irena from Grantorto, but his time with Radigund makes him late, nearly subverting his quest. And he is ultimately unable to complete the work of justice in Irena's kingdom:

> But ere he could reforme it thoroughly,
>   He through occasion called was away,
>   To Faerie Court, that of necessity
>   His course of Justice he was forst to stay.   (xii.27.1–4)

Although Artegall's status as an allegorical figure for Justice and his education with Astraea might lead us to assume that he is a representation of perfect justice, he is far from the ideal. Astraea is the ideal, and she has left earth (i.11). Artegall is a figure for humans, striving toward her Justice in the challenging circumstances of the world. As such, he is clearly flawed and, in many ways, easy to dislike. But Artegall also frequently shows flashes of personality—anger at Braggadochio (iii.36), pity for Radigund (v.13), impatience for Burbon's temporizing (xi.55–56)—that make the allegorical figure somewhat human. In a world "runne quite out of square," anyone so fully devoted to justice is worthy of a sympathetic reading even when he errs. See Anderson, Aptekar, Dunseath, Stump 2001, and *SE*: "Artegall."

5. Talus

The greatest obstacle to reading Artegall as a figure for ideal justice is his close association with Talus, the iron man who uses a flail to beat Faerie

Land into submission. Talus is chilling for his robotic and unstoppable violence—he is "Immoveable, resistlesse, without end" (i.12.7), and has a tendency to leave "heapes" of dead (v.19.6; vii.36.4). However, he is a gift from Astraea, and central to justice in Book Five. He serves as Artegall's "gard and government" (iv.3.9), providing both protection and the muscle to carry out his judgments, like the police force relative to the courts. To what extent Talus is the justifiable arm of the law, and to what extent he embodies police brutality, is one of the fundamental questions of social justice in the poem. Talus raises another problem of particular importance to empires: his effectiveness allows us to assume that, once justice has decided on the best solution, there are no practical concerns about its ability to exert its will. Such a fantasy of invincibility leads to idealized versions of justice, as if the decision making is all that matters, and the practical implementation of our decisions cannot go awry. Justice requires much more nuance, however, if force cannot assure outcomes, as both modern examples and the Elizabethan experience in Ireland show. Talus is also a figure of abiding fascination in his own right. Fletcher calls him a "perfect allegorical agent," which has interesting implications for Spenserian allegory (1964, 55). And Spenser gives him a tantalizing bit of interiority and therefore humanity. At the embarrassing moment when he must tell Britomart that Artegall has been imprisoned by Radigund, Talus stands mute and "with conscience / Of his ill newes, did inly chill and quake" (vi.9.5–6). In some fashion the robot has a conscience. In the aftermath of Artegall's humiliating rescue, at Artegall's weakest moment, Talus even leads him forward on the quest as "The true guide of his way and vertuous government" (viii.3.9). Perhaps this shows the resourcefulness of Talus, and perhaps it is an emblem for that frightening moment when, in the name of virtue, torturers become leaders. See Fletcher 1971 (137–46), Greenblatt 1983, Wagner, and *Variorum* (276–80).

6. Britomart

Britomart is the Knight of Chastity in Book Three, and then in Book Four becomes engaged to Artegall, establishing her future as the matriarch of the British monarchy. Her destiny accounts for the first half of her name, and the second half, suggestive of Mars and things martial, reflects that she is a woman warrior. It is in this capacity especially that Britomart appears in Book Five, heroically pursuing her own quest in the middle cantos. Britomart's quest is to clean up Artegall's mess. Alerted by Talus, she sets off in Canto Six to rescue Artegall, only to find herself nearly trapped by Dolon. Dolon has mistaken Britomart for Artegall and seeks revenge for the death of his son, whom Artegall summarily dispatched in Canto Two (vi.33). Britomart is paying for Artegall's violence in the early cantos, just as she must exert herself to correct his negligence in falling to the Amazon Radigund. Britomart defeats Radigund through military prowess—"She with one stroke both head and helmet cleft" (vii.34.6)—and through exemplary understanding. While Artegall foolishly agrees to be bound to Radigund's "lore" if he loses (iv.49.3), forsaking Astraea's "righteous lore" (i.4.9), Britomart refuses all conditions. She not only frees Artegall to resume his original quest, she seems to impart crucial wisdom, humanizing justice in Book Five. It is just after her victory over Radigund that Britomart, demonstrating equity and mercy, becomes the first to limit Talus:

> Yet when she saw the heapes, which he did make,
> Of slaughtred carkasses, her heart did quake
> For very ruth, which did it almost rive,
> That she his fury willed him to slake.   (vii.36.4–7)

Of all the figures in Book Five, Britomart is also the one given the most inward complexity, departing from allegory's tendency toward flat characters. Artegall's imprisonment, with its cross-dressing and its descent into romantic melodrama in Canto Five, is laced with overtones of sexual dalliance. Britomart responds with a fit of jealousy worthy of the stage (vi.12–15), as well as a remarkably complex set of motivations in her quest, leading to the psychologically subtle moment when, seeing Artegall in women's clothes, "with secrete shame, / She turnd her head aside" (vii.38.3–4). In addition, Britomart finds Artegall only after a deeply introspective trial of her own, at the temple of Isis. There she is confronted by the mysteries of pagan iconography, as well as by a dream, which stands at the center of her quest and at the center of Book Five. Britomart's dream is overdetermined with symbols, but reveals thoughts of power, sex, and violence—it has royal emblems, raging fires, and a crocodile that first threatens to eat Britomart, and then impregnates her (vii.12–16). A priest interprets the dream in terms of the larger allegory of Book Five, identifying her with equity and tying her to Artegall in his project of justice. But the psychological strangeness of Britomart's dream and the depth of her character exceed all simple allegorical tags. See Bieman, Bowman, Walker, and SE: "Britomart" and "Isis Church."

7. Elizabeth, Britomart, Radigund

One of the most challenging aspects of Britomart's quest is its conclusion when, after defeating Radigund's Amazon rule, she reestablishes the politics of female subjugation. Britomart becomes the princess of the city

Radegone, "And changing all that forme of common weale," repeals female liberty and restores women "To mens subjection" (vii.42). Although she is a female hero for most of Book Five, Britomart suddenly finishes as a preserver of the masculinist order, turning power over to Artegall and then disappearing from the text as her man leaves on his quest. This contradictory blend of female power and patriarchal ideology is best understood as a feature of Elizabethan England, where a deeply masculine society was ruled for 45 years by a queen. For the queen and her subjects, gender relations required subtle negotiations, such as Spenser attempts in his description of Radigund's polity:

> Such is the crueltie of womenkynd,
>   When they have shaken off the shamefast band,
>   With which wise Nature did them strongly bynd,
>   T'obay the heasts of mans well ruling hand,
>   That then all rule and reason they withstand,
>   To purchase a licentious libertie.
>   But vertuous women wisely understand,
>   That they were borne to base humilitie,
> Unlesse the heavens them lift to lawfull soveraintie. (v.25)

Deeply chauvinist in the first eight lines, he suddenly changes his tune in the alexandrine, clearly referring to Elizabeth. In this remarkable stanza, Spenser simultaneously preserves patriarchal ideologies and, through the logic of a divine exception, makes room for his queen. The pairing of Britomart and Radigund across Cantos Four through Six may be read as a similar negotiation—the intertwined narratives of the two woman warriors meditate on female power in general and on Elizabeth in particular.

Spenser has to be especially careful in such matters, since his entire poem is dedicated to "the most high, mightie, and magnificent empresse" Elizabeth. Furthermore, in the "Letter to Raleigh," Spenser identifies Gloriana as a figure for his queen—the Faerie Queen *is* Elizabeth. Spenser made no secret of his pursuit of court favor and did not hesitate to flatter, so much so that Stephen Greenblatt says frankly that Spenser "worships power" (174). But the poet has many resources and can blend critique into praise. In the last stanza of the Proem, he celebrates Elizabeth's transcendent justice and admits his own status as "basest thrall." And then he asks pardon for discoursing on "thy great justice praysed over all: / The instrument whereof loe here thy *Artegall*" (Proem 11). Spenser presents Book Five as "thy" justice and its knight as "thy Artegall"—a move that sounds like an elaborate compliment, until we enter into the poem and discover how frequently disfunctional Artegall and his justice can be.

For further reading on representations of Elizabeth, see Graziani, Quilligan, Stump 2001, Wells, Woods, and *SE*: "Elizabeth, images of."

8. Mercilla

The most direct representation of Elizabeth in Book Five is Mercilla, who presides over the trial of Duessa—transparently a figure for Mary, Queen of Scots. In this episode Spenser dares to take on the most controversial and spectacular issue in Elizabeth's reign. Mary was Catholic with claims on the throne, making her a threat to both Protestant and Elizabeth's rule. She had plotted against Elizabeth, had perhaps killed her own husband, and was perceived as a beautiful temptress—and yet, for years Elizabeth held her prisoner and refused execution. Finally in 1587, again with much controversy, Mary was tried and executed. Spenser reconfigures these messy events into a highly orderly scene, with the Court of Mercilla populated by allegorical personifications such as Awe, Order, and Zele. He accentuates Elizabeth's justice by making her a commanding presence in the courtroom—when in fact Elizabeth was absent—and by politely hiding the execution itself from the narrative. This neat scene is qualified, however, by the very disturbing two stanzas that precede it: as Arthur and Artegall enter Mercilla's court, they see a poet with his tongue nailed to a post, punished for criticizing the Queen (ix.25–26). Is Spenser emphasizing that he, unlike the bad poet Malfont, is being a good poet? Is he protesting against state censorship? Is he hinting that his portrayal of Mary's trial is subversive? The stanzas were prescient: Mary's son James (later King James I) took offense at Canto Nine and tried, unsuccessfully, to have Spenser punished. Malfont is particularly hard to interpret, but he serves to raise our awareness of the difficulty of writing poetry about recent political events. Spenser inserts him just as he is turning to Mary, Queen of Scots, and to the several historical allegories that dominate the end of Book Five. On Mercilla and Mary, see Gallagher, Goldberg, McCabe, *Variorum,* 319–24; and *SE*: "Mary, Queen of Scots" and "Mercilla."

9. Historical Allegory

While much of Book Five pertains to Ireland, Mercilla marks a turn in the final cantos to explicit and extended historical allegory. In Canto Eight Arthur defeats Mercilla's enemy, the Souldan. The Souldan is commonly read as a figure for Philip II, King of Spain, and his fearsome chariot recalls the Spanish Armada. After representing Mary, Queen of Scots in Canto Nine, Spenser takes on the English intervention in the Netherlands, through Arthur's aid to Belge in Cantos Ten and Eleven. Then Artegall's rescue of Burbon clearly alludes to Henry Bourbon of Navarre, the

French King who broke Protestant faith. And Book Five concludes with Artegall freeing Irena, finishing the allegorical treatment of Ireland. These cantos are full of specific historical allusions, which have led Spenserians to many different decipherings—for examples beyond this volume's notes, see *Variorum*, 299–335. At times Spenser is rewriting history, not merely reporting it. Arthur saves Belge in the poem, but the English adventure to the Netherlands in fact failed militarily; rather than the heroic celebration Arthur receives, the earl of Leicester was politically humiliated. Spenser is also organizing events, providing, as only literature can, an imaginative lens with which to view recent history. Grantorto, the villain behind both Burbon's and Irena's difficulties, represents the political force of Philip II and Catholic Spain. Spain is also behind the enemy in the Netherlands and, more indirectly, Mary's resistance to Elizabeth. The final cantos, then, are unified by their representation of the epochal struggle between English Protestantism and Catholicism. As Kenneth Borris argues, this confrontation was often cast in apocalyptic terms, with the Pope as the Antichrist in the English imagination. Justice becomes deeply intertwined in Protestant apocalyptic thinking, so that current politics become a phantasmagoria of giants and monsters and chivalric heroes. Book Five's final cantos serve as an example of how malleable history can be when worked upon by the persuasive imagination of a poet. See Borris, Gregory, Mallette, Prescott, and *SE*: "allegory, historical."

10. Book Five's Characters in Other Books

After Artegall and Britomart, who have already been discussed, the main character with an earlier history is Arthur. Spenser picks up his story when Arthur is a knight, before becoming king. Rather than matching him with Guinevere, Spenser adopts the alternate tradition that Arthur became romantically involved with fairies. Spenser's Arthur had a dream in which he saw and fell in love with the Faerie Queen, Gloriana, and vowed upon waking to seek her out (I.ix.13–15). This quest leads him across the Faerie landscape and into the narrative of each of Spenser's six books. Arthur generally shows up in the later cantos as a kind of *deus ex machina,* setting things right and enabling the titular knight to continue the quest. If *The Faerie Queene* had been finished, presumably Arthur would have taken part in all twelve books, knitting together all twelve virtues to become the true hero of the entire poem. We can guess that, in Book Twelve, Arthur would finally meet Gloriana, fulfilling his role as an emblem for "magnificence" ("Letter to Raleigh").

Another figure with a long prehistory is Duessa. Although a clear figure for Mary, Queen of Scots in Book Five, in Book One she plays a more theological role as the witch seductress of the Knight of Holinesse.

Set off against the maiden Una, the pure figure of oneness and truth, Duessa embodies doubleness and falsehood. She appears beautiful, but proves to be "A loathly, wrinckled hag" (I.viii.46.8). Duessa makes several more appearances throughout *The Faerie Queene*. Canto Three, telling of the wedding of Florimell, has a number of characters from earlier books. At the center are Marinell and Florimell, whose love is left unfulfilled in Book Four. We also meet Guyon, the Knight of Temperance in Book Two, and Braggadochio, a parodic knight who bedevils Guyon and others throughout the earlier books. Florimell is especially noteworthy for her endless persecution and victimhood, and the comic resolution of her narrative, as well as Braggadochio's unmasking, suggests the possibility of happy and just endings in general—as befits the legend of Justice. But Canto Three stands in contrast to the narrative of Artegall and Britomart, whose love affair is left unresolved when Artegall leaves his betrothed to continue his quest. Resistance to closure is especially felt in Canto Twelve, where Artegall is last seen hounded by the Blatant Beast, a doglike creature who spreads infamy and discourtesy. In the tradition of romance, this narrative thread continues beyond Book Five, as the Blatant Beast continues to run barking throughout Book Six.

11. Language, Sources, Annotations

Like Shakespeare, Spenser is free and inventive with language. He is also intentionally archaic, arousing the sense of a past chivalry and a lost golden age. Although *The Faerie Queene* may therefore feel doubly archaic to the modern reader, this edition preserves most of Spenser's idiosyncrasies. Punctuation is not standardized, and spelling is especially variable—so a word may be spelled two ways in a single line, as in: "He could his weapon shift from side to syde" (xi.6.5). The stanza of *The Faerie Queene,* a variation on the Italian ottava rima, is unique to Spenser and has since become eponymous—the Spenserian stanza. It has eight lines of iambic pentameter, punctuated in unusual style by a twelve-syllable alexandrine. And it has a complicated, interwoven rhyme scheme: *ababbcbcc*. Spenser's debts to romance and epic traditions are clear, as he points out in "The Letter to Raleigh." He also draws on a wide set of sources for his mythology, although he often submits the myths to his own invention, making it difficult to trace these exactly. He frequently seems to be working from the Italian mythographers, especially Natale Conti's *Mythologiae* (1567), but because Conti is not readily available in a complete translation, this volume's annotations refer to Ovid's *Metamorphoses* and other common texts for further research. (For Conti's influence on Spenser, see Lotspeich.) The reader will also find assistance in the Glossary and Index of Characters at the back.

THE FAERIE
QVEENE.

Difpofed into twelue bookes,

Fashioning

XII. Morall vertues.

LONDON
Printed for VVilliam Ponfonbie.

1 5 9 6.

Title page to the 1596 edition of *The Faerie Queene* (STC 23082)

TO
THE MOST HIGH,
MIGHTIE
And
MAGNIFICENT
EMPRESSE RENOVV-
MED FOR PIETIE, VER-
TVE, AND ALL GRATIOVS
GOVERNMENT ELIZABETH BY
THE GRACE OF GOD QVEENE
OF ENGLAND FRAVNCE AND
IRELAND AND OF VIRGI-
NIA, DEFENDOVR OF THE
FAITH, &c. HER MOST
HVMBLE SERVAVNT
EDMVND SPENSER
DOTH IN ALL HV-
MILITIE DEDI-
CATE, PRE-
SENT
AND CONSECRATE THESE
HIS LABOVRS TO LIVE
VVITH THE ETERNI-
TIE OF HER
FAME.

THE FIFTH
BOOKE OF THE
FAERIE QVEENE.

Contayning,
THE LEGEND OF ARTEGALL
OR
OF IVSTICE.

1   So oft as I with state of present time,
     The image of the antique world compare,
     When as mans age was in his freshest prime,
     And the first blossome of faire vertue bare,
     Such oddes[1] I finde twixt those, and these which are,
     As that, through long continuance of his course,
     Me seemes the world is runne quite out of square,
     From the first point of his appointed sourse,
   And being once amisse growes daily wourse and wourse.

2   For from the golden age, that first was named,
     It's now at earst[2] become a stonie one;
     And men themselves, the which at first were framed
     Of earthly mould, and form'd of flesh and bone,
     Are now transformed into hardest stone:
     Such as behind their backs (so backward bred)
     Were throwne by *Pyrrha* and *Deucalione*.[3]
     And if then those may any worse be red,[4]
   They into that ere long will be degendered.

3   Let none then blame me, if in discipline[5]
     Of vertue and of civill uses lore,[6]
     I doe not forme them to the common line
     Of present dayes, which are corrupted sore,

---

[1] **oddes:** difference.

[2] **at earst:** in time. For the Golden Age and succeeding ages, see *Metamorphoses,* 1.89–150. Spenser invents the age of stone, even worse than iron.

[3] After Zeus punished humankind with a flood, only Deucalion and his wife Pyrrha survived. Themis bade them throw stones, being the bones of Mother Earth, over their shoulders. From the stones sprang people (*Metamorphoses,* 1.347–415).

[4] **red:** supposed.

[5] **discipline:** instruction, practice. See "Letter to Raleigh."

[6] **civill uses lore:** wisdom in political use or practice.

But to the antique use, which was of yore,
When good was onely for it selfe desyred,
And all men sought their owne, and none no more;
When Justice was not for most meed outhyred,[1]
But simple Truth did rayne, and was of all admyred.

4 For that which all men then did vertue call,
Is now cald vice; and that which vice was hight,[2]
Is now hight vertue, and so us'd of all:
Right now is wrong, and wrong that was is right,
As all things else in time are chaunged quight.
Ne wonder; for the heavens revolution
Is wandred farre from, where it first was pight,[3]
And so doe make contrarie constitution[4]
Of all this lower world, toward his dissolution.

5 For who so list into the heavens looke,
And search the courses of the rowling spheares,[5]
Shall find that from the point, where they first tooke
Their setting forth, in these few thousand yeares
They all are wandred much; that plaine appeares.
For that same golden fleecy Ram, which bore
Phrixus and *Helle* from their stepdames feares,
Hath now forgot, where he was plast of yore,
And shouldred hath the Bull, which fayre *Europa* bore.[6]

---

[1] **meed outhyred:** hired out with a payment or bribe.

[2] **hight:** called.

[3] **pight:** placed.

[4] **constitution:** organizing or framing structure. Spenser adopts the astrological notion that the moral order of the world depends upon the movement of the stars, as designed in God's creation. So chaotic or "contrarie" movements in the heavens cause chaos in the lower world. The following stanzas describe such a departure from the original order of things. On Spenser's use of the stars in the Proem, see Fowler, 192–96.

[5] In Ptolemaic astronomy, the planets and stars were thought to move within concentric spheres.

[6] Within the inexactitude of the Ptolemaic system, the signs of the zodiac, by the sixteenth century, had shifted away from their original constellations. So, the constellation Aries (ram) had moved into the place of Taurus (bull). Spenser links the ram to the myth of Phrixus and Helle, as told by Boccaccio (*De Genealogia Deorum*, 13.68). He links the bull to the myth of Europa (*Metamorphoses*, 2.833–875). Spenser makes the same associations in *The Mutabilitie Cantos* (VII.vii.32–33).

6   And eke the Bull hath with his bow-bent horne
        So hardly butted those two twinnes of *Jove,*
        That they have crusht the Crab, and quite him borne
        Into the great *Nemaean* lions grove.[1]
        So now all range, and doe at randon rove
        Out of their proper places farre away,
        And all this world with them amisse doe move,
        And all his creatures from their course astray,
    Till they arrive at their last ruinous decay.

7   Ne is that same great glorious lampe of light,[2]
        That doth enlumine all these lesser fyres,
        In better case, ne keepes his course more right,
        But is miscaried with the other Spheres.
        For since the terme of fourteene hundred yeres,
        That learned *Ptolomae* his hight did take,
        He is declyned from that marke of theirs,
        Nigh thirtie minutes to the Southerne lake;[3]
    That makes me feare in time he will us quite forsake.

8   And if to those Aegyptian wisards old,
        Which in Star-read[4] were wont have best insight,
        Faith may be given, it is by them told,
        That since the time they first tooke the Sunnes hight,
        Foure times his place he shifted hath in sight,
        And twice hath risen, where he now doth West,
        And wested twice, where he ought rise aright.[5]
        But most is *Mars* amisse of all the rest,
    And next to him old *Saturne,* that was wont be best.[6]

---

[1] Aries crowds Gemini (twins), who crush Cancer (crab), which is carried into Leo (lion). Spenser links Gemini to the twins Castor and Pollux, sometimes considered sons of Jove. He links Leo to the Nemean Lion, which Hercules killed in his first labor.

[2] The sun, thought to illuminate the stars and planets (the lesser fires). This stanza describes how measurements revealed that the sun had shifted southward slightly since Ptolemy, although thirty minutes is incorrect. See *Variorum,* 158.

[3] **Southerne lake:** the oceans of the southern hemisphere.

[4] **Star-read:** star lore, astronomy.

[5] Egyptian astronomers had observed these anomalies, according to Herodotus (2.142). See *Variorum,* 159.

[6] Before Kepler in 1609, astronomers assumed circular rather than elliptical orbits. But they worried about the planets' observed departures from the circle, and Mars and Saturn were examples of obvious eccentricity.

9   For during *Saturnes* ancient raigne it's sayd,
         That all the world with goodnesse did abound:
         All loved vertue, no man was affrayd
         Of force, ne fraud in wight[1] was to be found:
         No warre was knowne, no dreadfull trompets sound,
         Peace universall rayn'd mongst men and beasts,
         And all things freely grew out of the ground:
         Justice sate high ador'd with solemne feasts,
     And to all people did divide her dred beheasts.[2]

10   Most sacred vertue she of all the rest,
         Resembling God in his imperiall might;
         Whose soveraine powre is herein most exprest,
         That both to good and bad he dealeth right,
         And all his workes with Justice hath bedight.[3]
         That powre he also doth to Princes lend,
         And makes them like himselfe in glorious sight,
         To sit in his owne seate, his cause to end,[4]
     And rule his people right, as he doth recommend.

11   Dread Soverayne Goddesse,[5] that doest highest sit
         In seate of judgement, in th'Almighties place,[6]
         And with magnificke might and wondrous wit
         Doest to thy people righteous doome[7] aread,
         That furthest Nations filles with awfull dread,
         Pardon the boldnesse of thy basest thrall,
         That dare discourse of so divine a read,[8]
         As thy great justice praysed over all:
     The instrument whereof loe here thy *Artegall.*

---

[1] **wight:** person.

[2] **divide:** dispense; **beheasts:** commands.

[3] **bedight:** equipped.

[4] **end:** fulfill.

[5] Spenser speaks directly to Queen Elizabeth.

[6] The 1609 edition changes "place" to "stead" in order to preserve the rhyme.

[7] **doome:** judgment.

[8] **read:** subject.

Canto One

Artegall trayn'd in Justice lore[1]
Irenaes quest pursewed,
He doeth avenge on Sanglier
his Ladies bloud embrewed.

1 Though vertue then were held in highest price,
    In those old times, of which I doe intreat,[2]
    Yet then likewise the wicked seede of vice
    Began to spring which shortly grew full great,
    And with their boughes the gentle plants did beat.
    But evermore some of the vertuous race
    Rose up, inspired with heroicke heat,
    That cropt the branches of the sient base,[3]
And with strong hand their fruitfull rancknes[4] did deface.

2 Such first was *Bacchus*,[5] that with furious might
    All th'East before untam'd did overronne,
    And wrong repressed, and establisht right,
    Which lawlesse men had formerly fordonne.[6]
    There Justice first her princely rule begonne.
    Next *Hercules* his like ensample shewed,
    Who all the West with equall conquest wonne,
    And monstrous tyrants with his club subdewed;
The club of Justice dread, with kingly powre endewed.

3 And such was he, of whom I have to tell,
    The Champion of true Justice *Artegall*.
    Whom (as ye lately mote remember well)[7]

---

[1] **lore:** wisdom.

[2] **intreat:** treat.

[3] **sient base:** base shoots.

[4] **rancknes:** ranks—used for rows of trees and soldiers, and to indicate social level and luxuriant or corrupt growth.

[5] Bacchus conquered the east, spreading justice and civilization as well as the cultivation of the vine. He is often paired with Hercules, who subdued monsters and established cities in the west; e.g., Horace, *Odes*, 3.3.

[6] **fordonne:** done in.

[7] In IV.vi.42, Artegall left his fiancée, Britomart, just after wooing her, to pursue his quest. For Artegall's name, see Introduction, 4.

An hard adventure, which did then befall,
Into redoubted perill forth did call;
That was to succour a distressed Dame,
Whom a strong tyrant did unjustly thrall,[1]
And from the heritage, which she did clame,
Did with strong hand withhold: *Grantorto*[2] was his name.

4   Wherefore the Lady, which *Eirena* hight,[3]
Did to the Faery Queene her way addresse,
To whom complayning her afflicted plight,
She her besought of gratious redresse.[4]
That soveraine Queene, that mightie Emperesse,
Whose glorie is to aide all suppliants pore,
And of weake Princes to be Patronesse,
Chose *Artegall* to right her to restore;
For that to her he seem'd best skild in righteous lore.[5]

5   For *Artegall* in justice was upbrought
Even from the cradle of his infancie,
And all the depth of rightfull doome[6] was taught
By faire *Astraea*,[7] with great industrie,
Whilest here on earth she lived mortallie.
For till the world from his perfection fell
Into all filth and foule iniquitie,
Astraea here mongst earthly men did dwell,
And in the rules of justice them instructed well.

6   Whiles through the world she walked in this sort,
Upon a day she found this gentle childe,
Amongst his peres playing his childish sport:
Whom seeing fit, and with no crime defilde,
She did allure with gifts and speaches milde,

[1] **thrall:** subjugate, enslave.

[2] In Italian, "great wrong." A general figure for tyranny, he is associated variously with the King of Spain, the Irish rebel, the Earl of Desmond, and papal power.

[3] *Eirena* **hight:** is called Eirena. Refers to *Éire,* Gaelic for "Ireland," and *Ierne,* the traditional name in Greek. Also suggests the Greek word for "peace."

[4] She begged the Queen for gracious help.

[5] **lore:** wisdom.

[6] **doome:** judgment.

[7] Daughter of Zeus and Themis, the goddess of justice. See *Metamorphoses,* 1.149–50. Upon leaving earth, Astraea was transformed into the constellation Virgo. In naming the zodiac, the Proem leaves off at Leo; Virgo, or Astraea, is the next sign. Also see Yates.

To wend[1] with her. So thence him farre she brought
Into a cave from companie exilde,
In which she noursled him, till yeares he raught,[2]
And all the discipline of justice there him taught.

7   There she him taught to weigh both right and wrong
In equall ballance with due recompence,
And equitie to measure out along,
According to the line of conscience,
When so it needs with rigour to dispence.[3]
Of all the which, for want there of mankind,
She caused him to make experience
Upon wyld beasts, which she in woods did find,
With wrongfull powre oppressing others of their kind.

8   Thus she him trayned, and thus she him taught,
In all the skill of deeming wrong and right,
Untill the ripenesse of mans yeares he raught;
That even wilde beasts did feare his awfull sight,
And men admyr'd his overruling might;
Ne any liv'd on ground, that durst withstand
His dreadfull heast,[4] much lesse him match in fight,
Or bide the horror of his wreakfull[5] hand,
When so he list in wrath lift up his steely brand.[6]

9   Which steely brand, to make him dreaded more,
She gave unto him, gotten by her slight[7]
And earnest search, where it was kept in store
In *Joves* eternall house, unwist of wight,[8]
Since he himselfe it us'd in that great fight
Against the *Titans,* that whylome[9] rebelled

---

[1] **wend:** go.

[2] **noursled:** nurtured; **raught:** reached (mature) years.

[3] Two contrary readings are possible: equity either administers rigor or does without it. For equity and justice, see Introduction, 2.

[4] **heast:** command.

[5] **wreakfull:** vengeful.

[6] **brand:** sword.

[7] **slight:** trickery. Hamilton notes the possible irony of the knight of justice wielding a stolen sword.

[8] **unwist of wight:** unknown by any creature.

[9] **whylome:** in the past. For the Titans, see Hesiod, *Theogony,* 617–735; and *Metamorphoses,* 1.151–53.

Gainst highest heaven; *Chrysaor*[1] it was hight;
Chrysaor that all other swords excelled,
Well prov'd in that same day, when *Jove* those Gyants quelled.

10   For of most perfect metall it was made,
Tempred with Adamant[2] amongst the same,
And garnisht all with gold upon the blade
In goodly wise, whereof it tooke his name,
And was of no lesse vertue, then of fame.
For there no substance was so firme and hard,
But it would pierce or cleave, where so it came;
Ne any armour could his dint out ward,[3]
But wheresoever it did light, it throughly shard.[4]

11   Now when the world with sinne gan to abound,
Astraea loathing lenger here to space[5]
Mongst wicked men, in whom no truth she found,
Return'd to heaven, whence she deriv'd her race;
Where she hath now an everlasting place,
Mongst those twelve signes, which nightly we doe see
The heavens bright-shining baudricke to enchace;[6]
And is the *Virgin*, sixt in her degree,
And next her selfe her righteous ballance hanging bee.[7]

12   But when she parted hence, she left her groome
An yron man, which did on her attend
Alwayes, to execute her stedfast doome,[8]
And willed him with *Artegall* to wend,[9]
And doe what ever thing he did intend.
His name was *Talus*,[10] made of yron mould,

---

[1] In Greek, "golden sword." See Hesiod, *Theogony*, 281.

[2] Mythical substance, sometimes associated with diamond or steel, of unsurpassed strength.

[3] **out ward:** fend off.

[4] **shard:** cut.

[5] **space:** roam.

[6] **baudricke:** a richly jeweled belt, here a metaphor for the zodiac; **enchace:** adorn.

[7] Virgo, the sixth sign in the zodiac, is next to the constellation Libra, the scales.

[8] **doome:** judgment.

[9] **wend:** go.

[10] Modeled after Talos, a mythological man of bronze who traveled around Crete carrying tablets inscribed with the laws. For the many sources, see *Variorum*, 165–66. Talus may also suggest "talon," for its sharp violence, or, as Hamilton suggests, the Latin *talio*, as in retaliation. See Introduction, 5.

Immoveable, resistlesse, without end.
Who in his hand an yron flale did hould,
With which he thresht out falshood, and did truth unfould.

13   He now went with him in this new inquest,[1]
        Him for to aide, if aide he chaunst to neede,
        Against that cruell Tyrant, which opprest
        The faire *Irena* with his foule misdeede,
        And kept the crowne in which she should succeed.
        And now together on their way they bin,[2]
        When as they saw a Squire in squallid weed,[3]
        Lamenting sore his sorowfull sad tyne,[4]
With many bitter teares shed from his blubbred eyne.

14   To whom as they approched, they espide
        A sorie sight, as ever seene with eye;
        An headlesse Ladie lying him beside,
        In her owne blood all wallow'd wofully,
        That her gay clothes did in discolour die.
        Much was he moved at that ruefull sight;
        And flam'd with zeale of vengeance inwardly,
        He askt, who had that Dame so fouly dight;[5]
Or whether his owne hand, or whether other wight?

15   "Ah woe is me, and well away" (quoth hee)
        Bursting forth teares, like springs out of a banke,
        "That ever I this dismall day did see:
        Full farre was I from thinking such a pranke;
        Yet litle losse it were, and mickle[6] thanke,
        If I should graunt that I have doen the same,
        That I mote drinke the cup, whereof she dranke:
        But that I should die guiltie of the blame,
The which another did, who now is fled with shame."

16   "Who was it then" (sayd *Artegall*) "that wrought?
        And why? doe it declare unto me trew."
        "A knight" (said he) "if knight he may be thought,

---

[1] **inquest:** quest, judicial inquiry.
[2] **bin:** were.
[3] **weed:** clothing.
[4] **tyne:** trouble.
[5] **dight:** treated.
[6] **mickle:** much.

That did his hand in Ladies bloud embrew,[1]
And for no cause, but as I shall you shew.
This day as I in solace[2] sate hereby
With a fayre love, whose losse I now do rew,
There came this knight, having in companie
This lucklesse Ladie, which now here doth headlesse lie.

17   "He, whether mine seem'd fayrer in his eye,
Or that he wexed[3] weary of his owne,
Would change with me; but I did it denye;
So did the Ladies both, as may be knowne,
But he, whose spirit was with pride upblowne,
Would not so rest contented with his right,
But having from his courser her downe throwne,
Fro me reft mine away by lawlesse might,
And on his steed her set, to beare her out of sight.

18   "Which when his Ladie saw, she follow'd fast,
And on him catching hold, gan loud to crie
Not so to leave her, nor away to cast,
But rather of his hand besought to die.
With that his sword he drew all wrathfully,
And at one stroke cropt off her head with scorne,
In that same place, whereas it now doth lie.
So he my love away with him hath borne,
And left me here, both his and mine owne love to morne."

19   "Aread"[4] (sayd he) "which way then did he make?
And by what markes may he be knowne againe?"
"To hope" (quoth he) "him soone to overtake,
That hence so long departed, is but vaine:
But yet he pricked[5] over yonder plaine,
And as I marked, bore upon his shield,
By which it's easie him to know againe,
A broken sword within a bloodie field;
Expressing well his nature, which the same did wield."

---

[1] **embrew:** soak.

[2] **solace:** pleasure, comfort.

[3] **wexed:** grew.

[4] **Aread:** declare.

[5] **pricked:** spurred a horse. Recalls the opening of *The Faerie Queene*, "A Gentle Knight was pricking on the plaine" (I.i.1).

20 No sooner sayd, but streight he after sent
    His yron page, who him pursew'd so light,
    As that is seem'd above the ground he went:
    For he was swift as swallow in her flight,[1]
    And strong as Lyon in his Lordly might.
    It was not long, before he overtooke
    Sir *Sanglier;*[2] (so cleeped was that Knight)
    Whom at the first he ghessed by his looke,
And by the other markes, which of his shield he tooke.

21 He bad him stay, and backe with him retire;
    Who full of scorne to be commaunded so,
    The Lady to alight did eft[3] require,
    Whilest he reformed that uncivill fo:
    And streight at him with all his force did go.
    Who mov'd no more therewith, then when a rocke
    Is lightly stricken with some stones throw;
    But to him leaping, lent him such a knocke,
That on the ground he layd him like a sencelesse blocke.[4]

22 But ere he could him selfe recure againe,
    Him in his iron paw he seized had;
    That when he wak't out of his warelesse[5] paine,
    He found him selfe unwist, so ill bestad,[6]
    That lim he could not wag. Thence he him lad,
    Bound like a beast appointed to the stall:
    The sight whereof the Lady sore adrad,
    And fain'd[7] to fly for feare of being thrall;
But he her quickly stayd, and forst to wend withall.

23 When to the place they came, where *Artegall*
    By that same carefull[8] Squire did then abide,
    He gently gan him to demaund of all,

---

[1] Talus has superhuman speed, and so overtakes Sir Sanglier despite the latter's head start.

[2] In French, "wild boar." Artegall has in fact already beaten him in a tournament (IV.iv.40).

[3] **eft:** then.

[4] I.e., Sir Sanglier is knocked out.

[5] **warelesse:** unconscious or without wariness.

[6] **unwist:** unknowing how; **bestad:** situated.

[7] **fain'd:** attempted.

[8] **carefull:** full of cares and worries.

That did betwixt him and that Squire betide.[1]
Who with sterne countenance and indignant pride
Did aunswere, that of all he guiltlesse stood,
And his accuser thereuppon defide:[2]
For neither he did shed that Ladies bloud,
Nor tooke away his love, but his owne proper good.[3]

24   Well did the Squire perceive him selfe too weake,
      To aunswere his defiaunce in the field,
      And rather chose his challenge off to breake,
      Then to approve[4] his right with speare and shield.
      And rather guilty chose him selfe to yield.
      But *Artegall* by signes perceiving plaine,
      That he it was not, which that Lady kild,
      But that strange Knight, the fairer love to gaine,
Did cast about by sleight[5] the truth thereout to straine.

25   And sayd, "Now sure this doubtfull causes right
      Can hardly but by Sacrament[6] be tride,
      Or else by ordele,[7] or by blooddy fight;
      That ill perhaps mote fall to either side.
      But if ye please, that I your cause decide,
      Perhaps I may all further quarrell end,
      So ye will sweare my judgement to abide."
      Thereto they both did franckly condiscend,[8]
And to his doome with listfull[9] eares did both attend.

26   "Sith then" (sayd he) "ye both the dead deny,
      And both the living Lady claime your right,
      Let both the dead and living equally
      Devided be betwixt you here in sight,
      And each of either take his share aright.[10]

---

[1] **betide:** happen.

[2] Sanglier defies the Squire to prove his story by means of combat. The knight with justice on his side, according to the notion of judicial combat, gains victory through God's intervention.

[3] **proper good:** possession.

[4] **approve:** prove.

[5] **sleight:** trick.

[6] **Sacrament:** solemn oath.

[7] A physical ordeal, by fire or water, meant to determine guilt.

[8] **condiscend:** consent.

[9] **listfull:** carefully listening.

[10] Recalling the judgment of Solomon (1 Kings 3.16–28).

But looke who does dissent from this my read,[1]
He for a twelve moneths day shall in despight
Beare for his penaunce that same Ladies head;
To witnesse to the world, that she by him is dead."[2]

27 Well pleased with that doome was *Sangliere*,
And offred streight the Lady to be slaine.
But that same Squire, to whom she was more dere,
When as he saw she should be cut in twaine,
Did yield, she rather should with him[3] remaine
Alive, then to him selfe be shared dead;
And rather then his love should suffer paine,
He chose with shame to beare that Ladies head.
True love despiseth[4] shame, when life is cald in dread.

28 Whom when so willing *Artegall* perceaved;
"Not so thou Squire," (he sayd) "but thine I deeme
The living Lady, which from thee he reaved:[5]
For worthy thou of her doest rightly seeme.
And you, Sir Knight, that love so light esteeme,
As that ye would for little leave the same,
Take here your owne, that doth you best beseeme,
And with it beare the burden of defame;
Your owne dead Ladies head, to tell abrode your shame."

29 But *Sangliere* disdained much his doome,
And sternly gan repine at his beheast;[6]
Ne would for ought obay, as did become,[7]
To beare that Ladies head before his breast.
Untill that *Talus* had his pride represt,
And forced him, maulgre,[8] it up to reare.
Who when he saw it bootelesse to resist,
He tooke it up, and thence with him did beare,
As rated Spaniell takes his burden up for feare.[9]

---

[1] **read:** judgment.

[2] Cf. Malory, *Le Morte D'Arthur,* 6.17.

[3] I.e., Sanglier.

[4] **despiseth:** disregards.

[5] **reaved:** robbed.

[6] **beheast:** promise.

[7] **as did become:** as was appropriate.

[8] **maulgre:** reluctantly.

[9] Spenser makes frequent use of dog similes: ii.25; vi.26; viii.7, 22, 36, 49; ix.6; xi.12; xii.38.

30   Much did that Squire Sir *Artegall* adore,
         For his great justice, held in high regard;
         And as his Squire him offred evermore
         To serve, for want of other meete reward,
         And wend with him on his adventure hard.
         But he thereto would by no meanes consent;
         But leaving him forth on his journey far'd:
         Ne wight with him but onely *Talus* went.
      They two enough t'encounter an whole Regiment.

Canto Two

Artegall heares of Florimell,
Does with the Pagan fight:
Him slaies, drownes Lady Munera,
Does race her castle quight.

1   Nought is more honorable to a knight,
      Ne better doth beseeme[1] brave chevalry,
    Then to defend the feeble in their right,
    And wrong redresse in such as wend awry.
    Whilome[2] those great Heroes got thereby
    Their greatest glory, for their rightfull deedes,
    And place deserved with the Gods on hy.
    Herein the noblesse of this knight exceedes,
Who now to perils great for justice sake proceedes.

2   To which as he now was uppon the way,
      He chaunst to meet a Dwarfe in hasty course;
    Whom he requir'd[3] his forward hast to stay,
    Till he of tidings mote with him discourse.
    Loth was the Dwarfe, yet did he stay perforse,
    And gan of sundry[4] newes his store to tell,
    As to his memory they had recourse:
    But chiefly of the fairest *Florimell,*
How she was found againe, and spousde to *Marinell.*[5]

---

[1] **beseeme:** suit.

[2] **Whilome:** in the past.

[3] **requir'd:** requested.

[4] **sundry:** various.

[5] The story of Florimell unfolds in Books Three and Four. The beautiful and virginal Florimell was raised by the Graces, whence she received her girdle, endowed with chastity and much sought (IV.v.1–6). She loves Marinell, a sea nymph's son, but hears in the Faerie Court that he is dead (III.v.3–11). She is chased and harassed throughout Books Three and Four, and finally imprisoned by Proteus under the sea (III.viii.29–43). Meanwhile a witch creates the "False Florimell" out of snow (III.viii.5–10). The False Florimell is passed from knight to knight, ending up with Braggadocchio (IV.v.14–27). The real Florimell is sought by Satyrane and other knights of the Faerie Court, and, at the end of Book Four, is saved from Proteus and betrothed to Marinell (IV.xii.28–35).

3   For this was *Dony, Florimels* owne Dwarfe,
  Whom having lost (as ye have heard whyleare)
  And finding in the way the scattred scarfe,[1]
  The fortune of her life long time did feare.
  But of her health when *Artegall* did heare,
  And safe returne, he was full inly glad,
  And askt him where, and when her bridale cheare
  Should be solemniz'd: for if time he had,
He would be there, and honor to her spousall ad.

4   "Within three daies" (quoth hee) "as I do here,
  It will be at the Castle of the strond;[2]
  What time if naught me let,[3] I will be there
  To doe her service, so as I am bond.
  But in my way a little here beyond
  A cursed cruell Sarazin doth wonne,[4]
  That keepes a Bridges passage by strong hond,
  And many errant Knights hath there fordonne;
That makes all men for feare that passage for to shonne."[5]

5   "What mister wight"[6] (quoth he) "and how far hence
  Is he, that doth to travellers such harmes?"
  "He is" (said he) "a man of great defence;
  Expert in battell and in deedes of armes;
  And more emboldned by the wicked charmes,
  With which his daughter doth him still support;
  Having great Lordships[7] got and goodly farmes,
  Through strong oppression of his powre extort;[8]
By which he stil them holds, and keepes with strong effort.

6   "And dayly he his wrongs encreaseth more,
  For never wight he lets to passe that way;
  Over his Bridge, albee he[9] rich or poore,

---

[1] In a conversation with Arthur, Dony tells of losing Florimell (III.v.3–12). The scarf is Florimell's girdle, dropped while she is fleeing a hyena (III.vii.31). "Dony" recalls the Italian word for "squire."

[2] Marinell lives on a seacoast called the Rich Strond (III.iv.20).

[3] **let:** prevent.

[4] **Sarazin:** pagan; **wonne:** dwell.

[5] For similar episodes, see Malory, *Morte D'Arthur,* 6.10; and *Orlando,* 29.33.

[6] **What mister wight:** what kind of person, what rank or occupation.

[7] **Lordships:** estates.

[8] **extort:** extorted. This archaic participle also may recall the tyrant Grantorto.

[9] **albee he:** although he is.

But he him makes his passage-penny pay:
Else he doth hold him backe or beat away.
Thereto he hath a groome of evill guize,
Whose scalp is bare, that bondage doth bewray,[1]
Which pols and pils[2] the poore in piteous wize;
But he him selfe uppon the rich doth tyrannize.

7   "His name is hight *Pollente*,[3] rightly so
For that he is so puissant and strong,
That with his powre he all doth overgo,
And makes them subject to his mighty wrong;
And some by sleight he eke doth underfong.[4]
For on a Bridge he custometh to fight,
Which is but narrow, but exceeding long;
And in the same are many trap fals pight,[5]
Through which the rider downe doth fall through oversight.

8   "And underneath the same a river flowes,
That is both swift and dangerous deepe withall;
Into the which whom so he overthrowes,
All destitute of helpe doth headlong fall,
But he him selfe, through practise usuall,
Leapes forth into the floud, and there assaies[6]
His foe confused through his sodaine fall,
That horse and man he equally dismaies,
And either both them drownes, or trayterously slaies.

9   "Then doth he take the spoile of them at will,
And to his daughter brings, that dwels thereby:
Who all that comes doth take, and therewith fill
The coffers of her wicked threasury;

---

[1] **bewray:** reveal.

[2] **pols and pils:** plunders and pillages. There are several puns here: "poll" also means a bare head, and "to pill" is also to shave or to remove the skin of the scalp—hence the groom's bare scalp "doth bewray" his actions. "To poll" is also to tax, as they are doing to travelers crossing the bridge. Spenser alludes to the common abuse of tolls and monopolies in general. See *Variorum*, 170–71.

[3] From the Latin word for "power," and the Italian word for "powerful." The name continues the pun on "poll," which reaches a climax in 19.4.

[4] **underfong:** entrap.

[5] **trap fals pight:** falsely placed traps—i.e., trapdoors.

[6] **assaies:** attacks.

Which she with wrongs hath heaped up so hy,
That many Princes she in wealth exceedes,
And purchast all the countrey lying ny
With the revenue of her plenteous meedes,[1]
Her name is *Munera*,[2] agreeing with her deedes.

10   "Thereto she is full faire, and rich attired,
     With golden hands and silver feete beside,
     That many Lords have her to wife desired:
     But she them all despiseth for great pride."
     "Now by my life" (sayd he) "and God to guide,
     None other way will I this day betake,
     But by that Bridge, whereas he doth abide:
     Therefore me thither lead." No more he spake,
But thitherward forthright his ready way did make.

11   Unto the place he came within a while,
     Where on the Bridge he ready armed saw
     The Sarazin, awayting for some spoile.
     Who as they to the passage gan to draw,
     A villaine to them came with scull all raw,
     That passage money did of them require,
     According to the custome of their law.
     To whom he aunswerd wroth, "Loe there thy hire;"[3]
And with that word him strooke, that streight he did expire.

12   Which when the Pagan saw, he wexed[4] wroth,
     And streight him selfe unto the fight addrest,
     Ne was Sir *Artegall* behinde: so both
     Together ran with ready speares in rest.
     Right in the midst, whereas they brest to brest
     Should meete, a trap was letten downe to fall
     Into the floud: streight leapt the Carle[5] unblest,
     Well weening that his foe was falne withall:
But he[6] was well aware, and leapt before his fall.

---

[1] **meedes:** dishonest gains.

[2] From the Latin word for "profit." Munera has been likened to Langland's Lady Meed in *Piers Plowman* (2.5–17).

[3] **hire:** payment.

[4] **wexed:** grew.

[5] **Carle:** churl, villain.

[6] I.e. Artegall.

13 There being both together in the floud,
   They each at other tyrannously flew;
   Ne ought the water cooled their whot bloud,
   But rather in them kindled choler[1] new.
   But there the Paynim,[2] who that use well knew
   To fight in water, great advantage had,
   That oftentimes him nigh he overthrew:[3]
   And eke the courser, whereuppon he rad,
  Could swim like to a fish, whiles he his backe bestrad.

14 Which oddes when as Sir *Artegall* espide,
   He saw no way, but close with him in hast;
   And to him driving strongly downe the tide,
   Uppon his iron coller griped fast,
   That with the straint his wesand nigh he brast.[4]
   There they together strove and struggled long,
   Either the other from his steede to cast;
   Ne ever *Artegall* his griple[5] strong
  For any thing wold slacke, but still upon him hong.

15 As when a Dolphin and a Sele are met,
   In the wide champian[6] of the Ocean plaine:
   With cruell chaufe[7] their courages they whet,
   The maysterdome of each by force to gaine,
   And dreadfull battaile twixt them do darraine:[8]
   They snuf, they snort, they bounce, they rage, they rore,
   That all the sea disturbed with their traine,[9]
   Doth frie with fome above the surges hore.[10]
  Such was betwixt these two the troublesome uprore.

16 So *Artegall* at length him forst forsake
   His horses backe, for dread of being drownd,
   And to his handy swimming him betake.
   Eftsoones[11] him selfe he from his hold unbownd,

---

[1] **choler:** anger.

[2] **Paynim:** pagan.

[3] I.e., Pollente almost overthrew Artegall.

[4] **wesand:** wind-pipe; **brast:** burst.

[5] **griple:** grip.

[6] **champian:** flat expanse.

[7] **chaufe:** chafing, rage.

[8] **darraine:** wage.

[9] **traine:** wake.

[10] **hore:** white.

[11] **Eftsoones:** soon after.

And then no ods[1] at all in him he fownd:
For *Artegall* in swimming skilfull was,
And durst the depth of any water sownd.
So ought each Knight, that use[2] of perill has,
In swimming be expert through waters force to pas.

17   Then very doubtfull was the warres event,[3]
        Uncertaine whether[4] had the better side.
        For both were skild in that experiment,[5]
        And both in armes well traind and throughly tride.
        But *Artegall* was better breath'd beside,
        And towards th'end, grew greater in his might,
        That his faint foe no longer could abide
        His puissance, ne beare him selfe upright,
But from the water to the land betooke his flight.

18   But *Artegall* pursewd him still so neare,
        With bright Chrysaor in his cruell hand,
        That as his head he gan a litle reare
        Above the brincke, to tread upon the land,
        He smote it off, that tumbling on the strand
        It bit the earth for very fell despight,[6]
        And gnashed with his teeth, as if he band[7]
        High God, whose goodnesse he despaired quight,
Or curst the hand, which did that vengeance on him dight.[8]

19   His corps was carried downe along the Lee,[9]
        Whose waters with his filthy bloud it stayned:
        But his blasphemous head, that all might see,
        He pitcht upon a pole on high ordayned;
        Where many years it afterwards remayned,
        To be a mirrour to all mighty men,

---

[1] **ods:** advantage—Pollente cannot gain the upper hand.

[2] **use:** usual experience.

[3] **event:** outcome.

[4] **whether:** which.

[5] **experiment:** trial.

[6] Hamilton points out that this image recalls the curse that the serpent shall eat dust (Gen. 3.14), and is repeated at xi.14 and xii.23.

[7] **band:** cursed.

[8] **dight:** execute.

[9] May refer to the Irish river Lee. In 1581, the body of the defeated rebel Sir John of Desmond was hung above the river Lee in Cork. See *Variorum*, 173.

In whose right hands great power is contayned,
That none of them the feeble overren,
But alwaies doe their powre within just compasse pen.

20   That done, unto the Castle he did wend,
      In which the Paynims[1] daughter did abide,
      Guarded of many which did her defend:
      Of whom he entrance sought, but was denide,
      And with reprochfull blasphemy defide,
      Beaten with stones downe from the battilment,
      That he was forced to withdraw aside;
      And bad his servant *Talus* to invent
Which way he enter might, without endangerment.

21   Eftsoones[2] his Page drew to the Castle gate,
      And with his iron flale at it let flie,
      That all the warders it did sore amate,[3]
      The which erewhile[4] spake so reprochfully,
      And made them stoupe, that looked earst[5] so hie.
      Yet still he bet, and bounst uppon the dore,
      And thundred strokes thereon so hideouslie,
      That all the peece[6] he shaked from the flore,
And filled all the house with feare and great uprore.

22   With noise whereof the Lady forth appeared
      Uppon the Castle wall, and when she saw
      The daungerous state, in which she stood, she feared
      The sad effect of her neare overthrow;
      And gan entreat that iron man below,
      To cease his outrage, and him faire besought,
      Sith neither force of stones which they did throw,
      Nor powr of charms, which she against him wrought,
Might otherwise prevaile, or make him cease for ought.

23   But when as yet she saw him to proceede,
      Unmov'd with praiers, or with piteous thought,
      She ment him to corrupt with goodly meede;[7]

[1] **Paynims:** pagan's.

[2] **Eftsoones:** soon after.

[3] **amate:** dismay.

[4] **erewhile:** formerly.

[5] **earst:** earlier, once.

[6] **peece:** fortress.

[7] **meede:** bribes.

And causde great sackes with endlesse riches fraught,
Unto the battilment to be upbrought,
And powred forth over the Castle wall,
That she might win some time, though dearly bought
Whilest he to gathering of the gold did fall.
But he was nothing mov'd, nor tempted therewithall.

24   But still continu'd his assault the more,
And layd on load with his huge yron flaile,
That at the length he has yrent[1] the dore,
And made way for his maister to assaile.
Who being entred, nought did then availe
For wight, against his powre them selves to reare:
Each one did flie; their hearts began to faile,
And hid them selves in corners here and there;
And eke their dame halfe dead did hide her self for feare.

25   Long they her sought, yet no where could they finde her,
That sure they ween'd she was escapt away:
But *Talus,* that could like a limehound[2] winde her,
And all things secrete wisely could bewray,[3]
At length found out, whereas she hidden lay
Under an heape of gold. Thence he her drew
By the faire lockes, and fowly did array,
Withouten pitty of her goodly hew,[4]
That *Artegall* him selfe her seemelesse[5] plight did rew.

26   Yet for no pitty would he change the course
Of Justice, which in *Talus* hand did lye;
Who rudely hayld[6] her forth without remorse,
Still holding up her suppliant hands on hye,
And kneeling at his feete submissively.
But he her suppliant hands, those hands of gold,
And eke her feete, those feete of silver trye,[7]
Which sought unrighteousnesse, and justice sold,
Chopt off, and nayld on high, that all might them behold.

---

[1] **yrent:** torn apart.
[2] **limehound:** hound for hunting boars.
[3] **bewray:** reveal.
[4] **hew:** appearance.
[5] **seemelesse:** unseemly.
[6] **hayld:** dragged.
[7] **silver trye:** choice silver.

27 Her selfe then tooke he by the sclender wast,
       In vaine loud crying, and into the flood
       Over the Castle wall adowne her cast,
       And there her drowned in the durty mud:
       But the streame washt away her guilty blood.
       Thereafter all that mucky pelfe[1] he tooke,
       The spoile of peoples evill gotten good,
       The which her sire had scrap't by hooke and crooke,
And burning all to ashes, powr'd it downe the brooke.[2]

28 And lastly all that Castle quite he raced,[3]
       Even from the sole of his foundation,
       And all the hewen stones thereof defaced,
       That there mote be no hope of reparation,
       Nor memory thereof to any nation.
       All which when *Talus* throughly had perfourmed,
       Sir *Artegall* undid the evill fashion,
       And wicked customes of that Bridge refourmed.
Which done, unto his former journey he retourned.

29 In which they measur'd mickle[4] weary way,
       Till that at length nigh to the sea they drew;
       By which as they did travell on a day,
       They saw before them, far as they could vew,
       Full many people gathered in a crew;
       Whose great assembly they did much admire.
       For never there the like resort[5] they knew.
       So towardes them they coasted,[6] to enquire
What thing so many nations met, did there desire.

30 There they beheld a mighty Gyant[7] stand
       Upon a rocke, and holding forth on hie
       An huge great paire of ballance in his hand,
       With which be boasted in his surquedrie,[8]

[1] **pelfe:** stolen property.
[2] See Deut. 9.21.
[3] **raced:** razed.
[4] **mickle:** much.
[5] **resort:** assemblage.
[6] **coasted:** approached.

[7] Often called the Egalitarian Giant or the Giant with the scales, he espouses a revolutionary social program like the communism associated with early modern groups such as the Anabaptists. See *Variorum,* 336–41; and SE, "radicalism in Spenser."
[8] **surquedrie:** pride, arrogance.

That all the world he would weigh equallie,
   If ought he had the same to counterpoys.
   For want whereof he weighed vanity,[1]
   And fild his ballaunce full of idle toys:
Yet was admired much of fooles, women, and boys.

31   He sayd that he would all the earth uptake,
        And all the sea, devided each from either:
        So would he of the fire one ballaunce make,
        And one of th'ayre, without or wind, or wether:
        Then would he ballaunce heaven and hell together,
        And all that did within them all containe;
        Of all whose weight, he would not misse a fether.
        And looke what surplus did of each remaine,
     He would to his[2] owne part restore the same againe.

32   For why,[3] he sayd they all unequall were,
        And had encroched uppon others share,
        Like as the sea (which plaine he shewed there)
        Had worne the earth, so did the fire the aire,
        So all the rest did others parts empaire.
        And so were realmes and nations run awry.
        All which he undertooke for to repaire,
        In sort[4] as they were formed aunciently;
     And all things would reduce unto equality.

33   Therefore the vulgar did about him flocke,
        And cluster thicke unto his leasings[5] vaine,
        Like foolish flies about an hony crocke,
        In hope by him great benefite to gaine,
        And uncontrolled freedome to obtaine.
        All which when *Artegall* did see, and heare,
        How he mis-led the simple peoples traine,[6]
        In sdeignfull[7] wize he drew unto him neare,
     And thus unto him spake, without regard or feare.

---

[1] See Ps. 62.9.

[2] **his:** its. The Gyant promises to redistribute all things equally.

[3] **For why:** because.

[4] **In sort:** in the manner.

[5] **leasings:** lies, with a secondary meaning of gleanings.

[6] **traine:** course of life, properly ordered sequence.

[7] **sdeignfull:** disdainful.

34   "Thou that presum'st to weigh the world anew,
        And all things to an equall to restore,
        In stead of right me seemes great wrong dost shew,
        And far above thy forces pitch to sore.[1]
        For ere thou limit what is lesse or more
        In every thing, thou oughtest first to know,
        What was the poyse[2] of every part of yore:
        And looke then how much it doth overflow,
Or faile thereof, so much is more then just to trow.[3]

35   "For at the first they all created were
        In goodly measure, by their Makers might,
        And weighed out in ballaunces so nere,
        That not a dram was missing of their right,[4]
        The earth was in the middle centre pight,[5]
        In which it doth immoveable abide,
        Hemd in with waters like a wall in sight;
        And they with aire, that not a drop can slide:
Al which the heavens containe, and in their courses guide.[6]

36   "Such heavenly justice doth among them raine,
        That every one doe know their certaine bound,
        In which they doe these many yeares remaine,
        And mongst them al no change hath yet beene found.[7]
        But if thou now shouldst weigh them new in pound,
        We are not sure they would so long remaine:
        All change is perillous, and all chaunce unsound.
        Therefore leave off to weigh them all againe,
Till we may be assur'd they shall their course retaine."

---

[1] Artegall charges that the Giant soars above the height his intellectual force can reach.

[2] **poyse:** weight.

[3] I.e., the Giant's measurements will be off because he made arbitrary assumptions as to the original weights, according to Gough (187).

[4] See Job 38.4–6; Isa. 40.12; 2 Esd. 4.36.

[5] **pight:** placed.

[6] Artegall's argument relies on Ptolemy's geocentric theory, even though Coperni-cus challenged it 50 years before the writing of Book Five. The heliocentric theory was slow to gain acceptance, although we cannot say whether or not Spenser agreed with Artegall's position.

[7] Artegall seems to be contradicted by Proem, 4. Gough points out that, in Artegall's time, the corruption of the heavenly bodies was just beginning. But the Giant's argument in stanza 32 comes very near to the Proem's claim that current instabilities in nature parallel a degradation of justice.

37   "Thou foolishe Elfe" (said then the Gyant wroth)
        "Seest not, how badly all things present bee,
        And each estate quite out of order goth?[1]
        The sea it selfe doest though not plainely see
        Encroch uppon the land there under thee;
        And th'earth it selfe how daily its increast,
        By all that dying to it turned be?
        Were it not good that wrong were then surceast,[2]
And from the most, that some were given to the least?

38   "Therefore I will throw downe these mountaines hie,
        And make them levell[3] with the lowly plaine:
        These towring rocks, which reach unto the skie,
        I will thrust downe into the deepest maine,
        And as they were, them equalize againe.
        Tyrants that make men subject to their law,
        I will suppresse, that they no more may raine;
        And Lordings curbe, that commons[4] over-aw;
And all the wealth of rich men to the poore will draw."

39   "Of things unseene how canst thou deeme[5] aright,"
        Then answered the righteous *Artegall*,
        "Sith thou misdeem'st so much of things in sight?
        What though the sea with waves continuall
        Doe eate the earth, it is no more[6] at all:
        Ne is the earth the lesse, or loseth ought,
        For whatsoever from one place doth fall,
        Is with the tide unto an other brought:
For there is nothing lost, that may be found, if sought.

40   "Likewise the earth is not augmented more,
        By all that dying into it doe fade.
        For of the earth they formed were of yore,
        How ever gay their blossome or their blade
        Doe flourish now, they into dust shall vade.[7]

---

[1] **goth:** goes.

[2] **surceast:** stopped.

[3] Perhaps alluding to the emerging term for radical political change. During the Civil War, the Levellers were a political group that sought to level hierarchical society.

[4] **commons:** the common people.

[5] **deeme:** interpret.

[6] **no more:** not increased.

[7] **vade:** vanish. See Job 14.2; Isa. 40.6–8.

What wrong then is it, if that when they die,
They turne to that, whereof they first were made?
All in the powre of their great Maker lie:
All creatures must obey the voice of the most hie.

41   "They live, they die, like as he doth ordaine,
Ne ever any asketh reason why.
The hils doe not the lowly dales disdaine;
The dales doe not the lofty hils envy.
He maketh Kings to sit in soverainty;
He maketh subjects to their powre obay;[1]
He pulleth downe, he setteth up on hy;
He gives to this, from that he takes away.
For all we have is his: what he list doe, he may.[2]

42   "What ever thing is done, by him is donne,
Ne any may his mighty will withstand;
Ne any may his soveraine power shonne,
Ne loose that he hath bound with stedfast band.
In vaine therefore doest thou now take in hand,
To call to count, or weigh his workes anew,
Whose counsels depth thou canst not understand,
Sith of things subject to thy daily vew
Thou doest not know the causes, nor their courses dew.[3]

43   "For take thy ballaunce, if thou be so wise,
And weigh the winde, that under heaven doth blow;[4]
Or weigh the light, that in the East doth rise;
Or weigh the thought, that from mans mind doth flow.
But if the weight of these thou canst not show,
Weigh but one word which from thy lips doth fall.
For how canst thou those greater secrets know,
That doest not know the least thing of them all?
Ill can he rule the great, that cannot reach the small."

---

[1] As Todd says, "Indeed this and the next stanza are formed entirely from Holy Writ" (*Variorum*, 179). Here Spenser echoes several Biblical passages that give divine authority to monarchs, including Prov. 8.15–16; Rom. 13.1–5.

[2] See Job 42.2; 1 Sam. 2.6–8.

[3] **courses dew:** just result.

[4] See Job 28.25, 2 Esd. 4.5.

44   Therewith the Gyant much abashed sayd;
        That he of little things made reckoning light,
        Yet the least word that ever could be layd
        Within his ballaunce, he could way aright.
        "Which is" (sayd he[1]) "more heavy then in weight,
        The right or wrong, the false or else the trew?"
        He answered, that he would try it streight,
        So he the words into his ballaunce threw,
    But streight the winged words out of his ballaunce flew.

45   Wroth wext he then, and sayd, that words were light,[2]
        Ne would within his ballaunce well abide.
        But he could justly weigh the wrong or right.
        "Well then," sayd *Artegall*, "let it be tride.
        First in one ballance set the true aside."
        He did so first; and then the false he layd
        In th'other scale; but still it downe did slide,
        And by no meane could in the weight[3] be stayd.
    For by no meanes the false will with the truth be wayd.

46   "Now take the right likewise," sayd *Artegale*,
        "And counterpeise[4] the same with so much wrong."
        So first the right he put into one scale;
        And then the Gyant strove with puissance strong
        To fill the other scale with so much wrong.
        But all the wrongs that he therein could lay,
        Might not it peise; yet did he labour long,
        And swat, and chauf'd, and proved[5] every way:
    Yet all the wrongs could not a litle right downe way.

47   Which when he saw, he greatly grew in rage,
        And almost would his balances have broken:
        But *Artegall* him fairely gan asswage,
        And said; "Be not upon thy balance wroken:[6]
        For they doe nought but right or wrong betoken;[7]
        But in the mind the doome of right must bee;

---

[1] I.e., Artegall.

[2] **wext:** grew; **light:** unimportant.

[3] **weight:** scales.

[4] **counterpeise:** counterpoise or counter-balance.

[5] **swat, and chauf'd, and proved:** sweated and chafed and tried.

[6] **wroken:** avenged.

[7] **betoken:** signify—objectively, without the mental judgment of the next line.

And so likewise of words, the which be spoken,
The eare must be the ballance, to decree
And judge, whether with truth or falshood they agree.

48   "But set the truth and set the right aside,
     For they with wrong or falshood will not fare;
     And put two wrongs together to be tride,
     Or else two falses, of each equall share;
     And then together doe them both compare.
     For truth is one, and right is ever one."
     So did he, and then plaine it did appeare,
     Whether of them the greater were attone.[1]
     But right sate in the middest of the beame alone.[2]

49   But he the right from thence did thrust away,
     For it was not the right, which he did seeke;
     But rather strove extremities to way,
     Th'one to diminish, th'other for to eeke.[3]
     For of the meane he greatly did misleeke.
     Whom when so lewdly minded *Talus* found,
     Approching nigh unto him cheeke by cheeke,
     He shouldered him from off the higher ground,
     And down the rock him throwing, in the sea him dround.[4]

50   Like as a ship, whom cruell tempest drives
     Upon a rocke with horrible dismay,
     Her shattered ribs in thousand peeces rives,[5]
     And spoyling all her geares and goodly ray,[6]
     Does make her selfe misfortunes piteous pray.
     So downe the cliffe the wretched Gyant tumbled;
     His battred ballances in peeces lay,
     His timbered bones all broken rudely rumbled,
     So was the high aspyring with huge ruine humbled.

51   That when the people, which had there about
     Long wayted, saw his sudden desolation,

---

[1] **Whether:** which; **attone:** at once—i.e., in comparison.

[2] According to Gough, Artegall demonstrates the Aristotelian argument that right and wrong cannot be weighed, for there are infinite degrees of falsehood, but truth is one. Only two wrongs can be weighed, and between these excesses lies the mean. See Aristotle, *The Nicomachean Ethics*, 2.6.

[3] **eeke:** increase.

[4] Talus' action resembles Aries, who "shouldred hath the Bull" (Proem, 5).

[5] **rives:** breaks.

[6] **ray:** array.

They gan to gather in tumultuous rout,[1]
And mutining, to stirre up civill faction,
For certaine losse of so great expectation.
For well they hoped to have got great good;
And wondrous riches by his innovation.
Therefore resolving to revenge his blood,
They rose in armes, and all in battell order stood.

52   Which lawlesse multitude him comming too
        In warlike wise, when *Artegall* did vew,
        He much was troubled, ne wist[2] what to doo.
        For loth he was his noble hands t'embrew[3]
        In the base blood of such a rascall crew;
        And otherwise, if that he should retire,
        He fear'd least they with shame would him pursew.
        Therefore he *Talus* to them sent, t'inquire
The cause of their array, and truce for to desire.

53   But soone as they him nigh approching spide,
        They gan with all their weapons him assay,[4]
        And rudely stroke at him on every side:
        Yet nought they could him hurt, ne ought dismay.
        But when at them he with his flaile gan lay,
        He like a swarme of flyes them overthrew;
        Ne any of them durst come in his way,
        But here and there before his presence flew,
And hid themselves in holes and bushes from his view.

54   As when a Faulcon hath with nimble flight
        Flowne at a flush[5] of Ducks, foreby the brooke,
        The trembling foule dismayd with dreadfull sight
        Of death, the which them almost overtooke,
        Doe hide themselves from her astonying[6] looke,
        Amongst the flags[7] and covert round about.
        When *Talus* saw they all the field forsooke
        And none appear'd of all that raskall rout,[8]
To *Artegall* he turn'd, and went with him throughout.

---

[1] **rout:** mob.

[2] **wist:** knew.

[3] **embrew:** plunge into, stain.

[4] **assay:** attack.

[5] **flush:** flight of startled birds.

[6] **astonying:** petrifying.

[7] **flags:** reeds.

[8] **rout:** mob.

Canto Three

The spousals of faire Florimell,
where turney many knights:
There Braggadochio is uncas'd
in all the Ladies sights.

1   After long stormes and tempests overblowne,
        The sunne at length his joyous face doth cleare:
        So when as fortune all her spight hath showne,
        Some blisfull houres at last must needes appeare;
        Else should afflicted wights oftimes despeire.
        So comes it now to *Florimell*[1] by tourne,
        After long sorrowes suffered whyleare,[2]
        In which captiv'd she many moneths did mourne,
    To tast of joy, and to wont[3] pleasures to retourne.

2   Who being freed from *Proteus*[4] cruell band
        By *Marinell,* was unto him affide,[5]
        And by him brought againe to Faerie land;
        Where he her spous'd, and made his joyous bride.
        The time and place was blazed farre and wide;
        And solemne feasts and giusts[6] ordain'd therefore.
        To which there did resort from every side
        Of Lords and Ladies infinite great store;
    Ne any Knight was absent, that brave courage bore.

3   To tell the glorie of the feast that day,
        The goodly service, the devicefull sights,[7]
        The bridegromes state, the brides most rich aray,

---

[1] Recalling Flora, the goddess of flowers, and the Latin word for honey, *mel.* For the background on Florimell and Marinell, see ii.2.9n.; and Introduction, 10.

[2] **whyleare:** formerly.

[3] **wont:** accustomed.

[4] A god of the sea, Proteus has the gifts of prophecy and changing shapes. See III.viii.30; and Homer, *Odyssey,* 4.351–93. Proteus imprisoned Florimell beneath the waves (III.viii.30–42) until she was released by command of Neptune (IV.xii.32).

[5] **affide:** betrothed.

[6] **giusts:** jousts.

[7] **devicefull sights:** sights full of devices, such as pageants and spectacles.

The pride of Ladies, and the worth of knights,
The royall banquets, and the rare delights
Were worke fit for an Herauld, not for me:
But for so much as to my lot here lights,
That with this present treatise doth agree,
True vertue to advance, shall here recounted bee.[1]

4   When all men had with full satietie
        Of meates and drinkes their appetites suffiz'd,
        To deedes of armes and proofe of chevalrie
        They gan themselves addresse, full rich aguiz'd,[2]
        As each one had his furnitures[3] deviz'd.
        And first of all issu'd Sir *Marinell,*
        And with him six knights more, which enterpriz'd
        To chalenge all in right of *Florimell,*
And to maintaine, that she all others did excell.[4]

5   The first of them was hight Sir *Orimont,*
        A noble Knight, and tride in hard assayes:
        The second had to name Sir *Bellisont,*
        But second unto none in prowesse prayse;
        The third was *Brunell,* famous in his dayes;
        The fourth *Ecastor,* of exceeding might;
        The fift *Armeddan,* skild in lovely layes;[5]
        The sixt was *Lansack,* a redoubted Knight:
All six well seene[6] in armes, and prov'd in many a fight.

6   And them against came all that list to giust,
        From every coast and countrie under sunne:
        None was debard, but all had leave that lust.[7]
        The trompets sound; then all together ronne.

---

[1] The herald traditionally describes the guests and the details of the festival. This is one of the rare instances in which the poet speaks in the first person. He distinguishes between his poem's moral aim of advancing virtue and the more frivolous details of chivalric romance.

[2] **aguiz'd:** arrayed.

[3] **furnitures:** armor and equipment.

[4] In the tournament the knights are fighting to prove who represents the most beautiful and virtuous lady. This tradition is based on the same logic as the trial by battle: heaven will assure a just conclusion.

[5] **layes:** love songs.

[6] **seene:** skilled. These knights may have been complimentary references to courtiers, according to Hamilton.

[7] **lust:** desired, chose.

Full many deedes of armes that day were donne,
And many knights unhorst, and many wounded,
As fortune fell; yet litle lost or wonne:
But all that day the greatest prayse redounded
To *Marinell,* whose name the Heralds loud resounded.

7   The second day, so soone as morrow light
Appear'd in heaven, into the field they came,
And there all day continew'd cruell fight,
With divers fortune fit for such a game,
In which all strove with perill to winne fame.
Yet whether side was victor, note[1] be ghest:
But at the last the trompets did proclame
That *Marinell* that day deserved best.
So they disparted were, and all men went to rest.

8   The third day came, that should due tryall lend
Of all the rest, and then this warlike crew
Together met, of all to make an end.
There *Marinell* great deeds of armes did shew;
And through the thickest like a Lyon flew,
Rashing off helmes, and ryving[2] plates a sonder,
That every one his daunger did eschew.
So terribly his dreadfull strokes did thonder,
That all men stood amaz'd, and at his might did wonder.

9   But what on earth can alwayes happie stand?
The greater prowesse greater perils find.
So farre he past amongst his enemies band,
That they have him enclosed so behind,
As by no meanes he can himselfe outwind.
And now perforce they have him prisoner taken;
And now they doe with captive bands him bind;
And now they lead him thence, of all forsaken,
Unlesse some succour had in time him overtaken.

10   It fortun'd whylest they were thus ill beset,
Sir *Artegall* into the Tilt-yard came,
With *Braggadochio,*[3] whom he lately met

---

[1] **whether:** which; **note:** could not.

[2] **Rashing:** slashing; **ryving:** tearing.

[3] Braggart or boaster, with an Italian suffix. Braggadochio is a parodic figure for

Upon the way, with that his snowy Dame.
Where when he understood by common fame,[1]
What evill hap to *Marinell* betid,
He much was mov'd at so unworthie shame,
And streight that boaster prayd, with whom he rid,
To change his shield with him, to be the better hid.

11   So forth he went, and soone them over hent,[2]
    Where they were leading *Marinell* away,
    Whom he assayld with dreadlesse hardiment,
    And forst the burden of their prize to stay.
    They were an hundred knights of that array;
    Of which th'one halfe upon himselfe did set,
    Th'other stayd behind to gard the pray.
    But he ere long the former fiftie bet;[3]
And from th'other fiftie soone the prisoner fet.[4]

12   So backe he brought Sir *Marinell* againe;
    Whom having quickly arm'd againe anew,
    They both together joyned might and maine,
    To set afresh on all the other crew.
    Whom with sore havocke soone they overthrew,
    And chaced quite out of the field, that none
    Against them durst his head to perill shew.
    So were they left Lords of the field alone:
So *Marinell* by him was rescu'd from his fone.[5]

13   Which when he had perform'd, then backe againe
    To *Braggadochio* did his shield restore:
    Who all this while behind him did remaine,
    Keeping there close with him in pretious store
    That his false Ladie,[6] as ye heard afore.
    Then did the trompets sound, and Judges rose,
    And all these knights, which that day armour bore,

---

knighthood who causes confusion in Books Two, Three, and Four. He appears at a tournament held by the knight Satyrane, where he gains the companionship of the False Florimell, an imposter made of snow (IV.v.26). Braggadochio resembles Ariosto's Martano (*Orlando*, 17–18).

[1] **fame:** report.

[2] **over hent:** overtook.

[3] **bet:** beat.

[4] **fet:** fetched.

[5] **fone:** foes.

[6] I.e., keeping the False Florimell hidden as a precious treasure.

Came to the open hall, to listen whose
The honour of the prize should be adjudg'd by those.

14 And thether also came in open sight
Fayre *Florimell*, into the common hall,
To greet his guerdon[1] unto every knight,
And best to him, to whom the best should fall.
Then for that stranger knight they loud did call,
To whom that day they should the girlond yield.
Who came not forth: but for Sir *Artegall*
Came *Braggadochio*, and did shew his shield,
Which bore the Sunne brode blazed in a golden field.

15 The sight whereof did all with gladnesse fill:
So unto him they did addeeme[2] the prise
Of all that Tryumph. Then the trompets shrill
Don *Braggadochios* name resounded thrise:
So courage lent a cloke to cowardise.
And then to him came fayrest *Florimell*,
And goodly gan to greet his brave emprise,[3]
And thousand thankes him yeeld, that had so well
Approv'd that day, that she all others did excell.

16 To whom the boaster, that all knights did blot,
With proud disdaine did scornefull answere make;
That what he did that day, he did it not
For her, but for his owne dear Ladies sake,
Whom on his perill he did undertake,
Both her and eke all others to excell:
And further did uncomely speaches crake.[4]
Much did his words the gentle Ladie quell,[5]
And turn'd aside for shame to heare, what he did tell.

17 Then forth he brought his snowy *Florimele*,
Whom *Trompart*[6] had in keeping there beside,
Covered from peoples gazement with a vele.

---

[1] **greet his guerdon:** celebrate the reward.

[2] **addeeme:** award.

[3] **emprise:** enterprise.

[4] **crake:** speak boastfully, speak in a grating cry as does a crow.

[5] **quell:** disconcert.

[6] Suggesting deception, from "trump," meaning to cheat. Also suggesting pomp and flattery, from "trumpet." Trompart swears allegiance to Braggadochio in Book Two and acts as his servant.

Whom when discovered they had throughly eide,
With great amazement they were stupefide;
And said, that surely *Florimell* it was,
Or if it were not *Florimell* so tride,[1]
That *Florimell* her selfe she then did pas.
So feeble skill[2] of perfect things the vulgar has.

18   Which when as *Marinell* beheld likewise,
      He was therewith exceedingly dismayd;
      Ne wist he what to thinke, or to devise,
      But like as one, whom feends had made affrayd,
      He long astonisht stood, ne ought he sayd,
      Ne ought he did, but with fast fixed eies
      He gazed still upon that snowy mayd;
      Whom ever as he did the more avize,[3]
The more to be true *Florimell* he did surmize.

19   As when two sunnes appeare in the azure skye,[4]
      Mounted in *Phoebus* charet fierie bright,
      Both darting forth faire beames to each mans eye,
      And both adorn'd with lampes of flaming light,
      All that behold so strange prodigious sight,
      Not knowing natures worke, nor what to weene,
      Are rapt with wonder, and with rare affright.
      So stood Sir *Marinell,* when he had seene
The semblant[5] of this false by his faire beauties Queene.

20   All which when *Artegall,* who all this while
      Stood in the preasse[6] close covered, well advewed,
      And saw that boasters pride and gracelesse guile,
      He could no longer beare, but forth issewed,
      And unto all himselfe there open shewed,
      And to the boaster said; "Thou losell[7] base,

---

[1] **so tride:** after an inspection.

[2] **skill:** power of discrimination.

[3] **avize:** look at.

[4] Referring to the phenomenon of the parhelion, intensified solar light that was taken to be a reflection of the sun, or a mock sun. It was thought to be an omen.

[5] **semblant:** appearance, resemblance.

[6] **preasse:** crowd.

[7] **losell:** scoundrel.

That hast with borrowed plumes thy selfe endewed,
And others worth with leasings[1] doest deface,
When they are all restor'd, thou shalt rest in disgrace.

21 "That shield, which thou doest beare, was it indeed,
Which this dayes honour sav'd to *Marinell;*
But not that arme, nor thou the man I reed,[2]
Which didst that service unto *Florimell.*
For proofe shew forth thy sword, and let it tell,
What strokes, what dreadfull stoure[3] it stird this day:
Or shew the wounds, which unto thee befell;
Or shew the sweat, with which thou diddest sway
So sharpe a battell, that so many did dismay.

22 "But this the sword, which wrought those cruell stounds,[4]
And this the arme, the which that shield did beare,
And these the signes," (so shewed forth his wounds)
"By which that glorie gotten doth appeare.
As for this Ladie, which he sheweth here,
Is not (I wager) *Florimell* at all;
But some fayre Franion, fit for such a fere,[5]
That by misfortune in his hand did fall."
For proofe whereof, he bad them *Florimell* forth call.

23 So forth the noble Ladie was ybrought,
Adorn'd with honor and all comely grace:
Whereto her bashfull shamefastnesse ywrought
A great increase in her faire blushing face;
As roses did with lillies interlace.
For of those words, the which that boaster threw,
She inly yet conceived great disgrace.
Whom when as all the people such did vew,
They shouted loud, and signes of gladnesse all did shew.

24 Then did he set her by that snowy one,
Like the true saint beside the image set,
Of both their beauties to make paragone,[6]

[1] **leasings:** lies.
[2] **reed:** judge.
[3] **stoure:** storm.
[4] **stounds:** fierce attacks.

[5] **Franion:** loose, wanton person; **fere:** companion, consort.
[6] **paragone:** comparison.

And triall, whether[1] should the honor get.
Streightway so soone as both together met,
Th'enchaunted Damzell vanisht into nought:
Her snowy substance melted as with heat,
Ne of that goodly hew[2] remayned ought,
But th'emptie girdle, which about her wast was wrought.[3]

25   As when the daughter of *Thaumantes* faire,[4]
Hath in a watry cloud displayed wide
Her goodly bow, which paints the liquid ayre;
That all men wonder at her colours pride;
All suddenly, ere one can looke aside,
The glorious picture vanisheth away,
Ne any token doth thereof abide:
So did this Ladies goodly forme decay,
And into nothing goe, ere one could it bewray.[5]

26   Which when as all that present were, beheld,
They stricken were with great astonishment,
And their faint harts with senselesse horrour queld,[6]
To see the thing, that seem'd so excellent,
So stolen from their fancies wonderment;
That what of it became, none understood.
And *Braggadochio* selfe[7] with dreriment
So daunted was in his despeyring mood,
That like a lifelesse corse immoveable he stood.

27   But *Artegall* that golden belt uptooke,
The which of all her spoyle was onely left;
Which was not hers, as many it mistooke,
But *Florimells* owne girdle, from her reft,[8]
While she was flying, like a weary weft,[9]
From that foule monster, which did her compell

---

[1] **whether:** which.

[2] **hew:** appearance.

[3] The False Florimell was awarded Florimell's girdle at Satyrane's tournament (IV.v.14). Given that only a chaste woman can wear the girdle, it is unclear how the False Florimell has it on.

[4] Iris, the rainbow goddess. See *Metamorphoses*, 11.647; Virgil, *Aeneid*, 9.5.

[5] **bewray:** point out.

[6] **queld:** quailed, withered.

[7] I.e., himself.

[8] **reft:** robbed. See ii.3.n.

[9] **weft:** waif, outcast, or homeless person.

To perils great; which he unbuckling eft,[1]
Presented to the fayrest *Florimell;*
Who round about her tender wast it fitted well.

28 Full many Ladies often had assayd,
About their middles that faire belt to knit;
And many a one suppos'd to be a mayd:
Yet it to none of all their loynes would fit,
Till *Florimell* about her fastned it.
Such power it had, that to no womans wast
By any skill or labour it would fit,
Unlesse that she were continent and chast,
But it would lose or breake, that many had disgrast.

29 Whilest thus they busied were bout *Florimell,*
And boastfull *Braggadochio* to defame,
Sir *Guyon* as by fortune then befell,
Forth from the thickest preasse of people came,
His owne good steed, which he had stolne, to clame;[2]
And th'one hand seizing on his golden bit,
With th'other drew his sword: for with the same
He ment the thiefe there deadly to have smit:
And had he not bene held, he nought had fayld of it.

30 Thereof great hurly burly moved was
Throughout the hall, for that same warlike horse.
For *Braggadochio* would not let him pas;
And *Guyon* would him algates[3] have perforse,
Or it approve[4] upon his carrion corse.
Which troublous stirre when *Artegall* perceived,
He nigh them drew to stay th'avengers forse,
And gan inquire, how was that steed bereaved,[5]
Whether by might extort, or else by slight deceaved.[6]

---

[1] **eft:** afterward.

[2] Sir Guyon is the hero of Book Two, the Legend of Temperaunce. Braggadochio steals his horse and spear (II.iii.4).

[3] **algates:** by all means.

[4] **approve:** prove, settle the score.

[5] **bereaved:** stolen.

[6] I.e., whether stolen by might or by deception.

31   Who all that piteous storie, which befell
        About that wofull couple, which were slaine,
        And their young bloodie babe to him gan tell;[1]
        With whom whiles he did in the wood remaine,
        His horse purloyned was by subtill traine:[2]
        For which he chalenged the thiefe to fight.
        But he for nought could him thereto constraine.
        For as the death he hated such despight,[3]
And rather had to lose, then trie in armes his right.

32   Which *Artegall* well hearing, though no more
        By law of armes there neede ones right to trie,
        As was the wont of warlike knights of yore,
        Then that his foe should him the field denie,[4]
        Yet further right by tokens to descrie,
        He askt, what privie tokens he did beare.[5]
        "If that" (said *Guyon*) "may you satisfie,
        Within his mouth a blacke spot doth appeare,
Shapt like a horses shoe, who list to seeke it there."

33   Whereof to make due tryall, one did take
        The horse in hand, within his mouth to looke:
        But with his heeles so sorely he him strake,
        That all his ribs he quite in peeces broke,
        That never word from that day forth he spoke.
        Another that would seeme to have more wit,
        Him by the bright embrodered hedstall[6] tooke:
        But by the shoulder him so sore he bit,
That he him maymed quite, and all his shoulder split.

34   Ne he his mouth would open unto wight,
        Untill that *Guyon* selfe unto him spake,
        And called *Brigadore*[7] (so was he hight)

[1] Guyon is giving aid to a babe soaked in the blood of his slaughtered parents when Braggadochio steals his horse (II.i.35–55).

[2] **traine:** trick.

[3] **despight:** open defiance—i.e., Guyon's challenge.

[4] According to the rules of chivalry, Braggadochio forfeits his claim when he refuses to fight.

[5] Although Braggadochio has lost his claim to the horse, Artegall seeks further evidence, just as he rejects the justice of combat conventions in i.25.

[6] **hedstall:** halter.

[7] A version of Orlando's horse, Brigliadoro, meaning, "bridle of gold" in Italian.

Whose voice so soone as he did undertake,[1]
Eftsoones[2] he stood as still as any stake,
And suffred all his secret marke to see:
And when as he him nam'd, for joy he brake
His bands, and follow'd him with gladfull glee,
And friskt, and flong aloft, and louted[3] low on knee.

35   Thereby Sir *Artegall* did plaine areed,[4]
     That unto him the horse belong'd, and sayd;
     "Lo there Sir *Guyon,* take to you the steed,
     As he with golden saddle is arayd;
     And let that losell,[5] plainely now displayd,
     Hence fare on foot, till he an horse have gayned."
     But the proud boaster gan his doome upbrayd,
     And him revil'd, and rated, and disdayned,
That judgement so unjust against him had ordayned.

36   Much was the knight incenst with his lewd word,
     To have revenged that his villeny;
     And thrise did lay his hand upon his sword,
     To have him slaine, or dearely doen aby.[6]
     But *Guyon* did his choler pacify,
     Saying, "Sir knight, it would dishonour bee
     To you, that are our judge of equity,
     To wreake your wrath on such a carle[7] as hee
It's punishment enough, that all his shame doe see."[8]

37   So did he mitigate Sir *Artegall,*
     But *Talus* by the backe the boaster hent,[9]
     And drawing him out of the open hall,
     Upon him did inflict this punishment.
     First he his beard did shave, and fowly shent:[10]

---

[1] **undertake:** hear.

[2] **Eftsoones:** immediately.

[3] **louted:** bowed.

[4] **areed:** judge.

[5] **losell:** scoundrel.

[6] **aby:** pay (a penalty).

[7] **carle:** churl.

[8] This is the only occasion in Book Five when Artegall has a personal interest in a judgment. He grows angry and seeks revenge, so that Guyon, the Knight of Temperance, must remind him to practice equity. On equity, see Introduction, 2.

[9] **hent:** seized.

[10] **shent:** disgraced, disfigured.

Then from him reft his shield, and it renverst,[1]
And blotted out his armes with falshood blent,
And himselfe baffuld, and his armes unherst,[2]
And broke his sword in twaine, and all his armour sperst.[3]

38   The whiles his guilefull groome was fled away:
        But vaine it was to thinke from him to flie.[4]
        Who overtaking him did disaray,
        And all his face deform'd with infamie,
        And out of court him scourged openly.
        So ought all faytours,[5] that true knighthood shame,
        And armes dishonour with base villanie,
        From all brave knights be banisht with defame:
For oft their lewdnes blotteth good deserts with blame.

39   Now when these counterfeits were thus uncased
        Out of the foreside[6] of their forgerie,
        And in the sight of all men cleane disgraced,
        All gan to jest and gibe full merilie
        At the remembrance of their knaverie.
        Ladies can[7] laugh at Ladies, Knights at Knights,
        To thinke with how great vaunt of braverie
        He them abused, through his subtill slights,
And what a glorious shew he made in all their sights.

40   There leave we them in pleasure and repast,
        Spending their joyous dayes and gladfull nights,
        And taking usurie of time forepast,[8]
        With all deare delices[9] and rare delights,
        Fit for such Ladies and such lovely knights:
        And turne we here to this faire furrowes end
        Our wearie yokes, to gather fresher sprights,[10]
        That when as time to *Artegall* shall tend,
We on his first adventure may him forward send.

---

[1] **renverst:** turned upside down.

[2] **baffuld:** dishonored—baffling was a ritu-
alistic way of shaming a knight; **unherst:**
disassembled.

[3] **sperst:** dispersed.

[4] Trompart escapes, but Braggadochio can-
not get away from Talus.

[5] **faytours:** imposters.

[6] **foreside:** façade, appearance.

[7] **can:** did.

[8] I.e., taking profit or reward from earlier
labors.

[9] **delices:** pleasures, delicacies.

[10] **sprights:** spirits.

Canto Four

Artegall dealeth right betwixt
two brethren that doe strive,
Saves Terpine from the gallow tree,
and doth from death reprive.

1   Who so upon him selfe will take the skill
      True Justice unto people to divide,[1]
      Had neede have mightie hands, for to fulfill
      That, which he doth with righteous doome decide,
      And for to maister wrong and puissant pride.
      For vaine it is to deeme of things aright,
      And makes wrong doers justice to deride,
      Unlesse it be perform'd with dreadlesse might.
  For powre is the right hand of Justice truely hight.

2   Therefore whylome to knights of great emprise[2]
      The charge of Justice given was in trust,
      That they might execute her judgements wise,
      And with their might beat downe licentious lust,
      Which proudly did impugne her sentence just.
      Whereof no braver president[3] this day
      Remaines on earth, preserv'd from yron rust
      Of rude oblivion, and long times decay,
  Then this of *Artegall*, which here we have to say.

3   Who having lately left that lovely payre,
      Enlincked fast in wedlockes loyall bond,
      Bold *Marinell* with *Florimell* the fayre,
      With whom great feast and goodly glee he fond,
      Departed from the Castle of the strond,
      To follow his adventures first intent,

---

[1] **divide:** dispense, sort out—but possibly with an underlying tone of violence.

[2] **emprise:** glory, prowess.

[3] **president:** precedent, example.

Which long agoe he taken had in hond:
Ne wight with him for his assistance went,
But that great yron groome, his gard and government.[1]

4   With whom as he did passe by the sea shore,
       He chaunst to come, whereas two comely Squires,
       Both brethren, whom one wombe together bore,
       But stirred up with different desires,
       Together strove, and kindled wrathfull fires:
       And them beside two seemely[2] damzels stood,
       By all meanes seeking to asswage their ires,
       Now with faire words; but words did little good,
Now with sharpe threats; but threats the more increast their mood.

5   And there before them stood a Coffer[3] strong,
       Fast bound on every side with iron bands,
       But seeming to have suffred mickle[4] wrong,
       Either by being wreckt uppon the sands,
       Or being carried farre from forraine lands.
       Seem'd that for it these Squires at ods did fall,
       And bent against them selves their cruell hands.
       But evermore, those Damzels did forestall
Their furious encounter, and their fiercenesse pall.[5]

6   But firmely fixt they were, with dint of sword,
       And battailes doubtfull proofe their rights to try,
       Ne other end their fury would afford,
       But what to them Fortune would justify.[6]
       So stood they both in readinesse: thereby
       To joyne the combate with cruell intent;
       When *Artegall* arriving happily,[7]
       Did stay a while their greedy bickerment,
Till he had questioned the cause of their dissent.

---

[1] **government:** means of governing or executing his justice. See viii.3.9.

[2] **seemely:** beautiful.

[3] **Coffer:** chest.

[4] **mickle:** much.

[5] **pall:** diminish.

[6] The brothers seek justice through ordeal by combat, which is called doubtful because it relies on Fortune or chance. Cf. i.25.

[7] **happily:** by good luck.

7　To whom the elder did this aunswere frame;
　　　"Then weete[1] ye Sir, that we two brethren be,
　　To whom our sire, *Milesio*[2] by name,
　　Did equally bequeath his lands in fee,[3]
　　Two Ilands, which ye there before you see
　　Not farre in sea; of which the one appeares
　　But like a little Mount of small degree;
　　　Yet was as great and wide ere many yeares,
As that same other Isle, that greater bredth now beares.[4]

8　"But tract of time, that all things doth decay,
　　　And this devouring Sea, that naught doth spare,
　　The most part of my land hath washt away,
　　And throwne it up unto my brothers share:
　　So his encreased, but mine did empaire.
　　Before which time I lov'd, as was my lot,
　　That further mayd, hight *Philtera*[5] the faire,
　　　With whom a goodly doure[6] I should have got,
And should have joyned bene to her in wedlocks knot.

9　"Then did my younger brother *Amidas*[7]
　　　Love that same other Damzell, *Lucy* bright,
　　To whom but little dowre allotted was;
　　Her vertue was the dowre, that did delight.
　　What better dowre can to a dame be hight?[8]
　　But now when *Philtra* saw my lands decay,
　　And former livelod[9] fayle, she left me quight,
　　　And to my brother did ellope streight way:
Who taking her from me, his owne love left astray.

10　"She seeing then her selfe forsaken so,
　　　Through dolorous despaire, which she conceyved,
　　Into the Sea her selfe did headlong throw,

[1] **weete:** know.

[2] Gough suggests a relation to Milesius of Irish legend. Milesius was a Scythian invader of Ireland, whose sons quarreled over the island.

[3] **in fee:** as a permanent inheritance.

[4] The brothers' two equal islands have become unequal through erosion. This judicial problem is called alluvion, in which the movement of water causes the formation of new land, setting off property disputes.

[5] Combining the Greek word for "love" with the Latin word for "land."

[6] **doure:** dowry.

[7] Combining Greek and Latin roots, suggests "fond of possessions."

[8] **hight:** promised.

[9] **livelod:** livelihood.

Thinking to have her griefe by death bereaved.
But see how much her purpose was deceaved.
Whilest thus amidst the billowes[1] beating of her
Twixt life and death, long to and fro she weaved,
She chaunst unwares to light uppon this coffer,
Which to her in that daunger hope of life did offer.

11   "The wretched mayd that earst[2] desir'd to die,
When as the paine of death she tasted had,
And but halfe seene his ugly visnomie,[3]
Gan to repent, that she had beene so mad,
For any death to chaunge life though most bad:
And catching hold of this Sea-beaten chest,
The lucky Pylot of her passage sad,
After long tossing in the seas distrest,
Her weary barke at last uppon mine Isle did rest.

12   "Where I by chaunce then wandring on the shore,
Did her espy, and through my good endevour
From dreadfull mouth of death, which threatned sore
Her to have swallow'd up, did helpe to save her.
She then in recompence of that great favour,
Which I on her bestowed, bestowed on me
The portion of that good, which Fortune gave her,
Together with her selfe in dowry free;
Both goodly portions, but of both the better she.[4]

13   "Yet in this coffer, which she with her brought,
Great threasure sithence[5] we did finde contained;
Which as our owne we tooke, and so it thought.
But this same other Damzell since hath fained,
That to her selfe that threasure appertained;
And that she did transport the same by sea,
To bring it to her husband new ordained,
But suffred cruell shipwracke by the way.
But whether it be so or no, I can not say.

---

[1] **billowes:** waves.

[2] **earst:** earlier.

[3] **visnomie:** physiognomy—face, appearance.

[4] This raises the judicial problem of salvage.

Under the laws of salvage, the older brother may claim the coffer as wreckage—and he seems justified in claiming Lucy by the same right.

[5] **sithence:** afterward.

14   "But whether it indeede be so or no,
     This doe I say, that what so good or ill
     Or God or Fortune unto me did throw,
     Not wronging any other by my will,
     I hold mine owne, and so will hold it still.
     And though my land he first did winne away,
     And then my love (though now it little skill,)[1]
     Yet my good lucke he shall not likewise pray;[2]
  But I will it defend, whilst ever that I may."

15   So having sayd, the younger did ensew;[3]
     "Full true it is, what so about our land
     My brother here declared hath to you:
     But not for it this ods twixt us doth stand,
     But for this threasure throwne uppon his strand;[4]
     Which well I prove, as shall appeare by triall,
     To be this maides, with whom I fastned hand,[5]
     Known by good markes, and perfect good espiall,[6]
  Therefore it ought be rendred her without deniall."

16   When they thus ended had, the Knight began;
     "Certes your strife were easie to accord,
     Would ye remit it to some righteous man."
     "Unto your selfe," said they, "we give our word,
     To bide what judgement ye shall us afford."
     "Then for assuraunce to my doome to stand,
     Under my foote let each lay downe his sword,
     And then you shall my sentence understand."
  So each of them layd downe his sword out of his hand.

17   Then *Artegall* thus to the younger sayd;
     "Now tell me *Amidas,* if that ye may,
     Your brothers land the which the sea hath layd
     Unto your part, and pluckt from his away,
     By what good right doe you withhold this day?"
     "What other right" (quoth he) "should you esteeme,

---

[1] **little skill:** little matters.

[2] **pray:** prey upon.

[3] **ensew:** follow.

[4] **strand:** beach.

[5] **fastned hand:** betrothed.

[6] **espiall:** observation.

But that the sea it to my share did lay?"
"Your right is good" (sayd he) "and so I deeme,
That what the sea unto you sent, your own should seeme."

18   Then turning to the elder thus he sayd;
      "Now *Bracidas*[1] let this likewise be showne.
      Your brothers threasure, which from him is strayd,
      Being the dowry of his wife well knowne,
      By what right doe you claime to be your owne?"
      "What other right" (quoth he) "should you esteeme,
      But that the sea hath it unto me throwne?"
      "Your right is good" (sayd he) "and so I deeme,
That what the sea unto you sent, your own should seeme.

19   "For equall right in equall things doth stand,
      For what the mighty Sea hath once possest,
      And plucked quite from all possessors hand,
      Whether by rage of waves, that never rest,
      Or else by wracke, that wretches hath distrest,
      He may dispose by his imperiall might,
      As thing at randon left, to whom he list.
      So *Amidas*, the land was yours first hight,
And so the threasure yours is *Bracidas* by right."

20   When he his sentence thus pronounced had,
      Both *Amidas* and *Philtra* were displeased:
      But *Bracidas* and *Lucy* were right glad,
      And on the threasure by that judgement seased.[2]
      So was their discord by this doome appeased,
      And each one had his right. Then *Artegall*
      When as their sharpe contention he had ceased,
        Departed on his way, as did befall,
To follow his old quest, the which him forth did call.

21   So as he travelled uppon the way,
      He chaunst to come, where happily[3] he spide
      A rout of many people farre away;

---

[1] The Greek roots mean "few possessions,"
as Hamilton suggests, or "possessions thrown
up" (from the sea). See *Variorum*, 195.

[2] **seased:** siezed.

[3] **happily:** by chance.

To whom his course he hastily applide,
To weete[1] the cause of their assemblaunce wide.
To whom when he approched neare in sight,
(An uncouth sight) he plainely then descride
To be a troupe of women warlike dight,[2]
With weapons in their hands, as ready for to fight.

22   And in the midst of them he saw a Knight,
      With both his hands behinde him pinnoed[3] hard,
      And round about his necke an halter tight,
      As ready for the gallow tree prepard:
      His face was covered, and his head was bar'd,
      That who he was, uneath[4] was to descry;
      And with full heavy heart with them he far'd,
      Griev'd to the soule, and groning inwardly,
That he of womens hands so base a death should dy.

23   But they like tyrants, mercilesse the more,
      Rejoyced at his miserable case,
      And him reviled, and reproched sore
      With bitter taunts, and termes of vile disgrace.
      Now when as *Artegall* arriv'd in place,
      Did aske, what cause brought that man to decay,
      They round about him gan to swarme apace,
      Meaning on him their cruell hands to lay,
And to have wrought unwares some villanous assay.[5]

24   But he was soone aware of their ill minde,
      And drawing backe deceived their intent;
      Yet though him selfe did shame on womankinde
      His mighty hand to shend,[6] he *Talus* sent
      To wrecke on them their follies hardyment:
      Who with few sowces[7] of his yron flale,

---

[1] **weete:** know.

[2] **dight:** dressed.

[3] **pinnoed:** pinned, pinioned.

[4] **uneath:** difficult.

[5] **assay:** attempt.

[6] **to shend:** to punish, injure—i.e., Artegall was ashamed to attack women with his own hand. However, the chivalric conviction later falls away (iv.41ff.).

[7] **sowces:** blows.

Dispersed all their troupe incontinent,[1]
And sent them home to tell a piteous tale,
Of their vaine prowesse, turned to their proper bale.[2]

25   But that same wretched man, ordaynd to die,
         They left behind them, glad to be so quit:
         Him *Talus* tooke out of perplexitie,
         And horrour of fowle death for Knight unfit,
         Who more then losse of life ydreaded it;[3]
         And him restoring unto living light,[4]
         So brought unto his Lord, where he did sit,
         Beholding all that womanish weake fight;
Whom soone as he beheld, he knew, and thus behight.[5]

26   "Sir *Turpine*,[6] haplesse man, what make you here?
         Or have you lost your selfe, and your discretion,
         That ever in this wretched case ye were?
         Or have ye yeelded you to proude oppression
         Of womens powre, that boast of mens subjection?
         Or else what other deadly dismall day
         Is falne on you, by heavens hard direction,
         That ye were runne so fondly far astray,
As for to lead your selfe unto your owne decay?"

27   Much was the man confounded in his mind,
         Partly with shame, and partly with dismay,
         That all astonisht he him selfe did find,
         And little had for his excuse to say,
         But onely thus; "Most haplesse well ye may
         Me justly terme, that to this shame am brought,
         And made the scorne of Knighthod this same day.
         But who can scape, what his owne fate hath wrought?
The worke of heavens will surpasseth humaine thought."[7]

---

[1] **incontinent:** immediately.

[2] **proper bale:** own suffering.

[3] Hanging was used with criminals, and so was especially disgraceful to knights.

[4] See Ps. 56.13.

[5] **behight:** addressed.

[6] Suggests the Latin word for "shameful."

[7] I.e., heaven's will surpasses human thought.

28   "Right true: but faulty[1] men use oftentimes
        To attribute their folly unto fate,
        And lay on heaven the guilt of their owne crimes.[2]
        But tell, Sir *Terpin*, ne let you amate[3]
        Your misery, how fell ye in this state."
        "Then sith ye needs" (quoth he) "will know my shame,
        And all the ill, which chaunst to me of late,
        I shortly will to you rehearse the same,
    In hope ye will not turne misfortune to my blame.

29   "Being desirous (as all Knights are woont)
        Through hard adventures deedes of armes to try,
        And after fame and honour for to hunt,
        I heard report that farre abrode did fly,
        That a proud Amazon did late defy
        All the brave Knights, that hold of Maidenhead,[4]
        And unto them wrought all the villany,
        That she could forge in her malicious head,
    Which some hath put to shame, and many done be dead.[5]

30   "The cause, they say, of this her cruell hate,
        Is for the sake of *Bellodant*[6] the bold,
        To whom she bore most fervent love of late,
        And wooed him by all the waies she could:
        But when she saw at last, that he ne would
        For ought or nought be wonne unto her will,
        She turn'd her love to hatred manifold,
        And for his sake vow'd to doe all the ill
    Which she could doe to Knights, which now she doth fulfill.

31   "For all those Knights, the which by force or guile
        She doth subdue, she fowly doth entreate.[7]
        First she doth them of warlike armes despoile,

---

[1] **faulty:** guilty.

[2] But Artegall will later do exactly this (xi.41). Also see *A View*, 11–12.

[3] **amate:** dismay—i.e., do not let your misery dismay you.

[4] I.e., that maintain allegiance to the Order of Maidenhead, the order of knights who serve Gloriana. See I.vii.46.

[5] I.e., put to death. Amazons appear throughout classical and medieval literature. Spenser borrows chiefly from Diodorus Siculus (*Bibliotheca Historica*, 2.4–6, 3.52–55) and from Ariosto's Amazon queen Orontea (*Orlando*, 20).

[6] Suggesting in Latin "one given to war."

[7] **entreate:** treat.

And cloth in womens weedes:[1] And then with threat
Doth them compell to worke, to earne their meat,
To spin, to card, to sew, to wash, to wring;
Ne doth she give them other thing to eat,
But bread and water, or like feeble thing,
Them to disable from revenge adventuring.[2]

32   "But if through stout disdaine of manly mind,
Any her proud observaunce[3] will withstand,
Uppon that gibbet,[4] which is there behind,
She causeth them be hang'd up out of hand;
In which condition I right now did stand.
For being overcome by her in fight,
And put to that base service of her band,[5]
I rather chose to die in lives despight,
Then lead that shamefull life, unworthy of a Knight."

33   "How hight that Amazon?" (sayd Artegall)
"And where, and how far hence does she abide?"
"Her name" (quoth he) "they *Radigund*[6] doe call,
A Princesse of great powre, and greater pride,
And Queene of Amazons, in armes well tride,
And sundry battels, which she hath atchieved
With great success, that her hath glorifide,
And made her famous, more then is believed;
Ne would I it have ween'd, had I not late it prieved."[7]

34   "Now sure" (said he) "and by the faith that I
To Maydenhead and noble knighthood owe,
I will not rest, till I her might doe trie,
And venge the shame, that she to Knights doth show.
Therefore Sir *Terpin* from you lightly throw

---

[1] **weedes:** clothes.
[2] Artegall's cross-dressing and spinning is a shame traditionally inflicted by Amazons. It also recalls Hercules under the influence of Omphale. See Ovid, *Fasti*, 2.305–58.
[3] **observaunce:** rule.
[4] **gibbet:** gallows.

[5] **band:** bond.
[6] May recall the Greek words for "reckless" and "woman," or the Latin word meaning "to offend." There is a St. Radigund, famous for preserving her chastity by refusing to marry a prince. See SE, "Radigund."
[7] **prieved:** proved.

This squalid weede,[1] the patterne of dispaire,
And wend with me, that ye may see and know,
How Fortune will your ruin'd name repaire,
And knights of Maidenhead, whose praise she would empaire."

35   With that, like one that hopelesse was repry'vd[2]
      From deathes dore, at which he lately lay,
      Those yron fetters, wherewith he was gyv'd,[3]
      The badges of reproch, he threw away,
      And nimbly did him dight[4] to guide the way
      Unto the dwelling of that Amazone.
      Which was from thence not past a mile or tway:
      A goodly citty and a mighty one,
The which of her owne name she called *Radegone*.[5]

36   Where they arriving, by the watchmen were
      Descried streight, who all the citty warned,
      How that three warlike persons did appeare,
      Of which the one him seem'd a Knight all armed,
      And th'other two well likely to have harmed.
      Eftsoones the people all to harnesse[6] ran,
      And like a sort of Bees in clusters swarmed:
      Ere long their Queene her selfe, halfe like a man[7]
Came forth into the rout,[8] and them t'array began.

37   And now the Knights being arrived neare,
      Did beat uppon the gates to enter in,
      And at the Porter, skorning them so few,
      Threw many threats, if they the towne did win,
      To teare his flesh in peeces for his sin.
      Which when as *Radigund* there comming heard,
      Her heart for rage did grate, and teeth did grin:[9]
      She bad that streight the gates should be unbard,
And to them way to make, with weapons well prepard.

---

[1] I.e., the noose and fetters Terpin is wearing.

[2] **repry'vd:** reprieved.

[3] **gyv'd:** shackled.

[4] **dight:** prepare.

[5] The "goodly city" is sometimes read as an image of Elizabeth's London. Spenser may be echoing Christine de Pisan's writings on the Amazon Penthesilea. See SE, "Christine de Pisan."

[6] **harnesse:** arms.

[7] The 1609 edition has "arm'd like a man."

[8] **rout:** crowd.

[9] **grin:** bare, grind.

38   Soone as the gates were open to them set,
          They pressed forward, entraunce to have made.
          But in the middle way they were ymet
          With a sharpe showre of arrowes, which them staid,
          And better bad advise, ere they assaid[1]
          Unknowen perill of bold womens pride.
          Then all that rout uppon them rudely laid,
          And heaped strokes so fast on every side,
      And arrowes haild so thicke, that they could not abide.

39   But *Radigund* her selfe, when she espide
          Sir *Terpin,* from her direfull doome acquit,
          So cruell doale amongst her maides divide,[2]
          T'avenge that shame, they did on him commit,
          All sodainely enflam'd with furious fit,
          Like a fell Lionesse at him she flew,
          And on his head-peece him so fiercely smit,
          That to the ground him quite she overthrew,
      Dismayd so with the stroke, that he no colours knew.

40   Soone as she saw him on the ground to grovell,
          She lightly to him leapt, and in his necke
          Her proud foote setting, at his head did levell,[3]
          Weening at once her wrath on him to wreake,
          And his contempt, that did her judg'ment breake.
          As when a Beare hath seiz'd her cruell clawes
          Uppon the carkasse of some beast too weake,
          Proudly stands over, and a while doth pause,
      To heare the piteous beast pleading her plaintiffe[4] cause.

41   Whom when as *Artegall* in that distresse
          By chaunce beheld, he left the bloudy slaughter,
          In which he swam, and ranne to his redresse.[5]
          There her assayling fiercely fresh, he raught her
          Such an huge stroke, that it of sence distraught[6] her:

---

[1] **bad:** bade; **assaid:** tested.

[2] **doale:** punishment, blows, grief; **divide:** distribute—picking up on the primary meaning of "dole" as a portion or a division of a whole.

[3] **levell:** aim a blow.

[4] **plaintiffe:** plaintive and plaintiff in the judicial sense.

[5] **redresse:** relief.

[6] **distraught:** deranged.

And had she not it warded warily,
It had depriv'd her mother of a daughter.
Nathlesse for all the powre she did apply,
It made her stagger oft, and stare with ghastly eye.[1]

42   Like to an Eagle in his kingly pride,
        Soring through his wide Empire of the aire,
        To weather his brode sailes,[2] by chaunce hath spide
        A Goshauke,[3] which hath seized for her share
        Uppon some fowle, that should her feast prepare;
        With dreadfull force he flies at her bylive,[4]
        That with his souce,[5] which none enduren dare,
        Her from the quarrey he away doth drive,
    And from her griping pounce[6] the greedy prey doth rive.

43   But soone as she her sence recover'd had,
        She fiercely towards him her selfe gan dight,[7]
        Through vengeful wrath and sdeignfull[8] pride half mad:
        For never had she suffred such despight.
        But ere she could joyne hand with him to fight,
        Her warlike maides about her flockt so fast,
        That they disparted them, maugre[9] their might,
        And with their troupes did far a sunder cast:
    But mongst the rest the fight did untill evening last.

44   And every while that mighty yron man,
        With his strange weapon, never wont in warre,
        Them sorely vext, and courst,[10] and overran,
        And broke their bowes, and did their shooting marre,
        That none of all the many once did darre
        Him to assault, nor once approach him nie,
        But like a sort[11] of sheepe dispersed farre
        For dread of their devouring enemie,
    Through all the fields and vallies did before him flie.

---

[1] The four feminine rhymes in this stanza (lines 2, 4, 5, and 7) add an element of comedy to this scene of female power and violence, as Quilligan suggests (1987, 168).

[2] **weather:** air out; **sailes:** wings.

[3] **Goshauke:** a large, short-winged hawk.

[4] **bylive:** suddenly.

[5] **souce:** swoop.

[6] **pounce:** talons.

[7] **dight:** direct.

[8] **sdeignfull:** disdainful.

[9] **disparted:** separated; **maugre:** despite.

[10] **courst:** thrashed, hunted.

[11] **sort:** flock.

45   But when as daies faire shinie-beame, yclowded
          With fearefull shadowes of deformed night,
          Warn'd man and beast in quiet rest be shrowded,
          Bold *Radigund* with sound of trumpe on hight,
          Causd all her people to surcease from fight,
          And gathering them unto her citties gate,
          Made them all enter in before her sight,
          And all the wounded, and the weake in state,[1]
      To be convayed in, ere she would once retrate.

46   When thus the field was voided all away,
          And all things quieted, the Elfin Knight
          Weary of toile and travell[2] of that day,
          Causd his pavilion to be richly pight
          Before the city gate, in open sight;
          Where he him selfe did rest in safety,
          Together with sir *Terpin* all that night:
          But *Talus* usde in times of jeopardy
      To keepe a nightly watch, for dread of treachery.

47   But *Radigund* full of heart-gnawing griefe,
          For the rebuke,[3] which she sustain'd that day,
          Could take no rest, ne would receive reliefe,
          But tossed in her troublous minde, what way
          She mote revenge that blot, which on her lay.
          There she resolv'd her selfe in single fight
          To try her Fortune, and his[4] force assay,
          Rather then see her people spoiled quight,
      As she had seene that day a disaventerous[5] sight.

48   She called forth to her a trusty mayd,
          Whom she thought fittest for that businesse,
          Her name was *Clarin*,[6] and thus to her sayd;
          "Goe damzell quickly, doe thy selfe addresse,
          To doe[7] the message, which I shall expresse.

---

[1] **state:** condition.

[2] **travell:** travail.

[3] **rebuke:** disgrace.

[4] I.e., Artegall's.

[5] **disaventerous:** disastrous.

[6] Short for Clarinda, suggesting in Latin "making known" and "loud." In Tasso's *Gersusalemme Liberata*, there is an Amazon named Clorinda (1.47).

[7] **doe:** deliver.

Goe thou unto that stranger Faery Knight,
Who yeester day drove us to such distresse,
Tell, that to morrow I with him wil fight,
And try in equall field, whether[1] hath greater might.

49 "But these conditions doe to him propound,
That if I vanquishe him, he shall obay
My law, and ever to my lore be bound,
And so will I, if me he vanquish may;
What ever he shall like to doe or say.[2]
Goe streight, and take with thee, to witnesse it,
Sixe of thy fellowes of the best array,
And beare with you both wine and juncates[3] fit,
And bid him eate, henceforth he oft shall hungry sit."

50 The Damzell streight obayd, and putting all
In readinesse, forth to the Towne-gate went,
Where sounding loud a Trumpet from the wall,
Unto those warlike Knights she warning sent.
Then *Talus* forth issuing from the tent,
Unto the wall his way did fearelesse take,
To weeten what that trumpets sounding ment:
Where that same Damzell lowdly him bespake,
And shew'd, that with his Lord she would emparlaunce[4] make.

51 So he them streight conducted to his Lord,
Who, as he could,[5] them goodly well did greete,
Till they had told their message word by word:
Which he accepting well, as he could weete,[6]
Them fairely entertaynd with curt'sies meete,
And gave them gifts and things of deare delight.
So backe againe they homeward turnd their feete.
But *Artegall* him selfe to rest did dight,[7]
That he mote fresher be against the next daies fight.

---

[1] **whether:** which of us.

[2] According to Hamilton, this is a "heads-I-win, tails-you-lose" proposition. Futhermore, if Artegall becomes bound to Radigund's "lore," he will be forsaking the "righteous lore" taught by Astraea (i.4.9).

[3] **juncates:** delicacies.

[4] **emparlaunce:** parley.

[5] I.e., as best he could.

[6] I.e., as well as he knew how.

[7] **dight:** prepare.

Canto Five

Artegall fights with Radigund
And is subdewd by guile:
He is by her emprisoned,
But wrought[1] by Clarins wile.

1   So soone as day forth dawning from the East,
      Nights humid curtaine from the heavens withdrew,
      And earely calling forth both man and beast,
      Comaunded them their daily workes renew,
      These noble warriors, mindefull to pursew
      The last daies purpose[2] of their vowed fight,
      Them selves thereto preparde in order dew;
      The Knight, as best was seeming for a Knight,
And th'Amazon, as best it likt her selfe to dight.[3]

2   All in a Camis[4] light of purple silke
      Woven uppon with silver, subtly wrought,
      And quilted uppon sattin white as milke,
      Trayled with ribbands diversly distraught[5]
      Like as the workeman had their courses taught;
      Which was short tucked for light motion
      Up to her ham, but when she list, it raught[6]
      Downe to her lowest heele, and thereuppon
She wore for her defence a mayled habergeon.[7]

3   And on her legs she painted buskins[8] wore,
      Basted[9] with bends of gold on every side,
      And mailes betweene, and laced close afore:

---

[1] **wrought:** worked over.

[2] **purpose:** resolution.

[3] **dight:** equip.

[4] **Camis:** a loose dress. The purple silk recalls Dido (Virgil, *Aeneid,* 4.139), as Hamilton points out.

[5] **distraught:** drawn in different directions.

[6] **raught:** reached.

[7] **habergeon:** armored coat.

[8] **buskins:** boots.

[9] **Basted:** stitched.

Uppon her thigh her Cemitare[1] was tide,
With an embrodered belt of mickell pride;
And on her shoulder hung her shield, bedeckt
Uppon the bosse with stones, that shined wide,
As the faire Moone in her most full aspect,
That to the Moone it mote be like in each respect.[2]

4   So forth she came out of the citty gate,
    With stately port and proud magnificence,
    Guarded with many damzels, that did waite
    Uppon her person for her sure defence,
    Playing on shaumes[3] and trumpets, that from hence
    Their sound did reach unto the heavens hight.
    So forth into the field she marched thence,
    Where was a rich Pavilion ready pight,
Her to receive, till time they should begin the fight.

5   Then forth came *Artegall* out of his tent,
    All arm'd to point, and first the Lists[4] did enter:
    Soone after eke[5] came she, with fell intent,
    And countenaunce fierce, as having fully bent her,
    That battels utmost triall to adventer.[6]
    The Lists were closed fast, to barre the rout
    From rudely pressing to the middle center;
    Which in great heapes them circled all about,
Wayting, how Fortune would resolve that daungerous dout.

6   The Trumpets sounded, and the field[7] began;
    With bitter strokes it both began, and ended.
    She at the first encounter on him ran
    With furious rage, as if she had intended
    Out of his breast the very heart have rended:
    But he that had like tempests often tride,[8]

---

[1] **Cemitare:** scimitar.

[2] Recalls the Amazon shields in Virgil (*Aeneid*, 1.490). This line may inspire Milton's depiction of Satan's shield (*Paradise Lost*, 1.286–91).

[3] **shaumes:** instruments similar to oboes.

[4] **to point:** completely; **Lists:** barriers enclosing the space for tilting.

[5] **eke:** and.

[6] **adventer:** venture.

[7] **field:** battle.

[8] **tride:** weathered.

From that first flaw[1] him selfe right well defended.
The more she rag'd, the more he did abide;
She hewd, she foynd, she lasht, she laid on every side.

7   Yet still her blowes he bore, and her forbore,[2]
        Weening[3] at last to win advantage new;
        Yet still her crueltie increased more,
        And though powre faild, her courage did accrew,
        Which[4] fayling he gan fiercely her pursew.
        Like as a Smith that to his cunning feat[5]
        The stubborne mettall seeketh to subdew,
        Soone as he feeles it mollifide[6] with heat,
    With his great yron sledge doth strongly on it beat.

8   So did Sir *Artegall* upon her lay,
        As if she had an yron andvile beene,
        That flakes of fire, bright as the sunny ray,
        Out of her steely armes were flashing seene,
        That all on fire ye would her surely weene.
        But with her shield so well her selfe she warded,
        From the dread daunger of his weapon keene,
        That all that while her life she safely garded:
    But he that helpe from her against her will discarded.

9   For with his trenchant[7] blade at the next blow
        Halfe of her shield he shared quite away,
        That halfe her side it selfe did naked show,
        And thenceforth unto daunger opened way.
        Much was she moved with the mightie sway
        Of that sad stroke, that halfe enrag'd she grew,
        And like a greedie Beare unto her pray,
        With her sharpe Cemitare at him she flew,
    That glauncing down his thigh,[8] the purple bloud forth drew.

---

[1] **flaw:** squall.

[2] **forbore:** spared.

[3] **weening:** expecting.

[4] I.e., her power.

[5] **feat:** art.

[6] **mollifide:** softened.

[7] **trenchant:** cutting.

[8] In romance, sometimes standing for a nearby part.

10   Thereat she gan to triumph with great boast,
      And to upbrayd[1] that chaunce, which him misfell,
      As if the prize she gotten had almost,
      With spightfull speaches, fitting with her well;
      That his great hart gan inwardly to swell
      With indignation, at her vaunting vaine,
      And at her strooke with puissance feareful fell;
      Yet with her shield she warded it againe,
That[2] shattered all to peeces round about the plaine.

11   Having her thus disarmed of her shield,
      Upon her helmet he againe her strooke,
      That downe she fell upon the grassie field,
      In sencelesse swoune, as if her life forsooke,
      And pangs of death her spirit overtooke.
      Whom when he saw before his foote prostrated,
      He to her lept with deadly dreadfull looke,
      And her sunshynie helmet soone unlaced,
Thinking at once both head and helmet to have raced.[3]

12   But when as he discovered had her face,
      He saw his senses straunge astonishment,
      A miracle of natures goodly grace,
      In her faire visage voide of ornament,
      But bath'd in bloud and sweat together ment;[4]
      Which in the rudenesse of that evill plight,
      Bewrayd[5] the signes of feature excellent:
      Like as the Moone in foggie winters night,
Doth seeme to be her selfe, though darkned be her light.

13   At sight thereof his cruell minded hart
      Empierced was with pittifull regard,
      That his sharpe sword he threw from him apart,
      Cursing his hand that had that visage mard:
      No hand so cruell, nor no hart so hard,
      But ruth of beautie will it mollifie.[6]

---

[1] **upbrayd:** talk up.

[2] I.e., her shield.

[3] **raced:** cut off, destroyed.

[4] **ment:** mingled.

[5] **Bewrayd:** revealed.

[6] In a similar manner, Artegall quits fighting when Britomart's face is revealed (IV.vi. 18–23). Achilles is similarly overwhelmed by the Amazon Penthesilea (Propertius, *Elegies*, 3.11.13–16). Also see Tasso, *Gerusalemme Liberata*, 3.21–28.

By this upstarting from her swoune, she star'd
A while about her with confused eye;
Like one that from his dreame is waked suddenlye.

14 Soone as the knight she there by her did spy,
        Standing with emptie hands all weaponlesse,
        With fresh assault upon him she did fly,
        And gan renew her former cruelnesse:
        And though he still retyr'd,[1] yet nathelesse
        With huge redoubled strokes she on him layd;
        And more increast her outrage mercilesse,
        The more that he with meeke intreatie prayd,
Her wrathful hand from greedy vengeance to have stayd.

15 Like as a Puttocke[2] having spyde in sight
        A gentle Faulcon sitting on an hill,
        Whose other wing, now made unmeete for flight,
        Was lately broken by some fortune ill;
        The foolish Kyte, led with licentious will,
        Doth beat upon the gentle bird in vaine,
        With many idle stoups[3] her troubling still:
        Even so did *Radigund* with bootlesse paine
Annoy this noble Knight, and sorely him constraine.

16 Nought could he do, but shun the dred despight
        Of her fierce wrath, and backward still retyre,
        And with his single shield,[4] well as he might,
        Beare off the burden of her raging yre;
        And evermore he gently did desyre,
        To stay her stroks, and he himselfe would yield:
        Yet nould she hearke, ne let him once respyre,[5]
        Till he to her delivered had his shield,
And to her mercie him submitted in plaine field.

17 So was he overcome, not overcome,
        But to her yeelded of his owne accord;
        Yet was he justly damned by the doome

---

[1] **retyr'd:** fell back.

[2] **Puttocke:** a bird of prey such as a kite. Often associated with ignobleness.

[3] **stoups:** swoops.

[4] **single shield:** shield alone.

[5] **nould:** would not; **respyre:** breathe.

Of his owne mouth, that spake so warelesse[1] word,
To be her thrall, and service[2] her afford.
For though that he first victorie obtayned,
Yet after by abandoning his sword,
He wilfull[3] lost, that he before attayned.
No fayrer[4] conquest, then that with goodwill is gayned.

18 Tho[5] with her sword on him she flatling strooke,
    In signe of true subjection to her powre,[6]
    And as her vassall him to thraldome tooke.
    But *Terpine* borne to'a more unhappy howre,
    As he, on whom the lucklesse starres did lowre,
    She causd to be attacht,[7] and forthwith led
    Unto the crooke t'abide the balefull stowre,[8]
    From which he lately had through reskew fled:
Where he full shamefully was hanged by the hed.

19 But when they thought on *Talus* hands to lay,
    He with his yron flaile amongst them thondred,
    That they were fayne[9] to let him scape away,
    Glad from his companie to be so sondred;
    Whose presence all their troups so much encombred
    That th'heapes of those, which he did wound and slay,
    Besides the rest dismayd, might not be nombred:
    Yet all that while he would not once assay,[10]
To reskew his owne Lord, but thought it just t'obay.[11]

20 Then tooke the Amazon this noble knight,
    Left to her will by his owne wilfull blame,
    And caused him to be disarmed quight,
    Of all the ornaments[12] of knightly name,
    With which whylome he gotten had great fame:

[1] **warelesse:** unwary.

[2] Includes sexual favors, according to Hamilton.

[3] **wilfull:** voluntarily. Also full of will, in the sense of sexual desire.

[4] "Fair" can signify pure and complete. But it may ironically be read as beautiful or just.

[5] **Tho:** then.

[6] Touching him with the flat of her sword, Radigund dubs Artegall as her vassal.

[7] **attacht:** arrested.

[8] **crooke:** gallows; **stowre:** painful struggle, storm.

[9] **fayne:** inclined.

[10] **assay:** attempt.

[11] Talus recognizes Artegall's vow (iv.49).

[12] **ornaments:** gear, equipment.

In stead whereof she made him to be dight[1]
In womans weedes, that is to manhood shame,
And put before his lap a napron[2] white,
In stead of Curiets and bases[3] fit for fight.

21   So being clad, she brought him from the field,
        In which he had bene trayned many a day,
        Into a long large chamber, which was sield[4]
        With moniments of many knights decay,
        By her subdewed in victorious fray:
        Amongst the which she causd his warlike armes
        Be hang'd on high, that mote his shame bewray;[5]
        And broke his sword, for feare of further harmes,
With which he wont to stirre up battailous alarmes.[6]

22   There entred in, he round about him saw
        Many brave knights, whose names right well he knew,
        There bound t'obay that Amazons proud law,
        Spinning and carding all in comely rew,[7]
        That his bigge hart loth'd so uncomely vew.
        But they were forst through penurie and pyne,[8]
        To doe those workes, to them appointed dew:
        For nought was given them to sup or dyne,
But what their hands could earne by twisting linnen twyne.

23   Amongst them all she placed him most low,
        And in his hand a distaffe to him gave,
        That he thereon should spin both flax and tow;[9]
        A sordid office for a mind so brave.
        So hard it is to be a womans slave.
        Yet he it tooke in his owne selfes despight,
        And thereto did himselfe right well behave,
        Her to obay, sith he his faith had plight,[10]
Her vassall to become, if she him wonne in fight.

---

[1] **dight:** dressed.

[2] **napron:** apron.

[3] **Curiets and bases:** body armor and mail.

[4] **sield:** lined.

[5] **bewray:** reveal.

[6] The breaking of Artegall's sword Chrysaor recalls Braggadocchio's (iii.37).

[7] **rew:** row.

[8] **penurie and pyne:** lack of food and pining or suffering.

[9] **tow:** the fibers of the flax.

[10] **plight:** pledged.

24   Who had him seene, imagine mote thereby,
        That whylome hath of *Hercules* bene told,
        How for *Iolas* sake he did apply
        His mightie hands, the distaffe vile to hold,
        For his huge club, which had subdew'd of old
        So many monsters, which the world annoyed;
        His Lyons skin chaungd to a pall[1] of gold,
        In which forgetting warres, he onely joyed
In combats of sweet love, and with his mistresse toyed.[2]

25   Such is the crueltie of womenkynd,
        When they have shaken off the shamefast band,
        With which wise Nature did them strongly bynd,
        T'obay the heasts[3] of mans well ruling hand,
        That then all rule and reason they withstand,
        To purchase a licentious libertie.
        But vertuous women wisely understand,
        That they were borne to base humilitie,
Unlesse the heavens them lift to lawfull soveraintie.[4]

26   Thus there long while continu'd *Artegall,*
        Serving proud *Radigund* with true subjection;
        How ever it his noble heart did gall,
        T'obay a womans tyrannous direction,
        That might have had of life or death election:[5]
        But having chosen, now he might not chaunge.
        During which time, the warlike Amazon,
        Whose wandring fancie after lust did raunge,
Gan cast a secret liking to this captive straunge.

27   Which long concealing in her covert brest,
        She chaw'd the cud of lovers carefull plight;[6]
        Yet could it not so thoroughly digest,
        Being fast fixed in her wounded spright,[7]

---

[1] **pall:** robe.

[2] Hercules was enslaved and forced to spin with a distaff by Omphale, here conflated or confused with his last lover, Iole. See Ovid, *Heroides*, 9.59–118. Hercules spinning was a common Renaissance emblem for the emasculating power of female sexuality and licentious male desire. See Aptekar, 171–200.

[3] **heasts:** commands, behests.

[4] Spenser makes an exception in the alexandrine for Elizabeth.

[5] I.e., Artegall might have chosen to die instead, as did Terpine (iv.32).

[6] This image returns in vi.19.

[7] **spright:** spirit.

But it tormented her both day and night:
Yet would she not thereto yeeld free accord,
To serve the lowly vassall of her might,
And of her servant make her soverayne Lord:
So great her pride, that she such basenesse much abhord.

28   So much the greater still her anguish grew,
      Through stubborne handling of her love-sicke hart;
      And still the more she strove it to subdew,
      The more she still augmented her owne smart,
      And wyder made the wound of th'hidden dart.
      At last when long she struggled had in vaine,
      She gan to stoupe,[1] and her proud mind convert
      To meeke obeysance[2] of loves mightie raine,
And him entreat for grace, that had procur'd her paine.

29   Unto her selfe in secret she did call
      Her nearest handmayd, whom she most did trust,
      And to her said; "*Clarinda* whom of all
      I trust a live, sith I thee fostred[3] first;
      Now is the time, that I untimely must
      Thereof make tryall,[4] in my greatest need:
      It is so hapned, that the heavens unjust,
      Spighting my happie freedome, have agreed,
To thrall my looser life, or my last bale[5] to breed."

30   With that she turn'd her head, as halfe abashed,
      To hide the blush which in her visage rose,
      And through her eyes like sudden lightning flashed,
      Decking her cheeke with a vermilion rose:
      But soone she did her countenance compose,
      And to her turning, thus began againe;
      "This griefes deepe wound I would to thee disclose,
      Thereto compelled through hart-murdring paine,
But dread of shame my doubtfull lips doth still restraine."

---

[1] **stoupe:** bow, submit.

[2] **obeysance:** obedience.

[3] **fostred:** brought up.

[4] I.e., make trial of that trust.

[5] **thrall:** enslave; **bale:** torment, death.

31   "Ah my deare dread"[1] (said then the faithfull Mayd)
      "Can dread of ought your dreadlesse hart withhold,
      That many hath with dread of death dismayd,
      And dare even deathes most dreadfull face behold?
      Say on my soverayne Ladie, and be bold;
      Doth not your handmayds life at your foot lie?"
      Therewith much comforted, she gan unfold
      The cause of her conceived maladie,
  As one that would confesse, yet faine[2] would it denie.

32   *"Clarin"* (sayd she) "thou seest yond Fayry Knight,
      Whom not my valour, but his owne brave mind
      Subjected hath to my unequall[3] might;
      What right is it, that he should thraldome find,
      For lending life to me a wretch unkind;
      That for such good him recompence with ill?
      Therefore I cast,[4] how I may him unbind,
      And by his freedome get his free goodwill;
  Yet so, as bound to me he may continue still.

33   "Bound unto me, but not with such hard bands
      Of strong compulsion, and streight violence,
      As now in miserable state he stands;
      But with sweet love and sure benevolence,
      Voide of malitious mind, or foule offence.
      To which if thou canst win him any way,
      Without discoverie of my thoughts pretence,[5]
      Both goodly meede[6] of him it purchase may,
  And eke with gratefull service me right well apay.

34   "Which that thou mayst the better bring to pas,
      Loe here this ring, which shall thy warrant bee,
      And token true to old *Eumenias,*[7]
      From time to time, when thou it best shalt see,
      That in and out thou mayst have passage free.
      Goe now, *Clarinda,* well thy wits advise,

---

[1] Clarinda puns on the many uses of dread, meaning extreme fear. Here it is an address to one held in reverence.

[2] **faine:** rather.

[3] **unequall:** unjust.

[4] **cast:** consider.

[5] **pretence:** purpose.

[6] **meede:** reward.

[7] Artegall's jailor, meaning "goodwill" in Greek.

And all thy forces gather unto thee;
Armies of lovely lookes, and speeches wise,
With which thou canst even *Jove* himselfe to love entise."

35   The trustie Mayd, conceiving her intent,
    Did with sure promise of her good indevour,
    Give her great comfort, and some harts content.
    So from her parting, she thenceforth did labour
    By all the meanes she might, to curry favour
    With th'Elfin Knight, her Ladies best beloved;
    With daily shew of courteous kind behaviour,
    Even at the markewhite of his hart she roved,[1]
And with wide glauncing words, one day she thus him proved.[2]

36   "Unhappie Knight, upon whose hopelesse state
    Fortune envying good, hath felly[3] frowned,
    And cruell heavens have heapt an heavy fate;
    I rew that thus thy better dayes are drowned
    In sad despaire, and all thy senses swowned
    In stupid sorow, sith thy juster merit
    Might else have with felicitie bene crowned:
    Looke up at last, and wake thy dulled spirit,
To thinke how this long death thou mightest disinherit."

37   Much did he marvell at her uncouth[4] speach,
    Whose hidden drift he could not well perceive;
    And gan to doubt, least she him sought t'appeach[5]
    Of treason, or some guilefull traine[6] did weave,
    Through which she might his wretched life bereave.
    Both which to barre, he with this answere met her;
    "Faire Damzell, that with ruth (as I perceave)
    Of my mishaps, art mov'd to wish me better,
For such your kind regard, I can but rest your detter.

---

[1] An extended archery metaphor: "marke-white" is the white bull's-eye; to "rove" is to shoot with a scattered aim intended to zero in on the mark; "glauncing" suggests words that either miss the target or, as in Hamilton, are indirect.

[2] **proved:** tested.

[3] **felly:** fiercely.

[4] **uncouth:** awkward, obscure.

[5] **t'appeach:** to accuse.

[6] **traine:** trick.

38   "Yet weet ye well, that to a courage great
      It is no lesse beseeming well, to beare
      The storme of fortunes frowne, or heavens threat,
      Then in the sunshine of her countenance cleare
      Timely to joy, and carrie comely cheare.
      For though this cloud have now me overcast,
      Yet doe I not of better times despeyre;
      And, though unlike,[1] they should for ever last,
  Yet in my truthes assurance I rest fixed fast."

39   "But what so stonie mind" (she then replyde)
      "But if in his owne powre occasion lay,
      Would to his hope a windowe open wyde,
      And to his fortunes helpe make readie way?"[2]
      "Unworthy sure" (quoth he) "of better day,
      That will not take the offer of good hope,
      And eke pursew, if he attaine it may."
      Which speaches she applying to the scope[3]
  Of her intent, this further purpose to him shope.[4]

40   "Then why doest not, thou ill advized man,
      Make meanes to win thy libertie forlorne,[5]
      And try if thou by faire entreatie, can
      Move *Radigund?* who though she still have worne
      Her dayes in warre, yet (weet thou) was not borne
      Of Beares and Tygres, nor so salvage mynded,
      As that, albe[6] all love of men she scorne,
      She yet forgets, that she of men was kynded:[7]
  And sooth oft seene, that proudest harts base[8] love hath blynded."

41   "Certes *Clarinda*,[9] not of cancred[9] will,"
      (Sayd he) "nor obstinate disdainefull mind,
      I have forbore this duetie to fulfill:
      For well I may this weene, by that I fynd,
      That she a Queene, and come of Princely kynd,

---

[1] **unlike:** unlikely.
[2] I.e., what mind would not seize the occasion?
[3] **scope:** goal.
[4] **shope:** shaped, framed.
[5] **forlorne:** lost.
[6] **albe:** although.
[7] **kynded:** begotten.
[8] **base:** humble.
[9] **cancred:** diseased.

Both worthie is for to be sewd[1] unto,
Chiefely by him, whose life her law doth bynd,
And eke of powre her owne doome to undo,
And als' of princely grace to be inclyn'd thereto.

42   "But want of meanes hath bene mine onely let,[2]
From seeking favour, where it doth abound;
Which if I might by your good office get,
I to your selfe should rest for ever bound,
And readie to deserve, what grace I found."
She feeling him thus bite upon the bayt,
Yet doubting least his hold was but unsound,
And not well fastened, would not strike him strayt,
But drew him on with hope, fit leasure to awayt.

43   But foolish Mayd, whyles heedlesse of the hooke,
She thus oft times was beating off and on,
Through slipperie footing, fell into the brooke,
And there was caught to her confusion.
For seeking thus to salve[3] the Amazon,
She wounded was with her deceipts owne dart,
And gan thenceforth to cast affection,
Conceived close in her beguiled hart,
To *Artegall,* through pittie[4] of his causeless smart.

44   Yet durst she not disclose her fancies wound,
Ne to himselfe, for doubt of being sdayned,[5]
Ne yet to any other wight on ground,[6]
For feare her mistresse shold have knowledge gayned,
But to her selfe it secretly retayned,
Within the closet of her covert brest:
The more thereby her tender hart was payned.
Yet to awayt fit time she weened best,
And fairely did dissemble her sad thoughts unrest.

45   One day her Ladie, calling her apart,
Gan to demaund of her some tydings good,
Touching her loves successe, her lingring smart.

---

[1] **sewd:** courted.
[2] **let:** hindrance.
[3] **salve:** heal.

[4] Echoing Artegall, v.13.
[5] **sdayned:** disdained.
[6] **on ground:** on earth.

Therewith she gan at first to change her mood,
As one adaw'd,[1] and halfe confused stood;
But quickly she it overpast, so soone
As she her face had wypt, to fresh her blood:
Tho gan she tell her all, that she had donne,
And all the wayes she sought, his love for to have wonne.

46 But sayd, that he was obstinate and sterne,
Scorning her offers and conditions vaine;
Ne would be taught with any termes, to lerne
So fond a lesson, as to love againe.[2]
Die rather would he in penurious paine,
And his abridged dayes in dolour wast,
Then his foes love or liking entertaine:
His resolution was both first and last,
His bodie was her thrall, his hart was freely plast.

47 Which when the cruell Amazon perceived,
She gan to storme, and rage, and rend her gall,[3]
For very fell despight, which she conceived,
To be so scorned of a base borne thrall,
Whose life did lie in her least eye-lids fall;
Of which[4] she vow'd with many a cursed threat,
That she therefore would him ere long forstall.
Nathlesse when calmed was her furious heat,
he chang'd that threatfull mood, and mildly gan entreat.

48 "What now is left *Clarinda?* what remaines,
That we may compasse[5] this our enterprize?
Great shame to lose so long employed paines,
And greater shame t'abide so great misprize,[6]
With which he dares our offers thus despize.
Yet that his guilt the greater may appeare,
And more my gratious mercie by this wize,
I will a while with his first folly beare,
Till thou have tride againe, and tempted him more neare.

[1] **adaw'd:** daunted.
[2] **againe:** in return.
[3] The gall bladder was considered the seat of anger—Radigund seems about to rupture it in a fit of rage.
[4] I.e., his life.
[5] **compasse:** accomplish.
[6] **misprize:** scorn.

49   "Say, and do all, that may thereto prevaile;
    Leave nought unpromist, that may him perswade,
    Life, freedome, grace, and gifts of great availe,[1]
    With which the Gods themselves are mylder made:
    Thereto adde art, even womens witty trade,
    The art of mightie words, that men can charme;
    With which in case thou canst him not invade,
    Let him feele hardnesse of thy heavie arme:
Who will not stoupe with good, shall be made stoupe with harme.

50   "Some of his diet doe from him withdraw;
    For I him find to be too proudly fed.
    Give him more labour, and with streighter[2] law,
    That he with worke may be forwearied.[3]
    Let him lodge hard, and lie in strawen bed,
    That may pull downe the courage of his pride;
    And lay upon him, for his greater dread,
    Cold yron chaines, with which let him be tide;
And let, what ever he desires, be him denide.

51   "When thou hast all this doen, then bring me newes
    Of his demeane:[4] thenceforth not like a lover,
    But like a rebell stout I will him use.
    For I resolve this siege not to give over,
    Till I the conquest of my will recover."
    So she departed, full of griefe and sdaine,[5]
    Which inly did to great impatience move her.
    But the false mayden[6] shortly turn'd againe
Unto the prison, where her hart did thrall remaine.

52   There all her subtill nets she did unfold,
    And all the engins[7] of her wit display;
    In which she meant him warelesse to enfold,
    And of his innocence to make her pray.
    So cunningly she wrought her crafts assay,

---

[1] **availe:** value.

[2] **streighter:** stricter.

[3] **forwearied:** exhausted.

[4] **demeane:** demeanor—meaning behav-ior, but retaining the related senses of "to rule" and "to treat badly."

[5] **sdaine:** disdaine.

[6] I.e., Clarinda.

[7] **engins:** snares.

That both her Ladie, and her selfe withall,
And eke the knight attonce she did betray:
But most the knight, whom she with guilefull call[1]
Did cast[2] for to allure, into her trap to fall.

53   As a bad Nurse, which fayning to receive
      In her owne mouth the food, ment for her chyld,
      Withholdes it to her selfe, and doeth deceive
      The infant, so for want of nourture spoyld:
      Even so *Clarinda* her owne Dame beguyld,
      And turn'd the trust, which was in her affyde,[3]
      To feeding of her private fire, which boyld
      Her inward brest, and in her entrayles fryde,
The more that she it sought to cover and to hyde.

54   For comming to this knight, she purpose fayned,[4]
      How earnest suit she earst for him had made
      Unto her Queene, his freedome to have gayned;
      But by no meanes could her thereto perswade:
      But that in stead thereof, she sternely bade
      His miserie to be augmented more,
      And many yron bands on him to lade.[5]
      All which nathlesse she for his love forbore:
So praying him t'accept her service evermore.

55   And more then that, she promist that she would,
      In case she might finde favour in his eye,
      Devize how to enlarge him out of hould.
      The Fayrie[6] glad to gaine his libertie,
      Can[7] yeeld great thankes for such her curtesie,
      And with faire words, fit for the time and place,

[1] A metaphor from the use of bird calls in hunting.

[2] **cast:** contrive. Also picks up on the image of the nets.

[3] **affyde:** confided.

[4] **purpose fayned:** feigned a discourse, made up a tale.

[5] **lade:** load.

[6] Spenser calls Artegall a fairy, although he is a human changeling (III.iii.26).

[7] **can:** did.

To feede the humour of her maladie;
Promist, if she would free him from that case,[1]
He wold by all good means he might, deserve such grace.

56   So daily he faire semblant[2] did her shew,
          Yet never meant he in his noble mind,
      To his owne absent love to be untrew:
      Ne ever did deceiptfull *Clarin* find
      In her false hart, his bondage to unbind;
      But rather how she mote him faster tye.
      Therefore unto her mistresse most unkind
      She daily told, her love he did defye,
And him she told, her Dame his freedome did denye.

57   Yet thus much friendship she to him did show,
          That his scarse diet somewhat was amended,
      And his worke lessened, that his love mote grow:
      Yet to her Dame him still she discommended,[3]
      That she with him mote be the more offended.
      Thus he long while in thraldome there remayned,
      Of both beloved well, but litle frended;
      Untill his owne true love his freedome gayned,
Which in an other Canto will be best contayned.

---

[1] The repetition of "case" in this stanza may suggest that Artegall is engaging in a kind of casuistry, or equivocation, when he makes his promise to Clarinda.

[2] **semblant:** appearance.

[3] **discommended:** found fault with.

Canto Six

Talus brings newes to Britomart,
of Artegals mishap,
She goes to seeke him, Dolon meetes,
who seekes her to entrap.

1   Some men, I wote, will deeme in *Artegall*
      Great weaknesse, and report of him much ill,
      For yeelding so himselfe a wretched thrall,
      To th'insolent commaund of womens will;
      That all his former praise doth fowly spill.[1]
      But he the man, that say or doe so dare,
      Be well adviz'd, that he stand stedfast still:
      For never yet was wight so well aware,
But he at first or last was trapt in womens snare.[2]

2   Yet in the streightnesse[3] of that captive state,
      This gentle knight himselfe so well behaved,
      That notwithstanding all the subtill bait,
      With which those Amazons his love still craved,
      To his owne love his loialtie he saved:
      Whose character[4] in th'Adamantine mould
      Of his true hart so firmely was engraved,
      That no new loves impression ever could
Bereave[5] it thence: such blot his honour blemish should.

3   Yet his owne love, the noble *Britomart,*[6]
      Scarse so conceived in her jealous thought,

---

[1] **spill:** spoil.

[2] Spenser adds a misogynistic sentiment to 1 Cor. 10.12.

[3] **streightnesse:** strictness.

[4] **character:** an engraved mark, also carrying the sense of distinguishing traits.

[5] **Bereave:** rob, strip.

[6] The hero of Book Three, a figure for Chastity, and a dominating female warrior. See Introduction, 6. Just after vowing to marry Britomart, Artegall departed on his quest, promising to return within three months (IV.vi.43). Britomart resembles Ariosto's Bradamante. For this episode, see *Orlando*, 30–32.

What time[1] sad tydings of his balefull smart
In womans bondage, *Talus* to her brought;
Brought in untimely houre, ere it was sought.
For after that the utmost date, assynde
For his returne, she waited had for nought,
She gan to cast in her misdoubtfull mynde
A thousand feares, that love-sick fancies faine to fynde.[2]

4   Sometime she feared, least some hard mishap
       Had him misfalne in his adventurous quest;
       Sometime least his false foe did him entrap
       In traytrous traine, or had unwares opprest:[3]
       But most she did her troubled mynd molest,
       And secretly afflict with jealous feare,
       Least some new love had him from her possest;
       Yet loth she was, since she no ill did heare,
To thinke of him so ill: yet could she not forbeare.

5   One while she blam'd her selfe; another whyle
       She him condemn'd, as trustlesse and untrew:
       And then, her griefe with errour to beguyle,
       She fayn'd[4] to count the time againe anew,
       As if before she had not counted trew.
       For houres but dayes; for weekes, that passed were,
       She told but moneths, to make them seeme more few:[5]
       Yet when she reckned them, still drawing neare,
Each hour did seeme a moneth, and every moneth a yeare.

6   But when as yet she saw him not returne,
       She thought to send some one to seeke him out;
       But none she found so fit to serve that turne,
       As her owne selfe, to ease her selfe of dout.
       Now she deviz'd amongst the warlike rout
       Of errant Knights, to seeke her errant[6] Knight;

---

[1] **What time:** when.

[2] **faine to fynde:** are quick to find.

[3] **traine:** trap; **opprest:** overcome.

[4] **fayn'd:** wished.

[5] I.e., she counts the passed time in days and months rather than hours and weeks, since three months sounds like less time than twelve weeks. But when reckoning time to come, each hour seems a month, etc.

[6] **errant:** traveling and erring—a play on the quintessentially Spenserian word.

And then againe resolv'd to hunt him out
Amongst loose Ladies, lapped[1] in delight:
And then both Knights envide, and Ladies eke did spight.[2]

7 One day, when as she long had sought for ease
In every place, and every place thought best,
Yet found no place, that could her liking please,
She to a window came, that opened West,
Towards which coast[3] her love his way addrest.
There looking forth, shee in her heart did find
Many vaine fancies, working her unrest;
And sent her winged thoughts, more swift then wind,
To beare unto her love the message of her mind.

8 There as she looked long, at last she spide
One comming towards her with hasty speede:
Well weend she then, ere him she plaine descride,
That it was one sent from her love indeede.
Who when he nigh approcht, shee mote arede[4]
That it was *Talus, Artegall* his groome;
Whereat her heart was fild with hope and drede;
Ne would she stay, till he in place could come,
But ran to meete him forth, to know his tidings somme.[5]

9 Even in the dore him meeting, she begun;
"And where is he thy Lord, and how far hence?
Declare at once; and hath he lost or wun?"
The yron man, albe[6] he wanted sence
And sorrowes feeling, yet with conscience[7]
Of his ill newes, did inly chill and quake,
And stood still mute, as one in great suspence,
As if that by his silence he would make
Her rather reade his meaning, then him selfe it spake.

---

[1] **lapped:** surrounded—but with the ladies' laps embedded in the word, as Hamilton points out.

[2] I.e., Britomart assumes the worst about Artegall and all knights and ladies.

[3] **coast:** region. Ireland lies to the west of England.

[4] **arede:** recognize.

[5] **his tidings somme:** the sum of his news.

[6] **albe:** although.

[7] **conscience:** awareness. In Spenser's period, the word simultaneously meant consciousness and conscience. The second meaning may be reinforced here by the suggestion of an inner life in Talus.

10   Till she again thus sayd; "*Talus* be bold,
        And tell what ever it be, good or bad,
        That from thy tongue thy hearts intent doth hold."
     To whom he thus at length. "The tidings sad,
        That I would hide, will needs, I see, be rad.[1]
     My Lord, your love, by hard mishap doth lie
     In wretched bondage, wofully bestad."[2]
        "Ay me" (quoth she) "what wicked destinie?
     And is he vanquisht by his tyrant enemy?"

11   "Not by that Tyrant, his intended foe;
        But by a Tyrannesse" (he then replide,)
     "That him captived hath in haplesse woe."
     "Cease thou bad newes-man, badly doest thou hide
     Thy maisters shame, in harlots bondage tide.
     The rest my selfe too readily can spell."[3]
     With that in rage she turn'd from him aside,
        Forcing[4] in vaine the rest to her to tell,
     And to her chamber went like solitary cell.

12   There she began to make her monefull plaint[5]
        Against her Knight, for being so untrew;
     And him to touch with falshoods fowle attaint,
     That all his other honour overthrew.
     Oft did she blame her selfe, and often rew,
     For yeelding to a straungers love so light,
     Whose life and manners straunge she never knew;
        And evermore she did him sharpely twight[6]
     For breach of faith to her, which he had firmely plight.

13   And then she in her wrathfull will did cast,
        How to revenge that blot of honour blent;[7]
     To fight with him, and goodly die her last:
     And then againe she did her selfe torment,
     Inflicting on her selfe his punishment.
     A while she walkt, and chauft;[8] a while she threw

[1] **rad:** discovered.
[2] **wofully bestad:** troubled. This dialogue is Talus' first speech. He begins haltingly, as if the iron jaw needs oiling.
[3] **spell:** infer.
[4] **Forcing:** striving.
[5] **plaint:** complaint.
[6] **twight:** blame.
[7] **blent:** blemished.
[8] **chauft:** chafed.

Her selfe uppon her bed, and did lament:
Yet did she not lament with loude alew,[1]
As women wont, but with deepe sighes, and singulfs[2] few.

14 Like as a wayward childe, whose sounder sleepe
Is broken with some fearefull dreames affright,
With froward will doth set him selfe to weepe;
Ne can be stild for all his nurses might,
But kicks, and squals, and shriekes for fell despight:
Now scratching her, and her loose locks misusing;
Now seeking darkenesse, and now seeking light;
Then craving sucke, and then the sucke refusing.
Such was this Ladies fit, in her loves fond[3] accusing.

15 But when she had with such unquiet fits
Her selfe there close afflicted long in vaine,
Yet found no easement in her troubled wits,
She unto *Talus* forth return'd againe,
By change of place seeking to ease her paine;
And gan enquire of him, with mylder mood,   ·
The certaine cause of *Artegals* detaine;
And what he did, and in what state he stood,
And whether he did woo, or whether he were woo'd.

16 "Ah wellaway" (sayd then the yron man,)
"That he is not the while in state[4] to woo;
But lies in wretched thraldome, weake and wan,
Not by strong hand compelled thereunto,
But his owne doome, that none can now undoo."
"Sayd I not then" (quoth shee) "erwhile[5] aright,
That this is things compacte betwixt you two,
Me to deceive of faith unto me plight,
Since that he was not forst, nor overcome in fight?"

17 With that he gan at large to her dilate[6]
The whole discourse of his captivance[7] sad,
In sort as ye have heard the same of late.

---

[1] **alew:** halloo—i.e., she did not wail.

[2] **singulfs:** sobs.

[3] **fond:** foolish.

[4] **state:** condition.

[5] **erwhile:** earlier.

[6] **dilate:** expand, relate.

[7] **captivance:** captivity.

All which when she with hard enduraunce had
Heard to the end, she was right sore bestad,[1]
With sodaine stounds of wrath and griefe attone:[2]
Ne would abide, till she had aunswere made,
But streight her selfe did dight,[3] and armor don;
And mounting to her steede, bad *Talus* guide her on.

18   So forth she rode uppon her ready way,
      To seeke her Knight, as *Talus* her did guide:
      Sadly she rode, and never word did say,
      Nor good nor bad, ne ever lookt aside,
      But still right downe, and in her thought did hide
      The felnesse[4] of her heart, right fully bent
      To fierce avengement of that womans pride,
      Which had her Lord in her base prison pent,
And so great honour with so fowle reproch had blent.[5]

19   So as she thus melancholicke did ride,
      Chawing the cud of griefe and inward paine,[6]
      She chaunst to meete toward th'even-tide
      A Knight, that softly paced on the plaine,
      As if him selfe to solace he were faine.[7]
      Well shot[8] in yeares he seem'd, and rather bent
      To peace, then needlesse trouble to constraine.
      As well by view of that his vestiment,[9]
As by his modest semblant,[10] that no evill ment.

20   He comming neare, gan gently her salute
      With curteous words, in the most comely wize;
      Who though desirous rather to rest mute,
      Then termes to entertaine of common guize,[11]
      Yet rather then she kindnesse would despize,
      She would her selfe displease, so him requite.[12]

---

[1] **bestad:** beset.

[2] **stounds:** pangs; **attone:** at once.

[3] **dight:** dress.

[4] **felnesse:** fierceness, cruelty.

[5] **blent:** blemished.

[6] See v.27.

[7] **faine:** desirous.

[8] **shot:** advanced.

[9] **vestiment:** clothing.

[10] **semblant:** demeanor.

[11] I.e., small talk, to which the knight is inclined.

[12] **requite:** return his courtesy.

Then gan the other further to devize
Of things abrode, as next to hand did light,
And many things demaund, to which she answer'd light.[1]

21   For little lust[2] had she to talke of ought,
     Or ought to heare, that mote delightfull bee;
     Her minde was whole possessed of one thought,
     That gave none other place. Which when as hee
     By outward signes, (as well he might) did see,
     He list no lenger to use lothfull speach,
     But her besought to take it well in gree,[3]
     Sith shady dampe had dimd the heavens reach,
To lodge with him that night, unles good cause empeach.[4]

22   The Championesse, now seeing night at dore,
     Was glad to yeeld unto his good request:
     And with him went without gaine-saying more.
     Not farre away, but little wide by West,
     His dwelling was, to which he him addrest;[5]
     Where soone arriving they received were
     In seemly wise, as them beseemed best:
     For he their host them goodly well did cheare,
And talk't of pleasant things, the night away to weare.

23   Thus passing th'evening well, till time of rest,
     Then *Britomart* unto a bowre[6] was brought;
     Where groomes awayted her to have undrest.
     But she ne would undressed be for ought,
     Ne doffe her armes, though he her much besought.
     For she had vow'd, she sayd, not to forgo
     Those warlike weedes, till she revenge had wrought
     Of a late wrong uppon a mortall foe;
Which she would sure performe, betide her wele or wo.

24   Which when their Host perceiv'd, right discontent
     In minde he grew, for feare least by that art[7]
     He should his purpose misse, which close[8] he ment:

---

[1] **light:** sparingly.

[2] **lust:** desire.

[3] **well in gree:** with goodwill.

[4] **empeach:** argues against.

[5] **him addrest:** directed himself.

[6] **bowre:** bedroom.

[7] **art:** means.

[8] **close:** secretly.

Yet taking leave of her, he did depart.
There all that night remained *Britomart,*
Restlesse, recomfortlesse, with heart deepe grieved,
Not suffering the least twinckling sleepe to start
Into her eye, which th'heart mote have relieved,
But if the least appear'd, her eyes she streight reprieved.[1]

25   "Ye guilty eyes" (sayd she) "the which with guyle
     My heart at first betrayd,[2] will ye betray
     My life now to, for which[3] a little whyle
     Ye will not watch? false watches, wellaway,
     I wote when ye did watch both night and day
     Unto your losse: and now needes will ye sleepe?
     Now ye have made my heart to wake alway,
     Now will ye sleepe?[4] ah wake, and rather weepe,
   To thinke of your nights want, that should yee waking keepe."

26   Thus did she watch, and weare the weary night
     In waylfull plaints, that none was to appease;
     Now walking soft, now sitting still upright,
     As sundry[5] chaunge her seemed best to ease.
     Ne lesse did *Talus* suffer sleepe to seaze
     His eye-lids sad, but watcht continually,
     Lying without her dore in great disease;[6]
     Like to a Spaniell wayting carefully
   Least any should betray his Lady treacherously.

27   What time the native Belman of the night,
     The bird, that warned *Peter* of his fall,[7]
     First rings his silver Bell t'each sleepy wight,
     That should their mindes up to devotion call,
     She heard a wondrous noise below the hall.
     All sodainely the bed, where she should lie,

---

[1] **reprieved:** reproved.

[2] Britomart fell in love with Artegall on seeing his image in a magic mirror (III.ii.24).

[3] **for which:** because.

[4] Britomart's three questions recall Matt. 26.40–44, as Hamilton points out.

[5] **sundry:** varying.

[6] **disease:** uneasiness.

[7] The cock. See Matt. 26.34, 74–75; Mark 14.30, 68–72.

By a false trap was let adowne to fall
Into a lower roome, and by and by
The loft[1] was raysd againe, that no man could it spie.

28 With sight whereof she was dismayd right sore,
Perceiving well the treason, which was ment:
Yet stirred not at all for doubt of more,
But kept her place with courage confident,
Wayting what would ensue of that event.
It was not long, before she heard the sound
Of armed men, comming with close intent
Towards her chamber; at which dreadfull stound[2]
She quickly caught her sword, and shield about her bound.

29 With that there came unto her chamber dore
Two Knights, all arm'd ready for to fight,
And after them full many other more,
A raskall rout, with weapons rudely dight.[3]
Whom soone as *Talus* spide by glims[4] of night,
He started up, there where on ground he lay,
And in his hand his thresher ready keight.[5]
They seeing that, let drive at him streight way,
And round about him preace[6] in riotous aray.

30 But soone as he began to lay about
With his rude yron flaile, they gan to flie,
Both armed Knights, and eke unarmed rout:
Yet *Talus* after them apace did plie,[7]
Where ever in the darke he could them spie;
That here and there like scattred sheepe they lay.
Then backe returning, where his Dame did lie,
He to her told the story of that fray,
And all that treason there intended did bewray.

31 Wherewith though wondrous wroth, and inly burning,
To be avenged for so fowle a deede,
Yet being forst to abide the daies returning,

---

[1] **loft**: floor.
[2] **stound**: decisive moment.
[3] **dight**: equipped.
[4] **glims**: glimpse.

[5] **keight**: caught.
[6] **preace**: press.
[7] **plie**: run, attack.

She there remain'd, but with right wary heede,
Least any more such practise[1] should proceede.
Now mote ye know (that which to *Britomart*
Unknowen was) whence all this did proceede,
And for what cause so great mischievous smart[2]
Was ment to her, that never evill ment in hart.

32   The goodman of this house was *Dolon*[3] hight,
     A man of subtill wit and wicked minde,
     That whilome in his youth had bene a Knight,
     And armes had borne, but little good could finde,
     And much lesse honour by that warlike kinde
     Of life: for he was nothing valorous,
     But with slie shiftes and wiles did underminde
     All noble Knights, which were adventurous,
And many brought to shame by treason treacherous.

33   He had three sonnes, all three like fathers sonnes,
     Like treacherous, like full of fraud and guile,
     Of all that on this earthly compasse wonnes:[4]
     The eldest of the which was slaine erewhile
     By *Artegall,* through his owne guilty wile;[5]
     His name was *Guizor,*[6] whose untimely fate
     For to avenge, full many treasons vile
     His father *Dolon* had deviz'd of late
With these his wicked sons, and shewd his cankred hate.

34   For sure he weend, that this his present guest
     Was *Artegall,* by many tokens plaine;
     But chiefly by that yron page he ghest,
     Which still was wont with *Artegall* remaine;
     And therefore ment him surely to have slaine.
     But by Gods grace, and her good heedinesse,[7]

---

[1] **practise:** plotting.

[2] **smart:** injury.

[3] In English, suggests dole: guile as well as sorrow. Also the name of the bumbling Trojan spy (Homer, *Iliad,* 10.313–481). This episode is often read as alluding to the numerous attempts on Elizabeth's life (*Variorum,* 211–12).

[4] I.e., they are the most fraudulent, etc., of all that live on earth.

[5] **wile:** trick.

[6] For Artegall's killing of Pollente's "groome of evill guize," see ii.6–11.

[7] **heedinesse:** heedfulness.

She was preserved from their traytrous traine.
Thus she all night wore out in watchfulnesse,
Ne suffred slothfull sleepe her eyelids to oppresse.

35   The morrow next, so soone as dawning houre
        Discovered had the light to living eye,
        She forth yssew'd out of her loathed bowre,
        With full intent t'avenge that villany,
        On that vilde man, and all his family.
        And comming down to seeke them, where they wond,[1]
        Nor sire, nor sonnes, nor any could she spie:
        Each rowme she sought, but them all empty fond:
        They all were fled for feare, but whether, nether kond.[2]

36   She saw it vaine to make there lenger stay,
        But tooke her steede, and thereon mounting light,
        Gan her addresse unto her former way.
        She had not rid the mountenance of a flight,[3]
        But that she saw there present in her sight,
        Those two false brethren, on that perillous Bridge,
        On which *Pollente* with *Artegall* did fight.
        Streight was the passage like a ploughed ridge,
        That if two met, the one mote needes fall over the lidge.[4]

37   There they did thinke them selves on her to wreake:
        Who as she nigh unto them drew, the one
        These vile reproches gan unto her speake;
        "Thou recreant false traytor, that with lone
        Of armes hast knighthood stolne, yet Knight art none,
        No more shall now the darkenesse of the night
        Defend thee from the vengeance of thy fone,[5]
        But with thy bloud thou shalt appease the spright
        Of *Guizor,* by thee slaine, and murdred by thy slight."

38   Strange were the words in *Britomartis* eare;
        Yet stayd she not for them, but forward fared,
        Till to the perillous Bridge she came, and there

---

[1] **wond:** lived.

[2] **whether, nether kond:** whither, neither knew.

[3] **mountenance of a flight:** extent of an arrow's flight.

[4] **lidge:** ledge.

[5] **fone:** foes.

Talus desir'd, that he might have prepared
The way to her, and those two losels[1] scared.
But she thereat was wroth, that for despight
The glauncing sparkles through her bever[2] glared,
And from her eies did flash out fiery light,
Like coles, that through a silver Censer[3] sparkle bright.

39   She stayd not to advise which way to take;
     But putting spurres unto her fiery beast,
     Thorough the midst of them she way did make.
     The one of them, which most her wrath increast,
     Uppon her speare she bore before her breast,
     Till to the Bridges further end she past,
     Where falling downe, his challenge he releast:[4]
     The other over side the Bridge she cast
Into the river, where he drunke his deadly last.[5]

40   As when the flashing Levin[6] haps to light
     Uppon two stubborne oakes, which stand so neare,
     That way betwixt them none appeares in sight;
     The Engin[7] fiercely flying forth, doth teare
     Th'one from the earth, and through the aire doth beare;
     The other it with force doth overthrow,
     Uppon one side, and from his rootes doth reare.
     So did the Championesse those two there strow,[8]
And to their sire their carcasses left to bestow.

---

[1] **losels:** scoundrels.
[2] **bever:** face guard.
[3] **Censer:** vessel for burning incense.
[4] I.e., he withdrew his challenge.
[5] See *Orlando,* 35.38–48.
[6] **Levin:** lightning.
[7] **Engin:** the lightning.
[8] **strow:** strew.

Canto Seven

Britomart comes to Isis Church,
Where shee strange visions sees:
She fights with Radigund, her slaies,
And Artegall thence frees.

1   Nought is on earth more sacred or divine,
      That Gods and men doe equally adore,
      Then this same vertue, that doth right define:
      For th'hevens themselves, whence mortal men implore
      Right in their wrongs, are rul'd by righteous lore
      Of highest Jove, who doth true justice deale
      To his inferiour Gods, and evermore
      Therewith containes his heavenly Common-weale:[1]
    The skill whereof to Princes hearts he doth reveale.

2   Well therefore did the antique world invent,
      That Justice was a God of soveraine grace,
      And altars unto him, and temples lent,
      And heavenly honours in the highest place;
      Calling him great *Osyris,* of the race
      Of th'old Aegyptian Kings, that whylome were;
      With fayned colours shading[2] a true case:
      For that *Osyris,* whilest he lived here,
    The justest man alive, and truest did appeare.[3]

3   His wife was *Isis,* whom they likewise made
      A Goddesse of great powre and soverainty,
      And in her person cunningly did shade

---

[1] I.e., Jove contains, or governs, his commonwealth with true justice. Cf. Proem, 10.

[2] **shading:** representing or symbolizing—suggesting the poet's task in shadowing forth allegory, or what Spenser calls "darke conceit" ("Letter to Raleigh").

[3] The human King Osiris and Queen Isis were deified for their virtues, becoming important Egyptian gods of justice. Much of the detail of this episode comes from Plutarch, *Isis and Osiris;* and Diodorus, *Bibliotheca Historica,* 1.11–25. For the distinction between justice and equity, see Introduction, 2.

That part of Justice, which is Equity,
Whereof I have to treat here presently.
Unto whose temple when as *Britomart*
Arrived, shee with great humility
Did enter in, ne would that night depart;
But *Talus* mote not be admitted to her part.[1]

4   There she received was in goodly wize
     Of many Priests, which duely did attend
     Uppon the rites and daily sacrifize,
     All clad in linnen robes with silver hemd;
     And on their heads with long locks comely kemd,[2]
     They wore rich Mitres shaped like the Moone,
     To shew that *Isis* doth the Moone portend;[3]
     Like as *Osyris* signifies the Sunne.
     For that they both like race in equall justice runne.[4]

5   The Championesse them greeting, as she could,
     Was thence by them into the Temple led;
     Whose goodly building when she did behould,
     Borne uppon stately pillours, all dispred[5]
     With shining gold, and arched over hed,
     She wondred at the workemans passing skill,
     Whose like before she never saw nor red;[6]
     And thereuppon long while stood gazing still,
     But thought, that she thereon could never gaze her fill.

6   Thence forth unto the Idoll they her brought,
     The which was framed all of silver fine,
     So well as could with cunning hand be wrought,
     And clothed all in garments made of line,[7]
     Hemd all about with fringe of silver twine.
     Uppon her head she wore a Crowne of gold,

---

[1] **part:** side.

[2] **kemd:** combed.

[3] **portend:** signify.

[4] I.e., the sun and moon move in equally regular courses. "Justice" also recalls the association of the movements of heavenly bodies with the state of human affairs in the Proem. Osiris and Isis were identified with the sun and moon, respectively.

[5] **dispred:** covered.

[6] **red:** conceived.

[7] **line:** linen.

To shew that she had powre in things divine;
And at her feete a Crocodile was rold,
That with her[1] wreathed taile her middle did enfold.

7   One foote was set uppon the Crocodile,
    And on the ground the other fast did stand,
    So meaning to suppresse both forged guile,
    And open force:[2] and in her other hand
    She stretched forth a long white sclender wand.
    Such was the Goddesse; whom when *Britomart*
    Had long beheld, her selfe uppon the land
    She did prostrate, and with right humble hart,
Unto her selfe her silent prayers did impart.

8   To which the Idoll as it were inclining,
    Her wand did move with amiable looke,
    By outward shew her inward sence desining.[3]
    Who well perceiving, how her wand she shooke,
    It as a token of good fortune tooke.
    By this the day with dampe[4] was overcast,
    And joyous light the house of *Jove* forsooke:
    Which when she saw, her helmet she unlaste,
And by the altars side her selfe to slumber plaste.

9   For other beds the Priests there used none,
    But on their mother Earths deare lap did lie,
    And bake[5] their sides upon the cold hard stone,
    T'enure them selves to sufferaunce thereby
    And proud rebellious flesh to mortify.
    For by the vow of their religion
    They tied were to stedfast chastity,
    And continence of life, that all forgon,
They mote the better tend to their devotion.

---

[1] Perhaps a printer's error, as the crocodile is male.

[2] Crocodiles were traditionally associated with guile and force, luring victims with feigned weeping, according to Gough. See Aptekar, 87–107.

[3] **desining:** signifying.

[4] **dampe:** fog.

[5] **bake:** harden.

10   Therefore they mote not taste of fleshly food,
    Ne feed on ought, the which doth bloud containe,
    Ne drinke of wine, for wine they say is blood,
    Even the bloud of Gyants, which were slaine,
    By thundring Jove in the Phlegrean plaine.[1]
    For which the earth (as they the story tell)
    Wroth with the Gods, which to perpetuall paine
    Had damn'd her sonnes, which gainst them did rebell,
With inward griefe and malice did against them swell.[2]

11   And of their vitall bloud, the which was shed
    Into her pregnant bosome, forth she brought
    The fruitfull vine, whose liquor blouddy red
    Having the mindes of men with fury fraught,
    Mote in them stirre up old rebellious thought,
    To make new warre against the Gods againe:
    Such is the powre of that same fruit, that nought
    The fell contagion may thereof restraine,
Ne within reasons rule, her madding mood containe.

12   There did the warlike Maide her selfe repose,
    Under the wings of *Isis* all that night,[3]
    And with sweete rest her heavy eyes did close,
    After that long daies toile and weary plight.
    Where whilest her earthly parts with soft delight
    Of sencelesse sleepe did deeply drowned lie,
    There did appeare unto her heavenly spright
    A wondrous vision, which did close[4] implie
The course of all her fortune and posteritie.

13   Her seem'd, as she was doing sacrifize
    To *Isis*, deckt with Mitre on her hed,
    And linnen stole after those Priestes guize,
    All sodainely she saw transfigured

---

[1] The Titans, giants and sons of Earth, warred against Jove and lost. See *Metamorphoses*, 1.151–62; and Hesiod, *Theogony*, 617–735. For the association of wine with Titan blood, see Plutarch, *Isis and Osiris*, 6.

[2] Earth swells with her malice, and, in the next stanza, with pregnancy and blood. The Phlegrean Fields in Italy are also volcanic (*Variorum*, 220).

[3] This image of protective wings appears frequently in the Psalms, e.g., 17.8, 36.7, 57.1.

[4] **close:** secretly.

Her linnen stole to robe of scarlet red,
And Moone-like Mitre to a Crowne of gold,
That even she her selfe much wondered
At such a chaunge, and joyed to behold
Her selfe, adorn'd with gems and jewels manifold.[1]

14 And in the midst of her felicity,
    An hideous tempest seemed from below,
    To rise through all the Temple sodainely,
    That from the Altar all about did blow
    The holy fire, and all the embers strow
    Uppon the ground, which kindled privily,
    Into outragious flames unwares did grow,[2]
    That all the Temple put in jeopardy
Of flaming, and her selfe in great perplexity.

15 With that the Crocodile, which sleeping lay
    Under the Idols feete in fearelesse bowre,[3]
    Seem'd to awake in horrible dismay,
    As being troubled with that stormy stowre;
    And gaping greedy wide, did streight devoure
    Both flames and tempest: with which growen great,
    And swolne with pride of his owne peerelesse powre,
    He gan to threaten her likewise to eat;
But that the Goddesse with her rod him backe did beat.

16 Tho turning all his pride to humblesse meeke,
    Him selfe before her feete he lowly threw,
    And gan for grace and love of her to seeke:
    Which she accepting, he so neare her drew,
    That of his game she soone enwombed grew,
    And forth did bring a Lion of great might;
    That shortly did all other beasts subdew.
    With that she waked, full of fearefull fright,
And doubtfully dismayd[4] through that so uncouth sight.

---

[1] In this stanza it becomes impossible to distinguish Britomart from Isis.

[2] In Book Three, Britomart twice describes her love for Artegall with images of flames (III.ii.37, 43), as Hamilton points out.

[3] **fearelesse bowre:** a safe sleeping place.

[4] With a pun on lost virginity.

17   So thereuppon long while she musing lay,
        With thousand thoughts feeding her fantasie,
        Untill she spide the lampe of lightsome day,
        Up-lifted in the porch of heaven hie.
        Then up she rose fraught with melancholy,
        And forth into the lower parts did pas;
        Whereas the Priestes she found full busily
        About their holy things for morrow Mas:[1]
    Whom she saluting faire, faire resaluted was.

18   But by the change of her unchearefull looke,
        They might perceive, she was not well in plight;[2]
        Or that some pensivenesse to heart she tooke.
        Therefore thus one of them, who seem'd in sight
        To be the greatest, and the gravest wight,
        To her bespake; "Sir Knight it seemes to me,
        That thorough evill rest of this last night,
        Or ill apayd,[3] or much dismayd ye be,
    That by your change of cheare is easie for to see."

19   "Certes" (sayd she) "sith ye so well have spide
        The troublous passion of my pensive mind,
        I will not seeke the same from you to hide,
        But will my cares unfolde, in hope to find
        Your aide, to guide me out of errour blind."
        "Say on" (quoth he) "the secret of your hart:
        For by the holy vow, which me doth bind,
        I am adjur'd, best counsell to impart
    To all, that shall require my comfort in their smart."

20   Then gan she to declare the whole discourse
        Of all that vision, which to her appeard,
        As well as to her minde it had recourse.
        All which when he unto the end had heard,
        Like to a weake faint-hearted man he fared,[4]
        Through great astonishment of that strange sight;

[1] **morrow Mas:** morning mass.
[2] **plight:** condition, mood.
[3] **Or ill apayd:** either ill satisfied.
[4] **fared:** behaved.

And with long locks up-standing, stifly stared
Like one adawed[1] with some dreadfull spright.
So fild with heavenly fury, thus he her behight.[2]

21   "Magnificke Virgin, that in queint[3] disguise
       Of British armes doest maske thy royall blood,
       So to pursue a perillous emprize,
       How could'st thou weene, through that disguized hood,
       To hide thy state from being understood?
       Can from th'immortall Gods ought hidden bee?
       They doe thy linage, and thy Lordly brood;[4]
       They doe thy sire, lamenting sore for thee;[5]
They doe thy love, forlorne in womens thraldome see.

22   "The end whereof, and all the long event,[6]
       They doe to thee in this same dreame discover.
       For that same Crocodile doth represent
       The righteous Knight, that is thy faithfull lover,
       Like to *Osyris* in all just endever.[7]
       For that same Crocodile *Osyris* is,
       That under *Isis* feete doth sleepe for ever:
       To shew that clemence oft in things amis,
Restraines those sterne behests,[8] and cruell doomes of his.

23   "That Knight shall all the troublous stormes asswage,
       And raging flames, that many foes shall reare,
       To hinder thee from the just heritage
       Of thy sires Crowne, and from thy countrey deare.
       Then shalt thou take him to thy loved fere,[9]
       And joyne in equall portion of thy realme:
       And afterwards a sonne to him shalt beare,
       That Lion-like shall shew his powre extreame.
So blesse thee God, and give thee joyance of thy dreame."[10]

[1] **adawed:** daunted.
[2] **fury:** prophetic furor; **behight:** hailed.
[3] **queint:** unusual, cunning, refined.
[4] **brood:** descendants.
[5] Britomart secretly left her father, King Ryence, to become a knight (III.ii–iii).
[6] **event:** outcome.
[7] Osiris was often associated with the crocodile. The priest blends Artegall into his interpretation as well.
[8] **behests:** commands.
[9] **fere:** husband.
[10] The priest foresees what Merlin has also prophesied (III.iii.24–30), that Artegall and Britomart will establish the line of British monarchs. The lion (16.6 and 23.8) is a traditional emblem of British kings.

24   All which when she unto the end had heard,
         She much was eased in her troublous thought,
         And on those Priests bestowed rich reward:
         And royall gifts of gold and silver wrought,
         She for a present to their Goddesse brought.
      Then taking leave of them, she forward went,
      To seeke her love, where he was to be sought;
      Ne rested till she came without relent
   Unto the land of Amazons, as she was bent.

25   Whereof when newes to *Radigund* was brought,
         Not with amaze, as women wonted bee,
         She was confused in her troublous thought,[1]
         But fild with courage and with joyous glee,
         As glad to heare of armes, the which now she
      Had long surceast, she bad to open[2] bold,
      That she the face of her new foe might see.
      But when they of that yron man had told,
   Which late her folke had slaine, she bad them forth to hold.[3]

26   So there without the gate (as seemed best)
         She caused her Pavilion be pight;
         In which stout *Britomart* her selfe did rest,
         Whiles *Talus* watched at the dore all night.
         All night likewise, they of the towne in fright,
      Uppon their wall good watch and ward did keepe.
      The morrow next, so soone as dawning light
      Bad doe away the dampe[4] of drouzie sleepe,
   The warlike Amazon out of her bowre did peepe.[5]

27   And caused streight a Trumpet loud to shrill,
         To warne her foe to battell soone be prest:[6]
         Who long before awoke (for she ful ill
         Could sleepe all night, that in unquiet brest
         Did closely harbour such a jealous guest)

---

[1] I.e., Radigund is not confused and amazed in womanly fashion.

[2] I.e., the gates.

[3] **forth to hold:** to march out.

[4] **dampe:** fog.

[5] Britomart's battle with Radigund resembles the fight between Ariosto's Marfisa and Bradamante (*Orlando*, 36.44–84). It is often read as an allegory for Elizabeth's ongoing confrontation with Mary, Queen of Scots (*Variorum*, 221, 316).

[6] **prest:** ready.

Was to the battell whilome ready dight.[1]
Eftsoones that warriouresse with haughty crest
Did forth issue, all ready for the fight:
On th'other side her foe appeared soone in sight.

28   But ere they reared hand, the Amazone
      Began the streight[2] conditions to propound,
      With which she used still to tye her fone;[3]
      To serve her so, as she the rest had bound.
      Which when the other heard, she sternly frownd
      For high disdaine of such indignity,
      And would no lenger treat, but bad them sound.[4]
      For her no other termes should ever tie
      Then what prescribed were by lawes of chevalrie.

29   The Trumpets sound, and they together run
      With greedy rage, and with their faulchins[5] smot;
      Ne either sought the others strokes to shun,
      But through great fury both their skill forgot,
      And practicke use in armes: ne spared not
      Their dainty parts, which nature had created
      So faire and tender, without staine or spot,
      For other uses, then they them translated;
      Which they now hackt and hewd, as if such use they hated,[6]

30   As when a Tygre and a Lionesse[7]
      Are met at spoyling of some hungry pray,
      Both challenge[8] it with equall greedinesse:
      But first the Tygre clawes thereon did lay;
      And therefore loth to loose her right away,
      Doth in defence thereof full stoutly stond:

Cat
fight.

---

[1] **dight:** equipped.

[2] **streight:** strict.

[3] **fone:** foes. In contrast, Artegall accepts Radigund's terms (iv.49–51).

[4] **sound:** blow the trumpet to begin combat.

[5] **faulchins:** curved swords.

[6] Their disdain for, and hacking of, their dainty parts recalls the tradition by which Amazons cut off one breast.

[7] Britomart is frequently associated with lions, as royal beasts, and Radigund fits the traditional cruelty of the tiger, forming in this stanza an allegory of their relationship to Artegall—as well as a cat fight.

[8] **challenge:** claim.

To which the Lion strongly doth gainesay,
That she to hunt the beast first tooke in hond;
And therefore ought it have, where ever she it fond.

31   Full fiercely layde the Amazon about,
    And dealt her blowes unmercifully sore:
    Which *Britomart* withstood with courage stout,
    And them repaide againe with double more.
    So long they fought, that all the grassie flore
    Was fild with bloud, which from their sides did flow,
    And gushed through their armes, that all in gore
    They trode, and on the ground their lives did strow,[1]
Like fruitles seede, of which untimely death should grow.

32   At last proud *Radigund* with fell despight,
    Having by chaunce espide advantage neare,
    Let drive at her with all her dreadfull might,
    And thus upbrayding said; "This token beare
    Unto the man, whom thou doest love so deare;
    And tell him for his sake thy life thou gavest."[2]
    Which spitefull words she sore engriev'd to heare,
    Thus answer'd; "Lewdly thou my love depravest,[3]
Who shortly must repent that now so vainely bravest."[4]

33   Nath'lesse that stroke so cruell passage found,
    That glauncing on her shoulder plate, it bit
    Unto the bone, and made a griesly wound,
    That she her shield through raging smart of it
    Could scarse uphold; yet soone she it requit.
    For having force increast through furious paine,
    She her[5] so rudely on the helmet smit,
    That it empierced to the very braine,
And her proud person low prostrated on the plaine.

---

[1] **strow:** strew.

[2] Radigund implies that she has killed Artegall, and that Britomart will see him in death.

[3] **depravest:** pervert, corrupt, defame. It is unclear whether Britomart is responding to Radigund's claim that she has killed Artegall, or to the assumption that she has seduced him.

[4] **bravest:** boasts.

[5] I.e., Britomart strikes Radigund.

34   Where being layd,[1] the wrothfull Britonesse
       Stayd not, till she came to her selfe againe,
       But in revenge both of her loves distresse,
       And her late vile reproch, though vaunted vaine,[2]
       And also of her wound, which sore did paine,
       She with one stroke both head and helmet cleft.
       Which dreadfull sight, when all her warlike traine
       There present saw, each one of sence bereft,
Fled fast into the towne, and her sole victor left.

35   But yet so fast they could not home retrate,
       But that swift *Talus* did the formost win;[3]
       And pressing through the preace unto the gate,
       Pelmell with them attonce did enter in.
       There then a piteous slaughter did begin:
       For all that ever came within his reach,
       He with his yron flale did thresh so thin,
       That he no worke at all left for the leach:[4]
Like to an hideous storme, which nothing may empeach.[5]

36   And now by this the noble Conqueresse
       Her selfe came in, her glory to partake;
       Where though revengefull vow she did professe,
       Yet when she saw the heapes, which he did make,
       Of slaughtred carkasses, her heart did quake
       For very ruth, which did it almost rive,[6]
       That she his fury willed him to slake:
       For else he sure had left not one alive,
But all in his revenge of spirite would deprive.[7]

37   Tho[8] when she had his execution stayd,
       She for that yron prison did enquire,
       In which her wretched love was captive layd:

---

[1] I.e., Radigund is laid on the plain.

[2] The vile reproach is Radigund's sugges-
tion that she has killed, and perhaps slept
with, Artegall—which is a vain boast.

[3] **the formost win:** overtake them.

[4] **leach:** doctor; also the blood-sucking
worm used by doctors, suggesting that
Talus has spilled all their blood.

[5] **empeach:** impede.

[6] **rive:** crack.

[7] Britomart calling Talus off is compared by
Hamilton to Elizabeth calling Lord Grey
back from Ireland. For Britomart's pity, see
Introduction, 2.

[8] **Tho:** then.

Which breaking open with indignant ire,
She entred into all the partes entire.[1]
Where when she saw that lothly uncouth sight,
Of men disguiz'd in womanishe attire,
Her heart gan grudge, for very deepe despight
Of so unmanly maske, in misery misdight.

38   At last when as to her owne Love she came,
    Whom like disguize no lesse deformed had,
    At sight thereof abasht with secrete shame,
    She turnd her head aside, as nothing glad,
    To have beheld a spectacle so bad:
    And then too well beleev'd, that which tofore
    Jealous suspect[2] as true untruely drad,
    Which vaine conceipt now nourishing no more,
She sought with ruth to salve his sad misfortunes sore.[3]

39   Not so great wonder and astonishment,
    Did the most chast *Penelope* possesse,
    To see her Lord, that was reported drent,[4]
    And dead long since in dolorous distresse,
    Come home to her in piteous wretchednesse,
    After long travell of full twenty yeares,
    That she knew not his favours likelynesse,[5]
    For many scarres and many hoary heares,
But stood long staring on him, mongst uncertaine feares.

40   "Ah my deare Lord, what sight is this" (quoth she)
    "What May-game[6] hath misfortune made of you?
    Where is that dreadfull manly looke? where be
    Those mighty palmes, the which ye wont t'embrew[7]
    In bloud of Kings, and great hoastes to subdew?
    Could ought on earth so wondrous change have wrought,

---

[1] **entire:** inner.

[2] **suspect:** suspicion.

[3] These complicated lines seem to say that, upon seeing Artegall, Britomart no longer believes her earlier jealous suspicions, and now seeks to soothe his misfortune.

[4] **drent:** drowned. For Penelope, see Homer, *Odyssey*, 23.92–102.

[5] **likelynesse:** likeness.

[6] Referring to the parodic tradition of dressing a man up as the May Queen in the spring festival.

[7] **t'embrew:** to soak, stain.

As to have robde you of that manly hew?[1]
Could so great courage stouped have to ought?
Then farewell fleshly force; I see thy pride is nought."

41 Thenceforth she streight into a bowre him brought,
  And causd him those uncomely weedes undight;[2]
  And in their steede for other rayment sought,
  Whereof there was great store, and armors bright,
  Which had bene reft[3] from many a noble Knight;
  Whom that proud Amazon subdewed had,
  Whilest Fortune favour her successe in fight,
  In which when as she him anew had clad,
She was reviv'd, and joyd much in his semblance glad.

42 So there a while they afterwards remained,
  Him to refresh, and her late wounds to heale:
  During which space she there as Princes[4] rained,
  And changing all that forme of common weale,
  The liberty of women did repeale,
  Which they had long usurpt; and them restoring
  To mens subjection, did true Justice deale:[5]
  That all they as a Goddesse her adoring,
Her wisedome did admire, and hearkned to her loring.[6]

43 For all those Knights, which long in captive shade
  Had shrowded bene, she did from thraldome free;
  And magistrates of all that city made,
  And gave to them great living and large fee:[7]
  And that they should for ever faithfull bee,
  Made them sweare fealty to *Artegall*.
  Who when him selfe now well recur'd did see,
  He purposd to proceed, what so be fall,
Uppon his first adventure, which him forth did call.

---

[1] **hew:** appearance.
[2] **undight:** take off.
[3] **reft:** robbed.
[4] **Princes:** Princess.
[5] See v.25. The problem of Elizabeth com-
plicates both passages. Also see Introduction, 7.
[6] **loring:** teaching of lore.
[7] **great living and large fee:** great estates and large wealth.

44   Full sad and sorrowfull was *Britomart*
        For his departure, her new cause of griefe;
        Yet wisely moderated her owne smart,
        Seeing his honor, which she tendred[1] chiefe,
        Consisted much in that adventures priefe.[2]
        The care whereof, and hope of his successe
        Gave unto her great comfort and reliefe,
        That womanish complaints she did represse,
And tempred for the time her present heavinesse.

45   There she continu'd for a certaine space,
        Till through his want[3] her woe did more increase:
        Then hoping that the change of aire and place
        Would change her paine, and sorrow somewhat ease,
        She parted thence, her anguish to appease.
        Meane while her noble Lord sir *Artegall*
        Went on his way, ne ever howre did cease,
        Till he redeemed had that Lady thrall:[4]
That for another Canto will more fitly fall.

---

[1] **tendred:** valued.
[2] **priefe:** proof.
[3] **want:** lack.
[4] I.e., Irena.

Canto Eight

Prince Arthure and Sir Artegall,
Free Samient from feare:
They slay the Soudan, drive his wife,
Adicia to despaire.

1   Nought under heaven so strongly doth allure
     The sence of man, and all his minde possesse,
     As beauties lovely baite, that doth procure[1]
     Great warriours oft their rigour to represse,
     And mighty hands forget their manlinesse;
     Drawne with the powre of an heart-robbing eye,
     And wrapt in fetters of a golden tresse,
     That can with melting pleasaunce mollifye
Their hardned hearts, enur'd to bloud and cruelty.

2   So whylome learnd that mighty Jewish swaine,[2]
     Each of whose lockes did match a man in might,
     To lay his spoiles before his lemans traine:[3]
     So also did that great Oetean Knight[4]
     For his loves sake his Lions skin undight:
     And so did warlike *Antony* neglect
     The worlds whole rule for *Cleopatras* sight.[5]
     Such wondrous powre hath wemens faire aspect,
To captive men, and make them all the world reject.

3   Yet could it not sterne *Artegall* retaine,
     Nor hold from suite[6] of his avowed quest,
     Which he had undertane to *Gloriane;*

[1] **procure:** cause, persuade, with the background sense of procuring sex.

[2] Samson, who revealed to Dalila that his strength lay in his hair. She called in the Philistines, who cut his hair. (Judg. 16).

[3] **lemans traine:** lover's snare.

[4] Hercules, who allowed Iole to wear his lion's skin when he took on women's clothing and spun on a distaff, as recounted in v.24.

[5] Spenser here follows Tasso, who places Hercules and Antony on the gates to Armida's palace (*Gerusalemme Liberata*, 16: 1–7).

[6] **suite:** pursuit.

But left his love, albe[1] her strong request,
Faire *Britomart* in languor and unrest,
And rode him selfe uppon his first intent:
Ne day nor night did ever idly rest;
Ne wight but onely *Talus* with him went,
The true guide of his way and vertuous government.[2]

4   So travelling, he chaunst far off to heed
      A Damzell, flying on a palfrey[3] fast
      Before two Knights, that after her did speed
      With all their powre, and her full fiercely chast
      In hope to have her overhent[4] at last:
      Yet fled she fast, and both them farre outwent,
      Carried with wings of feare, like fowle aghast,
      With locks all loose, and rayment all to rent;[5]
And ever as she rode, her eye was backeward bent.

5   Soone after these he saw another Knight,
      That after those two former rode apace,
      With speare in rest, and prickt[6] with all his might:
      So ran they all, as they had bene at bace,[7]
      They being chased, that did others chase.
      At length he saw the hindmost overtake
      One of those two, and force him turne his face;
      How ever loth he were his way to slake,
Yet mote he algates[8] now abide, and answere make.

6   But th'other still pursu'd the fearefull Mayd;
      Who still from him as fast away did flie,
      Ne once for ought her speedy passage stayd,
      Till that at length she did before her spie
      Sir *Artegall,* to whom she streight did hie
      With gladfull hast, in hope of him to get
      Succour against her greedy enimy:
      Who seeing her approch gan forward set,
To save her from her feare, and him from force to let.[9]

---

[1] **albe:** despite.

[2] See Introduction, 5.

[3] **palfrey:** a small horse for ladies.

[4] **overhent:** overtaken.

[5] **all to rent:** altogether torn.

[6] **prickt:** rode.

[7] **bace:** a children's game in which the chasers are alternately chased.

[8] **algates:** nevertheless.

[9] **let:** prevent.

7   But he like hound full greedy of his pray,
      Being impatient of impediment,
      Continu'd still his course, and by the way
      Thought with his speare him quight have overwent.
      So both together ylike felly[1] bent,
      Like fiercely met. But *Artegall* was stronger,
      And better skild in Tilt and Turnament,
      And bore him quite out of his saddle, longer
Then two speares length; So mischiefe overmatcht the wronger.

8   And in his fall misfortune him mistooke;[2]
      For on his head unhappily he pight,
      That his owne waight his necke asunder broke,
      And left there dead. Meane while the other Knight
      Defeated had the other faytour[3] quight,
      And all his bowels in his body brast:[4]
      Whom leaving there in that dispiteous[5] plight,
      He ran still on, thinking to follow fast
His other fellow Pagan, which before him past.

9   In stead of whom finding there ready prest[6]
      Sir *Artegall,* without discretion
      He at him ran, with ready speare in rest:
      Who seeing him come still so fiercely on,
      Against him made againe. So both anon
      Together met, and strongly either strooke
      And broke their speares; yet neither has forgon
      His horses backe, yet to and fro long shooke,
And tottred like two towres, which through a tempest quooke.

10   But when againe they had recovered sence,
      They drew their swords, in mind to make amends
      For what their speares had fayled of their pretence.[7]
      Which when the Damzell, who those deadly ends
      Of both her foes had seene, and now her frends
      For her beginning a more fearefull fray,

[handwritten annotation: lots of tempers]

---

[1] **ylike felly:** equally fiercely.

[2] **mistooke:** seized.

[3] **faytour:** miscreant.

[4] **brast:** burst.

[5] **dispiteous:** pitiless.

[6] **ready prest:** at hand, armed.

[7] **pretence:** intention.

She to them runnes in hast, and her haire rends,
Crying to them their cruell hands to stay,
Untill they both doe heare, what she to them will say.

11   They stayd their hands, when she thus gan to speake;
        "Ah gentle Knights, what meane ye thus unwise
        Upon your selves anothers wrong to wreake?
        I am the wrong'd, whom ye did enterprise[1]
        Both to redresse, and both redrest likewise:
        Witnesse the Paynims both, whom ye may see
        There dead on ground. What doe ye then devise
        Of more revenge? if more, then I am shee,
Which was the roote of all, end your revenge on mee."

12   Whom when they heard so say, they lookt about,
        To weete if it were true, as she had told;
        Where when they saw their foes dead out of doubt,
        Eftsoones they gan their wrothfull hands to hold,
        And Ventailes[2] reare, each other to behold.
        Tho when as *Artegall* did *Arthure*[3] vew,
        So faire a creature, and so wondrous bold,
        He much admired both his heart and hew,
And touched with intire affection, nigh him drew.

13   Saying, "Sir Knight, of pardon I you pray,
        That all unweeting[4] have you wrong'd thus sore,
        Suffring my hand against my heart to stray:
        Which if ye please forgive, I will therefore
        Yeeld for amends my selfe yours evermore,
        Or what so penaunce shall by you be red."[5]
        To whom the Prince; "Certes me needeth more
        To crave the same, whom errour so misled,
As that I did mistake the living for the ded.

14   "But sith ye please, that both our blames shall die,
        Amends may for the trespasse soone be made,
        Since neither is endamadg'd much thereby."

---

[1] **enterprise:** undertake.

[2] **Ventailes:** face mask of the helmet.

[3] The king of national legend, and an allegory of Magnificence, according to the

"Letter to Raleigh." Arthur is often called "The Prince." See Introduction, 10.

[4] **unweeting:** unknowing.

[5] **red:** declared. Artegall offers to do homage and to serve him.

So can they both them selves full eath[1] perswade
To faire accordaunce, and both faults to shade,
Either embracing other lovingly,
And swearing faith to either on his blade,
Never thenceforth to nourish enmity,
But either others cause to maintaine mutually.

15 Then *Artegall* gan of the Prince enquire,
  What were those knights, which there on ground were layd,
  And had receiv'd their follies worthy hire,[2]
  And for what cause they chased so that Mayd.
  "Certes I wote not well" (the Prince then sayd)
  "But by adventure[3] found them faring so,
  As by the way unweetingly I strayd,
  And lo the Damzell selfe, whence all did grow,
Of whom we may at will the whole occasion know."

16 Then they that Damzell called to them nie,
  And asked her, what were those two her fone,
  From whom she earst so fast away did flie;
  And what was she her selfe so woe begone,
  And for what cause pursu'd of them attone.[4]
  To whom she thus; "Then wote ye well, that I
  Doe serve a Queene, that not far hence doth wone,[5]
  A Princesse of great powre and majestie,
Famous through all the world, and honor'd far and nie.

17 "Her name *Mercilla*[6] most men use to call;
  That is a mayden Queene of high renowne,
  For her great bounty knowen over all,
  And soveraine grace, with which her royall crowne
  She doth support, and strongly beateth downe
  The malice of her foes, which her envy,
  And at her happinesse do fret and frowne:
  Yet she her selfe the more doth magnify,
And even to her foes her mercies multiply.

---

[1] **can**: did; **eath**: easily.

[2] **hire**: reward.

[3] **adventure**: chance.

[4] **attone**: both.

[5] **wone**: live.

[6] Celebrating mercy, Mercilla, the "mayden Queene," is perhaps the most extensively drawn figure for Elizabeth in *The Faerie Queene*. See Introduction, 8.

18   "Mongst many which maligne her happy state,
        There is a mighty man,[1] which wonnes here by
        That with most fell despight and deadly hate,
        Seekes to subvert her Crowne and dignity,
        And all his powre doth thereunto apply:
        And her good Knights, of which so brave a band
        Serves her, as any Princesse under sky,
        He either spoiles,[2] if they against him stand,
Or to his part allures, and bribeth under hand.

19   "Ne him sufficeth all the wrong and ill,
        Which he unto her people does each day,
        But that he seekes by traytrous traines to spill[3]
        Her person, and her sacred selfe to slay:
        That O ye heavens defend, and turne away
        From her, unto the miscreant him selfe,
        That neither hath religion nor fay,[4]
        But makes his God of his ungodly pelfe,[5]
And Idols serves; so let his Idols serve the Elfe.

20   "To all which cruell tyranny they say,
        He is provokt, and stird up day and night
        By his bad wife, that hight *Adicia*,[6]
        Who counsels him through confidence of might,
        To breake all bonds of law, and rules of right.
        For she her selfe professeth mortall foe
        To Justice, and against her still doth fight,
        Working to all, that love her, deadly woe,
And making all her Knights and people to doe so.

21   "Which my liege Lady seeing, thought it best,
        With that his wife in friendly wise to deale,
        For stint of strife, and stablishment of rest
        Both to her selfe, and to her common weale,
        And all forepast displeasures to repeale.

[1] Often read as a figure for King Philip of Spain, who opposed Elizabeth and whose Catholicism was frequently considered idolatrous by English Protestants.

[2] **spoiles:** destroys.

[3] **spill:** overthrow.

[4] **fay:** faith.

[5] **pelfe:** riches—Spain's plunder of the Indies, according to Gough.

[6] In Greek, "Injustice." Gough associates her with Spain's "inquisitous government" (258). Spenser links her most of all with pride.

So me in message unto her she sent,
To treat with her by way of enterdeale,[1]
Of finall peace and faire attonement,[2]
Which might concluded be by mutuall consent.

22   "All times have wont safe passage to afford
       To messengers, that come for causes just:
       But this proude Dame disdayning all accord,
       Not onely into bitter termes forth brust,[3]
       Reviling me, and rayling as she lust,[4]
       But lastly to make proofe of utmost shame,
       Me like a dog she out of dores did thrust,
       Miscalling me by many a bitter name,
That never did her ill, ne once deserved blame.

23   "And lastly, that no shame might wanting be,
       When I was gone, soone after me she sent
       These two false Knights, whom there ye lying see,
       To be by them dishonoured and shent:[5]
       But thankt be God, and your good hardiment,[6]
       They have the price of their owne folly payd."
       So said this Damzell, that hight *Samient*,[7]
       And to those knights, for their so noble ayd,
Her selfe most gratefull shew'd, and heaped thanks repayd.

24   But they now having throughly heard, and seene
       Al those great wrongs, the which that mayd complained
       To have bene done against her Lady Queene,
       By that proud dame, which her so much disdained,
       Were moved much thereat, and twixt them fained,[8]
       With all their force to worke avengement strong
       Uppon the Souldan[9] selfe, which it mayntained,
       And on his Lady, th'author of that wrong,
And upon all those Knights, that did to her belong.

---

[1] **enterdeale:** negotiation. Mercilla's attempt at peaceful relations celebrates Elizabeth's efforts to avoid open war with Spain.

[2] **attonement:** concord.

[3] **brust:** burst.

[4] **lust:** pleased.

[5] **shent:** defiled.

[6] **hardiment:** courage.

[7] Based on the obsolete English "sam," meaning together or mutually, means "bringing together."

[8] **fained:** desired.

[9] The "mighty man" of 18.2, here named the Souldan, or sultan, a pagan ruler. See Tasso, *Gerusalemme Liberata*, 9.

25   But thinking best by counterfet disguise
      To their deseigne to make the easier way,
      They did this complot¹ twixt them selves devise,
      First that sir *Artegall* should him array,
      Like one of those two Knights, which dead there lay.
      And then that Damzell, the sad *Samient,*
      Should as his purchast² prize with him convay
      Unto the Souldans court, her to present
Unto his scornefull Lady, that for her had sent.

26   So as they had deviz'd, sir *Artegall*
      Him clad in th'armour of a Pagan knight,
      And taking with him, as his vanquisht thrall,
      That Damzell, led her to the Souldans right.³
      Where soone as his proud wife of her had sight,
      Forth of her window as she looking lay,
      She weened streight, it was her Paynim Knight,
      Which brought that Damzell, as his purchast pray;
And sent to him a Page, that mote direct his way.

27   Who bringing them to their appointed place,
      Offred his service to disarme⁴ the Knight;
      But he refusing him to let unlace,
      For doubt to be discovered by his sight,
      Kept himselfe still in his straunge armour dight.⁵
      Soone after whom the Prince arrived there,
      And sending to the Souldan in despight
      A bold defyance, did of him requere
That Damzell, whom he held as wrongfull prisonere.

28   Wherewith the Souldan all with furie fraught,
      Swearing, and banning⁶ most blasphemously,
      Commaunded straight his armour to be brought,
      And mounting straight upon a charret⁷ hye,

¹ **complot:** joint plot.
² **purchast:** acquired.
³ **right:** territory.
⁴ **disarme:** undress.
⁵ **straunge:** belonging to another; **dight:** dressed.

⁶ **banning:** cursing.
⁷ **charret:** chariot. With its height and iron hooks, the Souldan's chariot resembles a Spanish galleon. Stanzas 28 to 45 are generally read as allegorizing the defeat of the Spanish Armada. See *Variorum,* 226–28. Also see 2 Macc. 13.2.

With yron wheeles and hookes arm'd dreadfully,
And drawne of cruell steedes, which he had fed
With flesh of men, whom through fell tyranny
He slaughtred had, and ere they were halfe ded,
Their bodies to his beasts for provender did spred.

29   So forth he came all in a cote of plate,
        Burnisht with bloudie rust, whiles on the greene[1]
        The Briton Prince him readie did awayte,
        In glistering armes right goodly well beseene,
        That shone as bright, as doth the heaven sheene;
        And by his stirrup *Talus* did attend,
        Playing his pages part, as he had beene
        Before directed by his Lord; to th'end
He should his flale to finall execution bend.

30   Thus goe they both together to their geare,[2]
        With like fierce minds, but meanings different:
        For the proud Souldan with presumpteous cheare,[3]
        And countenance sublime and insolent,
        Sought onely slaughter and avengement:
        But the brave Prince for honour and for right,
        Gainst tortious powre and lawlesse regiment,[4]
        In the behalfe of wronged weake did fight:
More in his causes truth he trusted then in might.

31   Like to the *Thracian* Tyrant, who they say
        Unto his horses gave his guests for meat,
        Till he himselfe was made their greedie pray,
        And torne in peeces by *Alcides* great.[5]
        So thought the Souldan in his follies threat,
        Either the Prince in peeces to have torne
        With his sharpe wheeles, in his first rages heat,
        Or under his fierce horses feet have borne
And trampled downe in dust his thoughts disdained scorne.[6]

---

[1] **greene:** a lawn, but alluding to the sea, as Hamilton suggests.

[2] **geare:** business.

[3] **cheare:** expression.

[4] **tortious:** wrongful; **regiment:** government.

[5] Diomedes, King of Thrace, fed his guests to his horses, and suffered the same end at the hands of Hercules. See *Metamorphoses,* 9.194–96.

[6] I.e., the Souldan would have trampled Arthur, who was his thoughts' disdained scorne.

32   But the bold child[1] that perill well espying,
    If he too rashly to his charet drew,
    Gave way unto his horses speedie flying,
    And their resistlesse rigour did eschew.
    Yet as he passed by, the Pagan threw
    A shivering dart with so impetuous force,
    That had he not it shun'd with heedfull vew,
    It had himselfe transfixed, or his horse,
Or made them both one masse withouten more remorse.

33   Oft drew the Prince unto his charret nigh,
    In hope some stroke to fasten on him neare;
    But he was mounted in his seat so high,
    And his wingfooted coursers him did beare
    So fast away, that ere his readie speare
    He could advance, he farre was gone and past.
    Yet still he him did follow every where,
    And followed was of him likewise full fast;
So long as in his steedes the flaming breath did last.

34   Againe the Pagan threw another dart,
    Of which he had with him abundant store,
    On every side of his embatteld[2] cart,
    And of all other weapons lesse or more,
    Which warlike uses had deviz'd of yore.
    The wicked shaft guyded through th'ayrie wyde,
    By some bad spirit, that it to mischiefe bore,
    Stayd not, till through his curat[3] it did glyde,
And made a griesly wound in his enriven[4] side.

35   Much was he grieved with that haplesse throe,[5]
    That opened had the welspring of his blood;
    But much the more that to his hatefull foe
    He mote not come, to wreake his wrathfull mood.
    That made him rave, like to a Lyon wood,[6]
    Which being wounded of the huntsmans hand

---

[1] A chivalric term for a knight or young nobleman. Spenser usually uses it for Arthur.

[2] **embatteld:** fortified, armored.

[3] **curat:** breastplate.

[4] **enriven:** torn.

[5] **throe:** the Souldan's throw as well as his own convulsion of pain.

[6] **wood:** mad.

Can not come neare him in the covert wood,
Where he with boughes hath built his shady stand,
And fenst himselfe about with many a flaming brand.

36   Still when he sought t'approch unto him ny,
      His charret wheeles about him whirled round,
      And made him backe againe as fast to fly;
      And eke his steedes like to an hungry hound,
      That hunting after game hath carrion found,
      So cruelly did him pursew and chace,
      That his good steed, all[1] were he much renound
      For noble courage, and for hardie race,
      Durst not endure their sight, but fled from place to place.

37   Thus long they trast,[2] and traverst to and fro,
      Seeking by every way to make some breach,
      Yet could the Prince not nigh unto him goe,
      That one sure stroke he might unto him reach,
      Whereby his strengthes assay[3] he might him teach.
      At last from his victorious shield he drew
      The vaile, which did his powrefull light empeach;[4]
      And comming full before his horses vew,
      As they upon him prest, it plaine to them did shew.[5]

38   Like lightening flash, that hath the gazer burned,
      So did the sight thereof their sense dismay,
      That backe againe upon themselves they turned,
      And with their ryder ranne perforce[6] away:
      Ne could the Souldan them from flying stay,
      With raynes, or wonted rule, as well he knew.
      Nought feared they, what he could do, or say,
      But th'onely feare, that was before their vew;[7]
      From which like mazed deare,[8] dismayfully they flew.

[handwritten note: why rather fig. than purely physical?]

[handwritten note: Shield as text / defensive weapon]

[handwritten note: everything mediated]

[1] **all:** although.

[2] **trast:** traced.

[3] **assay:** proof.

[4] **empeach:** block.

[5] In Book One, Arthur's shield is accidentally unveiled with equally potent effect (I.viii.19). In all other fights until now, Arthur keeps it covered. The ease with which Arthur's shield confuses and defeats the enemy is often likened to the miraculous destruction and burning of the Armada. Also see *Orlando*, 10.107–10; 22.85–87.

[6] **perforce:** forcibly.

[7] I.e., they feared nothing but what was in their view, the shield.

[8] **mazed deare:** terrified deer.

39   Fast did they fly, as them their feete could beare,
          High over hilles, and lowly over dales,
      As they were follow'd of their former feare.
      In vaine the Pagan bannes,[1] and sweares, and rayles,
      And backe with both his hands unto him hayles[2]
      The resty[3] raynes, regarded now no more:
      He to them calles and speakes, yet nought avayles;
      They heare him not, they have forgot his lore,[4]
   But go, which way they list, their guide they have forlore.[5]

40   As when the firie-mouthed steeds, which drew
          The Sunnes bright wayne[6] to *Phaetons* decay,
      Soone as they did the monstrous Scorpion vew,
      With ugly craples[7] crawling in their way,
      The dreadfull sight did them so sore affray,
      That their well knowne courses they forwent,
      And leading th'ever-burning lampe astray,
      This lower world nigh all to ashes brent,
   And left their scorched path yet in the firmament.[8]

41   Such was the furie of these head-strong steeds,
          Soone as the infants[9] sunlike shield they saw,
      That all obedience both to words and deeds
      They quite forgot, and scornd all former law;
      Through woods, and rocks, and mountaines they did draw
      The yron charet, and the wheeles did teare,
      And tost the Paynim, without feare or awe;
      From side to side they tost him here and there,
   Crying to them in vaine, that nould[10] his crying heare.

---

[1] **bannes:** curses.

[2] **hayles:** hauls.

[3] **resty:** resisting control.

[4] **lore:** training.

[5] **forlore:** abandoned.

[6] **wayne:** chariot. Phaethon, son of Helios the sun god, was allowed to drive the horses of the sun for one day, but lost control and set fire to the world. Along the way he en-countered the constellation Scorpio. See *Metamorphoses,* 1.748–2.332.

[7] **craples:** grapples, claws.

[8] I.e., the Milky Way. See Chaucer, *The House of Fame,* 2.935–56.

[9] As with "child," a chivalric term for Arthur.

[10] **nould:** would not. The horses toss the Souldan just as the Spanish Armada was se-verely damaged by storms.

42 Yet still the Prince pursew'd him close behind,
      Oft making offer him to smite, but found
      No easie meanes according to his mind.
      At last they have all overthrowne to ground
      Quite topside turvey, and the pagan hound
      Amongst the yron hookes and graples keene,
      Torne all to rags, and rent with many a wound,
      That no whole peece of him was to be seene,
But scattred all about, and strow'd upon the greene.

43 Like as the cursed sonne of *Theseus*,[1]
      That following his chace in dewy morne,
      To fly his stepdames love outrageous,
      Of his owne steedes was all to peeces torne,
      And his faire limbs left in the woods forlorne;
      That for his sake *Diana* did lament,
      And all the wooddy Nymphes did wayle and mourne.
      So was this Souldan rapt and all to rent,[2]
That of his shape appear'd no litle moniment.[3]

44 Onely his shield and armour, which there lay,
      Though nothing whole, but all to brusd and broken,
      He up did take, and with him brought away,
      That mote remaine for an eternall token
      To all, mongst whom this storie should be spoken,
      How worthily, by heavens high decree,
      Justice that day of wrong her selfe had wroken,[4]
      That all men which that spectacle did see,
By like ensample mote for ever warned bee.

45 So on a tree, before the Tyrants dore,
      He caused them be hung in all mens sight,
      To be a moniment for evermore.
      Which when his Ladie from the castles hight
      Beheld, it much appald her troubled spright:
      Yet not, as women wont in dolefull fit,

[1] Hippolytus, who was dragged to death by his own horses. He refused his stepmother Phaedra's advances, and she claimed that he had seduced her, leading Theseus to curse his son. See I.v.37–39 and *Metamorphoses*, 15.497–546.

[2] **rapt:** overwhelmed: **all to rent:** altogether torn.

[3] **moniment:** trace.

[4] **wroken:** avenged.

She was dismayd, or faynted through affright,   *aellera*
But gathered unto her her troubled wit,
And gan eftsoones devize to be aveng'd for it.

46   Streight downe she ranne, like an enraged cow,
        That is berobbed of her youngling dere,
        With knife in hand, and fatally did vow,
        To wreake her on that mayden messengere,
        Whom she had causd be kept as prisonere,
        By *Artegall*, misween'd[1] for her owne Knight,
        That brought her backe. And comming present there,
        She at her ran with all her force and might,
All flaming with revenge and furious despight.

47   Like raging *Ino*,[2] when with knife in hand
        She threw her husbands murdred infant out,
        Or fell *Medea*,[3] when on *Colchicke* strand
        Her brothers bones she scattered all about;
        Or as that madding mother,[4] mongst the rout
        Of *Bacchus* Priests her owne deare flesh did teare.
        Yet neither *Ino*, nor *Medea* stout,
        Nor all the *Maenades* so furious were,
As this bold woman, when she saw that Damzell there.

48   But *Artegall* being thereof aware,
        Did stay her cruell hand, ere she her raught,[5]
        And as she did her selfe to strike prepare,
        Out of her fist the wicked weapon caught:
        With that like one enfelon'd[6] or distraught,
        She forth did rome, whether[7] her rage her bore,
        With franticke passion, and with furie fraught;
        And breaking forth out at a posterne dore,[8]
Unto the wyld wood ranne, her dolours to deplore.

---

[1] **misween'd:** mistaken.

[2] Ino madly threw herself and her son from a cliff into the sea. See *Metamorphoses*, 4.512–42.

[3] Medea assisted Jason in obtaining the Golden Fleece from Colchis. She scattered parts of her brother's body as a ploy to escape from her father.

[4] Agave, who, in a frenzy, tore her son Pentheus to pieces. He was spying on her as she and other devotees (Maenades) worshipped Bacchus. See *Metamorphoses*, 3.701–33, and Euripides, *Bacchae*.

[5] **raught:** reached.

[6] **enfelon'd:** angered, made murderous.

[7] **whether:** whither.

[8] **posterne dore:** back door.

49   As a mad bytch, when as the franticke fit
        Her burning tongue with rage inflamed hath,
        Doth runne at randon, and with furious bit
        Snatching at every thing, doth wreake her wrath
        On man and beast, that commeth in her path.[1]
        There they doe say, that she transformed was
        Into a Tygre, and that Tygres scath[2]
        In crueltie and outrage she did pas,
    To prove her surname true, that she imposed has.

50   Then *Artegall* himselfe discovering plaine,
        Did issue forth gainst all that warlike rout
        Of knights and armed men, which did maintaine
        That Ladies part, and to the Souldan lout:[3]
        All which he did assault with courage stout,
        All were they nigh an hundred knights of name,
        And like wyld Goates them chaced all about,
        Flying from place to place with cowheard[4] shame,
    So that with finall force them all he overcame.

51   Then caused he the gates be opened wyde,
        And there the Prince, as victour of that day,
        With tryumph entertayn'd and glorifyde,
        Presenting him with all the rich array,
        And roiall pompe, which there long hidden lay,
        Purchast through lawlesse powre and tortious[5] wrong
        Of that proud Souldan, whom he earst did slay.
        So both for rest there having stayd not long,
    Marcht with that mayd, fit matter for another song.

---

[1] Cf. Hecuba's transformation to a dog (*Metamorphoses,* 13.533–75).

[2] **scath:** doing harm.

[3] **lout:** bow.

[4] **cowheard:** coward. The spelling evokes Artegall's herding of the knights like wild goats.

[5] **tortious:** hurtful.

Canto Nine

Arthur and Artegall catch Guyle
whom Talus doth dismay,
They to Mercillaes pallace come,
and see her rich array.

1 What Tygre, or what other salvage wight[1]
   Is so exceeding furious and fell,
   As wrong, when it hath arm'd it selfe with might?
   Not fit mongst men, that doe with reason mell,[2]
   But mongst wyld beasts and salvage woods to dwell;
   Where still the stronger doth the weake devoure,
   And they that most in boldnesse doe excell,
   Are dreadded most, and feared for their powre:
Fit for *Adicia*, there to build her wicked bowre.

2 There let her wonne[3] farre from resort of men,
   Where righteous *Artegall* her late exyled;
   There let her ever keepe her damned den,
   Where none may be with her lewd parts defyled,
   Nor none but beasts may be of her despoyled:
   And turne we to the noble Prince, where late
   We did him leave, after that he had foyled
   The cruell Souldan, and with dreadfull fate[4]
Had utterly subverted his unrighteous state.

3 Where having with Sir *Artegall* a space
   Well solast[5] in that Souldans late delight,
   They both resolving now to leave the place,
   Both it and all the wealth therein behight[6]
   Unto that Damzell in her Ladies right,
   And so would have departed on their way.

---

[1] **salvage wight:** savage creature.

[2] **mell:** associate.

[3] **wonne:** dwell.

[4] **fate:** judgment.

[5] **solast:** taken comfort.

[6] **behight:** granted.

But she them woo'd by all the meanes she might,
And earnestly besought, to wend that day
With her, to see her Ladie thence not farre away.

4   By whose entreatie both they overcommen,
       Agree to goe with her, and by the way,
       (As often falles) of sundry things did commen.[1]
       Mongst which that Damzell did to them bewray
       A straunge adventure, which not farre thence lay;
       To weet a wicked villaine, bold and stout,
       Which wonned in a rocke not farre away,
       That robbed all the countrie there about,
And brought the pillage home, whence none could get it out.

5   Thereto both his owne wylie wit, (she sayd)
       And eke the fastnesse[2] of his dwelling place,
       Both unassaylable, gave him great ayde:
       For he so crafty was to forge and face,[3]
       So light of hand, and nymble of his pace,
       So smooth of tongue, and subtile in his tale,
       That could deceive one looking in his face;
       Therefore by name *Malengin*[4] they him call,
Well knowen by his feates, and famous over all.

6   Through these his slights[5] he many doth confound,
       And eke the rocke, in which he wonts to dwell,
       Is wondrous strong, and hewen farre under ground
       A dreadfull depth, how deepe no man can tell;
       But some doe say, it goeth downe to hell.
       And all within, it full of wyndings is,
       And hidden wayes, that scarce an hound by smell
       Can follow out those false footsteps of his,
Ne none can backe returne, that once are gone amis.

---

[1] **commen:** commune.

[2] **fastnesse:** strength.

[3] **forge and face:** to forge mischief and present a false face.

[4] Suggesting in Latin evil machinations. Also called Guyle in the argument. Gough associates Malengin and his guile with the guerilla warfare of the Irish (271). See *A View*, 96.

[5] **slights:** tricks.

7   Which when those knights had heard, their harts gan earne,[1]
        To understand that villeins dwelling place,
        And greatly it desir'd of her to learne,
        And by which way they towards it should trace.[2]
        "Were not" (sayd she) "that it should let[3] your pace
        Towards my Ladies presence by you ment,[4]
        I would you guyde directly to the place."
        "Then let not that" (said they) "stay your intent;
    For neither will one foot, till we that carle have hent."[5]

8   So forth they past, till they approched ny
        Unto the rocke, where was the villains won,[6]
        Which when the Damzell neare at hand did spy,
        She warn'd the knights thereof: who thereupon
        Gan to advize, what best were to be done.
        So both agreed, to send that mayd afore,
        Where she might sit nigh to the den alone,
        Wayling, and raysing pittifull uprore,
    As if she did some great calamitie deplore.

9   With noyse whereof when as the caytive carle[7]
        Should issue forth, in hope to find some spoyle,
        They in awayt[8] would closely him ensnarle,
        Ere to his den he backward could recoyle,
        And so would hope him easily to foyle.
        The Damzell straight went, as she was directed,
        Unto the rocke, and there upon the soyle
        Having her selfe in wretched wize abjected,
    Gan weepe and wayle, as if great griefe had her affected.

10   The cry whereof entring the hollow cave,
        Eftsoones brought forth the villaine, as they ment,
        With hope of her some wishfull boot[9] to have.
        Full dreadfull wight he was, as ever went
        Upon the earth, with hollow eyes deepe pent,

[1] **earne:** yearn.

[2] **trace:** proceed.

[3] **let:** slow.

[4] **ment:** intended.

[5] I.e., neither will go farther until they have caught the villain.

[6] **won:** dwelling.

[7] **caytive carle:** wretched churl.

[8] **in awayt:** in ambush.

[9] **boot:** booty.

And long curld locks, that downe his shoulders shagged,
And on his backe an uncouth vestiment
Made of straunge stuffe, but all to[1] worne and ragged,
And underneath his breech was all to torne and jagged.[2]

11 And in his hand an huge long staffe he held,
Whose top was arm'd with many an yron hooke,
Fit to catch hold of all that he could weld,[3]
Or in the compasse[4] of his clouches tooke;
And ever round about he cast his looke.
Als at his backe a great wyde net he bore,
With which he seldome fished at the brooke,
But usd to fish for fooles on the dry shore,
Of which he in faire weather wont to take great store.[5]

12 Him when the damzell saw fast by her side,
So ugly creature, she was nigh dismayd,
And now for helpe aloud in earnest cride.
But when the villaine saw her so affrayd,
He gan with guilefull words her to perswade,
To banish feare, and with *Sardonian*[6] smyle
Laughing on her, his false intent to shade,
Gan forth to lay his bayte her to beguyle,
That from her self unwares he might her steale the whyle.

13 Like as the fouler on his guilefull pype
Charmes to the birds full many a pleasant lay,
That they the whiles may take lesse heedie keepe,[7]
How he his nets doth for their ruine lay:
So did the villaine to her prate and play,
And many pleasant trickes before her show,
To turne her eyes from his intent away:
For he in slights and jugling feates did flow,[8]
And of legierdemayne the mysteries did know.

why this line? common wl Merilla? (handwritten)

in btw. parts (handwritten)

---

[1] **all to:** entirely.

[2] Malengin resembles the Irish as Spenser describes them in *A View* (56), as Gough points out.

[3] **weld:** overcome.

[4] **compasse:** reach.

[5] See *Orlando,* 15.43–45.

[6] **Sardonian:** sardonic.

[7] **heedie keepe:** heedful care.

[8] **flow:** overflow.

14   To which whilest she lent her intentive[1] mind,
        He suddenly his net upon her threw,
        That oversprad her like a puffe of wind;
        And snatching her soone up, ere well she knew,
        Ran with her fast away unto his mew,[2]
        Crying for helpe aloud. But when as ny
        He came unto his cave, and there did vew
        The armed knights stopping his passage by,
     He threw his burden downe, and fast away did fly.

15   But *Artegall* him after did pursew,
        The whiles the Prince there kept the entrance still:
        Up to the rocke he ran, and thereon flew
        Like a wyld Gote, leaping from hill to hill,
        And dauncing on the craggy cliffes at will;
        That deadly daunger seem'd in all mens sight,
        To tempt such steps, where footing was so ill:
        Ne ought avayled for the armed knight,
     To thinke to follow him, that was so swift and light.

16   Which when he saw, his yron man he sent,
        To follow him; for he was swift in chace.
        He him pursewd, where ever that he went,
        Both over rockes, and hilles, and every place,
        Where so he fled, he followd him apace:
        So that he shortly forst him to forsake
        The hight, and downe descend unto the base.
     There he him courst[3] a fresh, and soone did make
     To leave his proper forme, and other shape to take.

17   Into a Foxe himselfe he first did tourne;
        But he him hunted like a Foxe full fast:
        Then to a bush himselfe he did transforme,
        But he the bush did beat, till that at last
        Into a bird it chaung'd, and from him past,
        Flying from tree to tree, from wand[4] to wand:

---

[1] **intentive:** attentive.   [3] **courst:** chased.
[2] **mew:** den, a cage for birds.   [4] **wand:** branch.

But he then stones at it so long did cast,
That like a stone it fell upon the land,
But he then tooke it up, and held fast in his hand.[1]

18   So he it brought with him unto the knights,
      And to his Lord Sir *Artegall* it lent,
      Warning him hold it fast, for feare of slights.
      Who whilest in hand it gryping hard he hent,[2]
      Into a Hedgehogge all unwares it went,
      And prickt him so, that he away it threw.
      Then gan it runne away incontinent,[3]
      Being returned to his former hew:[4]
But *Talus* soone him overtooke, and backward drew.

19   But when as he would to a snake againe
      Have turn'd himselfe, he with his yron flayle
      Gan drive at him, with so huge might and maine,
      That all his bones, as small as sandy grayle[5]
      He broke, and did his bowels disentrayle;
      Crying in vaine for helpe, when helpe was past.
      So did deceipt the selfe deceiver fayle,
      There they him left a carrion outcast;
For beasts and foules to feede upon for their repast.

20   Thence forth they passed with that gentle Mayd,
      To see her Ladie, as they did agree.
      To which when she approched, thus she sayd;
      "Loe now, right noble knights, arriv'd ye bee
      Nigh to the place, which ye desir'd to see:
      There shall ye see my soverayne Lady Queene
      Most sacred wight, most debonayre and free,
      That ever yet upon this earth was seene,
Or that with Diademe hath ever crowned beene."

21   The gentle knights rejoyced much to heare
      The prayses of that Prince[6] so manifold,
      And passing litle further, commen were,

---

[1] Malengin resembles the shape-changer Proteus. See Homer, *Odyssey,* 4.351–93. Also see III.viii.39.

[2] **hent:** grasped.

[3] **incontinent:** immediately.

[4] **hew:** shape.

[5] **grayle:** gravel.

[6] In the Renaissance, a queen could be called a prince.

Where they a stately pallace did behold,
Of pompous show, much more then she had told;
With many towres, and tarras[1] mounted hye,
And all their tops bright glistering with gold,
That seemed to outshine the dimmed skye,
And with their brightnesse daz'd the straunge beholders eye.

22   There they alighting, by that Damzell were
Directed in, and shewed all the sight:
Whose porch, that most magnificke did appeare,
Stood open wyde to all men day and night;
Yet warded well by one of mickle might,
That sate thereby, with gyantlike resemblance,
To keepe out guyle, and malice, and despight,
That under shew oftimes of fayned semblance,
Are wont in Princes courts to worke great scath[2] and hindrance.

23   His name was *Awe;* by whom they passing in
Went up the hall, that was a large wyde roome,
All full of people making troublous din,
And wondrous noyse, as if that there were some,
Which unto them was dealing righteous doome.[3]
By whom they passing, through the thickest preasse,
The marshall of the hall[4] to them did come;
His name hight *Order,* who commaunding peace,
Them guyded through the throng, that did their clamors ceasse.

24   They ceast their clamors upon them to gaze;
Whom seeing all in armour bright as day,
Straunge there to see, it did them much amaze,
And with unwonted terror halfe affray.
For never saw they there the like array.
Ne ever was the name of warre there spoken,
But joyous peace and quietnesse alway,
Dealing just judgements, that mote not be broken
For any brybes, or threates of any to be wroken.[5]

---

[1] **tarras**: terraces.

[2] **scath**: harm.

[3] **doome**: judgment.

[4] The officer in charge of formal ceremony at court.

[5] **wroken**: inflicted.

25   There as they entred at the Scriene,[1] they saw
        Some one, whose tongue was for his trespasse vyle
        Nayld to a post, adjudged so by law:
        For that therewith he falsely did revyle,
        And foule blaspheme that Queene for forged guyle,
        Both with bold speaches, which he blazed had,
        And with lewd poems, which he did compyle;
        For the bold title of a Poet bad
He on himselfe had ta'en, and rayling rymes had sprad.

26   Thus there he stood, whylest high over his head,
        There written was the purport of his sin,
        In cyphers strange, that few could rightly read,
        BON FONS: but *bon* that once had written bin,
        Was raced[2] out, and *Mal* was now put in.
        So now *Malfont*[3] was plainely to be red;
        Eyther for th'evill, which he did therein,
        Or that he likened was to a welhed
Of evill words, and wicked sclaunders by him shed.

27   They passing by, were guyded by degree
        Unto the presence of that gratious Queene:
        Who sate on high, that she might all men see,
        And might of all men royally be seene,
        Upon a throne of gold full bright and sheene,
        Adorned all with gemmes of endlesse price,
        As either might for wealth have gotten bene,
        Or could be fram'd by workmans rare device;
And all embost with Lyons and with Flourdelice.[4]

28   All over her a cloth of state was spred,
        Not of rich tissew, nor of cloth of gold,
        Nor of ought else, that may be richest red,
        But like a cloud, as likest may be told,
        That her brode spreading wings did wyde unfold;

[1] A screen was used to divide large halls.

[2] **raced:** erased.

[3] "Font" recalls the Latin word for "fountain" and the French word for "maker," as well as the font used in printing. For consistency with "Malfont," many editors emend "BON FONS" to "BON FONT"—but the inconsistency of the 1596 edition matches the deeply vexed nature of writing and interpretation in this stanza.

[4] The lion represents England and the fleur-de-lis France, which Elizabeth claimed.

Whose skirts were bordred with bright sunny beams,[1]
Glistring like gold, amongst the plights[2] enrold,
And here and there shooting forth silver streames,
Mongst which crept litle Angels through the glittering gleames.

29   Seemed those litle Angels did uphold
      The cloth of state, and on their purpled wings
      Did beare the pendants, through their nimblesse[3] bold:
      Besides a thousand more of such, as sings
      Hymnes to high God, and carols heavenly things,
      Encompassed the throne, on which she sate:
      She Angel-like, the heyre of ancient kings
      And mightie Conquerors, in royall state,
Whylest kings and kesars at her feet did them prostrate.[4]

30   Thus she did sit in soverayne Majestie,
      Holding a Scepter in her royall hand,
      The sacred pledge of peace and clemencie,
      With which high God had blest her happie land,
      Maugre[5] so many foes, which did withstand.
      But at her feet her sword was likewise layde,
      Whose long rest rusted the bright steely brand;
      Yet when as foes enforst, or friends sought ayde,
She could it sternely draw, that all the world dismayde.[6]

31   And round about, before her feet there sate
      A bevie of faire Virgins clad in white,
      That goodly seem'd t'adorne her royall state,
      All lovely daughters of high *Jove,* that hight
      Litae, by him begot in loves delight,
      Upon the righteous *Themis:*[7] those they say

---

[1] Recalls the theophany on Sinai (Exod. 24.16–18), as Hamilton suggests.

[2] **plights:** pleats.

[3] **nimblesse:** nimbleness.

[4] This stanza echoes Rev. 4.10, 7.11, and 15.3.

[5] **Maugre:** despite.

[6] For Elizabeth's rusty sword, see her poem, "The Doubt of Future Foes" (Marcus, 133–34).

[7] The Litae are personified prayers, mediating between humans and their father Jove (Homer, *Iliad,* 9.498–512). The daughters of Themis and Jove are the Horae (Hesiod, *Theogony,* 901–903). Spenser conflates the two different figures.

Upon *Joves* judgement seat wayt day and night,
And when in wrath he threats the worlds decay,
They doe his anger calme, and cruell vengeance stay.

32   They also doe by his divine permission
       Upon the thrones of mortall Princes tend,
       And often treat for pardon and remission
       To suppliants, through frayltie which offend.
       Those did upon *Mercillaes* throne attend:
       Just *Dice,* wise *Eunomie,* myld *Eirene,*[1]
       And them amongst, her glorie to commend,
       Sate goodly *Temperance* in garments clene,
And sacred *Reverence,* yborne of heavenly strene.[2]

33   Thus did she sit in royall rich estate,
       Admyr'd of many, honoured of all,
       Whylest underneath her feete, there as she sate,
       An huge great Lyon lay, that mote appall
       An hardie courage, like captived thrall,
       With a strong yron chaine and coller bound,
       That once he could not move, nor quich[3] at all;
       Yet did he murmure with rebellions sound,
And softly royne, when salvage choler[4] gan redound.

34   So sitting high in dreaded soverayntie,
       Those two strange knights were to her presence brought;
       Who bowing low before her Majestie,
       Did to her myld obeysance,[5] as they ought,
       And meekest boone, that they imagine mought.
       To whom she eke inclyning her withall,
       As a faire stoupe[6] of her high soaring thought,
       A chearefull countenance on them let fall,
Yet tempred with some majestie imperiall.

---

[1] The names of the Horae, according to Hesiod, meaning justice, good government, and peace, respectively.

[2] **strene:** strain, lineage.

[3] **quich:** stir.

[4] **royne:** growl; **salvage choler:** savage anger.

[5] **obeysance:** homage.

[6] **stoupe:** the swoop of a bird of prey.

35   As the bright sunne, what time his fierie teme
          Towards the westerne brim begins to draw,
          Gins to abate the brightnesse of his beme,
          And fervour of his flames somewhat adaw:[1]
          So did this mightie Ladie, when she saw
          Those two strange knights such homage to her make,
          Bate somewhat of that Majestie and awe,
          That whylome wont to doe[2] so many quake,
      And with more myld aspect those two to entertake.

36   Now at that instant, as occasion fell,
          When these two stranger knights arriv'd in place,
          She was about affaires of common wele,
          Dealing of Justice with indifferent[3] grace,
          And hearing pleas of people meane and base.
          Mongst which as then, there was for to be heard
          The tryall of a great and weightie case,
          Which on both sides was then debating hard:
      But at the sight of these,[4] those were a while debard.

37   But after all her princely entertayne,
          To th'hearing of that former cause in hand,
          Her selfe eftsoones she gan convert[5] againe;
          Which that those knights likewise mote understand,
          And witnesse forth aright in forrain land,[6]
          Taking them up unto her stately throne,
          Where they mote heare the matter throughly scand
          On either part, she placed th'one on th'one,
      The other on the other side, and neare them none.[7]

38   Then was there brought, as prisoner to the barre,
          A Ladie of great countenance and place,
          But that she it with foule abuse did marre;
          Yet did appeare rare beautie in her face,
          But blotted with condition vile and base,
          That all her other honour did obscure,

---

[1] **adaw:** subdue.

[2] **doe:** make.

[3] **indifferent:** unbiased.

[4] I.e., Artegall and Arthur.

[5] **convert:** turn.

[6] I.e., report abroad Mercilla's justice.

[7] Artegall and Arthur are positioned along-side Mercilla to hear the case as judges.

And titles of nobilitie deface:
Yet in that wretched semblant,[1] she did sure
The peoples great compassion unto her allure.[2]

39   Then up arose a person of deepe reach,
    And rare in-sight, hard matters to revele;
    That well could charme his tongue, and time his speach
    To all assayes;[3] his name was called *Zele:*
    He gan that Ladie strongly to appele[4]
    Of many haynous crymes, by her enured,[5]
    And with sharpe reasons rang her such a pele,
    That those, whom she to pitie had allured,
He now t'abhorre and loath her person had procured.

40   First gan he tell, how this that seem'd so faire
    And royally arayd, *Duessa*[6] hight
    That false *Duessa*, which had wrought great care,[7]
    And mickle mischiefe unto many a knight,
    By her beguyled, and confounded quight:
    But not for those she now in question came,
    Though also those mote question'd be aright,
    But for vyld treasons, and outrageous shame,
Which she against the dred *Mercilla* oft did frame.

41   For she whylome (as ye mote yet right well
    Remember) had her counsels false conspyred,
    With faithlesse *Blandamour* and *Paridell,*[8]
    (Both two her paramours, both by her hyred,
    And both with hope of shadowes vaine inspyred.)
    And with them practiz'd,[9] how for to depryve

---

[1] **semblant:** appearance.

[2] Spenser allegorizes Mary, Queen of Scots, who was at times able to win a great deal of public sympathy. See McCabe and Introduction, 8.

[3] **assayes:** proofs.

[4] **appele:** accuse.

[5] **enured:** committed.

[6] Duessa embodies falsehood and doubleness, from the Italian for "two." She villain-ously traps knights with her false appearances throughout *The Faerie Queene.* Here Spenser transforms her into a figure for Mary. See Introduction, 10.

[7] **care:** trouble.

[8] Debased and contentious knights who ally with Duessa in Book Four. Here accused of plotting against Mercilla, as certain noblemen plotted with Mary against Elizabeth.

[9] **practiz'd:** plotted.

Mercilla of her crowne, by her aspyred,
That she might it unto her selfe deryve,
And tryumph in their blood, whom she to death did dryve.

42   But through high heavens grace, which favour not
       The wicked driftes of trayterous desynes,
       Gainst loiall Princes, all this cursed plot,
       Ere proofe[1] it tooke, discovered was betymes,
       And th'actours won the meede[2] meet for their crymes.
       Such be the meede of all, that by such mene
       Unto the type[3] of kingdomes title clymes.
       But false *Duessa* now untitled Queene,[4]
     Was brought to her sad doome, as here was to be seene.

43   Strongly did *Zele* her haynous fact[5] enforce,
       And many other crimes of foule defame
       Against her brought, to banish all remorse,
       And aggravate the horror of her blame.
       And with him to make part against her, came
       Many grave persons, that against her pled;
       First was a sage old Syre, that had to name
       The *Kingdomes care*, with a white silver hed,
     That many high regards[6] and reasons gainst her red.

44   Then gan *Authority* her to appose[7]
       With peremptorie powre, that made all mute;
       And then the law of *Nations* gainst her rose,
       And reasons brought, that no man could refute;
       Next gan *Religion* gainst her to impute
       High Gods beheast, and powre of holy lawes;
       Then gan the Peoples cry and Commons sute,
       Importune care of their owne publicke cause;
     And lastly *Justice* charged her with breach of lawes.

---

[1] **proofe:** effect.

[2] **meede:** reward.

[3] **type:** highest.

[4] Mary abdicated the Scottish crown in 1567.

[5] **fact:** guilt.

[6] **regards:** considerations.

[7] **appose:** examine.

45 But then for her, on the contrarie part,
    Rose many advocates for her to plead:
    First there came *Pittie*, with full tender hart,
    And with her joyn'd *Regard* of womanhead;
    And then came *Daunger* threatning hidden dread,
    And high alliance unto forren powre;[1]
    Then came *Nobilitie* of birth, that bread
    Great ruth through her misfortunes tragicke stowre;
    And lastly *Griefe* did plead, and many teares forth powre.

46 With the neare touch whereof in tender hart
    The Briton Prince was sore empassionate,
    And woxe[2] inclined much unto her part,
    Through the sad terror of so dreadfull fate,
    And wretched ruine of so high estate,
    That for great ruth his courage gan relent.[3]
    Which when as *Zele* perceived to abate,
    He gan his earnest fervour to augment,
    And many fearefull objects to them to present.

47 He gan t'efforce[4] the evidence anew,
    And new accusements to produce in place:
    He brought forth that old hag of hellish hew,
    The cursed *Ate*,[5] brought her face to face,
    Who privie was, and partie in the case:
    She, glad of spoyle and ruinous decay,
    Did her appeach,[6] and to her more disgrace,
    The plot of all her practise[7] did display,
    And all her traynes, and all her treasons forth did lay.

48 Then brought he forth, with griesly grim aspect,
    Abhorred *Murder*, who with bloudie knyfe
    Yet dropping fresh in hand did her detect,[8]

[1] The execution of Mary was a challenge to Mary's son, James VI of Scotland, and to Spain, where she was considered heir to the crown of England.

[2] **woxe:** grew.

[3] In feeling pity (ruth) and fear (terror), Arthur reacts to Duessa as Aristotle says an audience reacts to tragedy, as Hamilton points out.

[4] **t'efforce:** to urge violently.

[5] Greek goddess of discord. Duessa raised her from hell (IV.i.19) and is now condemned as a result.

[6] **appeach:** accuse.

[7] **practise:** scheming.

[8] **detect:** expose. Mary was suspected of complicity in the murder of her husband, Lord Darnley, in 1567.

And there with guiltie bloudshed charged ryfe:[1]
Then brought he forth *Sedition,* breeding stryfe
In troublous wits, and mutinous uprore:
Then brought he forth *Incontinence* of lyfe,
Even foule *Adulterie* her face before,
And lewd *Impietie,* that her accused sore.

49   All which when as the Prince had heard and seene,
His former fancies ruth he gan repent,
And from her partie[2] eftsoones was drawen cleene.
But *Artegall* with constant firme intent,
For zeale of Justice was against her bent.
So was she guiltie deemed of them all.
Then *Zele* began to urge her punishment,
And to their Queene for judgement loudly call,
Unto *Mercilla* myld for Justice gainst the thrall.[3]

50   But she, whose Princely breast was touched nere
With piteous ruth of her so wretched plight,
Though plaine she saw by all, that she did heare,
That she of death was guiltie found by right,
Yet would not let just vengeance on her light;
But rather let in stead thereof to fall
Few perling drops from her faire lampes of light;
The which she covering with her purple pall[4]
Would have the passion hid, and up arose withall.

---

[1] **ryfe:** forcefully.
[2] **partie:** side.
[3] **thrall:** prisoner.
[4] **pall:** robe.

Canto Ten

Prince Arthur takes the enterprize
for Belgee for to fight,
Gerioneos Seneschall
he slayes in Belges right.

1   Some Clarkes[1] doe doubt in their devicefull art,
      Whether this heavenly thing, whereof I treat,
      To weeten *Mercie* be of Justice part,
      Or drawne forth from her by divine extreate.[2]
      This well I wote, that sure she is as great,
      And meriteth to have as high a place,
      Sith in th'Almighties everlasting seat[3]
      She first was bred, and borne of heavenly race;
    From thence pour'd down on men, by influence of grace.

2   For if that Vertue be of so great might,
      Which from just verdict will for nothing start,[4]
      But to preserve inviolated right,
      Oft spilles[5] the principall, to save the part;
      So much more then is that of powre and art,
      That seekes to save the subject of her skill,
      Yet never doth from doome of right depart:
      As it is greater prayse to save, then spill,
    And better to reforme, then to cut off the ill.[6]

3   Who then can thee, *Mercilla,* throughly prayse,
      That herein doest all earthly Princes pas?
      What heavenly Muse shall thy great honour rayse

---

[1] **Clarkes:** scholars.

[2] **extreate:** extraction.

[3] See Exod. 25.22; Lev. 16.2; Num. 7.89; Isa. 16.5, in which God's throne is the mercy seat. See ix.27.

[4] **start:** flinch.

[5] **spilles:** spoils.

[6] Much of the language is obscure in this stanza, but the sense is probably that Justice ("that Vertue"), by sticking to the letter of the law, often secures the good of the part at the expense of the whole. The great art of mercy, or equity, lies in saving the "subject," or the part, without departing from "doome of right"—i.e., without sacrificing the whole intent of the law.

Up to the skies, whence first deriv'd it was,
And now on earth it selfe enlarged has,
From th'utmost brinke of the *Armericke*[1] shore,
Unto the margent of the *Molucas*?[2]
Those Nations farre thy justice doe adore:
But thine owne people do thy mercy prayse much more.

4   Much more it praysed was of those two knights;
 The noble Prince, and righteous *Artegall*,
 When they had seene and heard her doome a rights
 Against *Duessa*, damned by them all;
 But by her tempred without griefe[3] or gall,
 Till strong constraint did her thereto enforce.[4]
 And yet even then ruing her wilfull fall,
 With more then needfull naturall remorse,
And yeelding the last honour to her wretched corse.

5   During all which, those knights continu'd there,
 Both doing and receiving curtesies,
 Of that great Ladie, who with goodly chere
 Them entertayn'd, fit for their dignities,
 Approving[5] dayly to their noble eyes
 Royall examples of her mercies rare,
 And worthie paterns of her clemencies;
 Which till this day mongst many living are,
Who them to their posterities doe still declare.

6   Amongst the rest, which in that space befell,
 There came two Springals[6] of full tender yeares,
 Farre thence from forrein land, where they did dwell,
 To seeke for succour of her and of her Peares,[7]
 With humble prayers and intreatfull teares;
 Sent by their mother, who a widow was,

---

[1] *Armericke*: American.

[2] Also known as the Spice Islands, the Moluccas were visited by Sir Francis Drake in 1579.

[3] **griefe**: anger.

[4] Although politely not said, Duessa has her head cut off here. The adverb "thereto" indicates that "strong constraint" was applied appropriately to "her." The understatement reflects Mercilla's reluctance, mirroring Elizabeth's seeming reluctance to execute Mary Queen of Scots.

[5] **approving**: demonstrating.

[6] **Springals**: youths.

[7] **Peares**: peers, nobles.

Wrapt in great dolours and in deadly feares,
By a strong Tyrant, who invaded has
Her land, and slaine her children ruefully alas.

7   Her name was *Belgae,*[1] who in former age
     A Ladie of great worth and wealth had beene,
     And mother of a frutefull heritage,
     Even seventeene goodly sonnes;[2] which who had seene
     In their first flowre, before this fatall teene[3]
     Them overtooke, and their faire blossomes blasted,
     More happie mother would her surely weene,
     Then famous *Niobe,* before she tasted
     Latonaes childrens wrath, that all her issue wasted.[4]

8   But this fell Tyrant, through his tortious[5] powre,
     Had left her now but five of all that brood:
     For twelve of them he did by times devoure,
     And to his Idols sacrifice their blood,
     Whylest he of none was stopped, nor withstood.
     For soothly he was one of matchlesse might,
     Of horrible aspect, and dreadfull mood,
     And had three bodies in one wast empight,[6]
     And th'armes and legs of three, to succour him in fight.

9   And sooth they say, that he was borne and bred
     Of Gyants race, the sonne of *Geryon,*[7]
     He that whylome in Spaine so sore was dred,
     For his huge powre and great oppression,
     Which brought that land to his subjection,
     Through his three bodies powre, in one combynd;

[1] Referring to Belgium, and the Low Countries as a whole, which were ruled by Spain and sought help from England. In 1585 Elizabeth sent an army under the rule of Leicester (represented here by Arthur), though with far worse results than Spenser's account implies. See Introduction, 9.

[2] Represents the seventeen provinces of the Low Countries.

[3] **teene:** injury.

[4] Niobe boasted of her seven sons and seven daughters until a jealous Latona ordered her own children, Phoebus and Diana, to kill them. See *Metamorphoses,* 6.146–312.

[5] **tortious:** wrongful, illegal.

[6] **empight:** implanted.

[7] Geryon was a triple-bodied giant who kept a herd of fierce, red cattle in Spain. They were tended by Eurytion and the two-headed dog Orthrus. Hercules' tenth labor was to steal the cattle (Diodorus Siculus, 4.17–18).

And eke all strangers in that region
Arryving, to his kyne[1] for food assynd;
The fayrest kyne alive, but of the fiercest kynd.

10   For they were all, they say, of purple hew,
      Kept by a cowheard, hight *Eurytion,*
      A cruell carle, the which all strangers slew,
      Ne day nor night did sleepe, t'attend them on,
      But walkt about them ever and anone,
      With his two headed dogge, that *Orthrus* hight;
      Orthrus begotten by great *Typhaon,*
      And foule *Echidna,* in the house of night;[2]
    But *Hercules* them all did overcome in fight.

11   His sonne was this, *Geryoneo*[3] hight,
      Who after that his monstrous father fell
      Under *Alcides*[4] club, streight tooke his flight
      From that sad land, where he his syre did quell,
      And came to this, where *Belge* then did dwell,
      And flourish in all wealth and happinesse,
      Being then new made widow (as befell)
      After her Noble husbands late decesse;
    Which gave beginning to her woe and wretchednesse.

12   Then this bold Tyrant, of her widowhed
      Taking advantage, and her yet fresh woes,
      Himselfe and service to her offered,
      Her to defend against all forrein foes,
      That should their powre against her right oppose.
      Whereof she glad, now needing strong defence,
      Him entertayn'd, and did her champion chose:
      Which long he us'd with carefull diligence,
    The better to confirme her fearelesse confidence.

13   By meanes whereof, she did at last commit
      All to his hands, and gave him soveraine powre
      To doe, what ever he thought good or fit.

[1] **kyne:** cows.

[2] The fearsome Typhon and Echidna give birth to many monsters, including Orthrus. See Hesiod, *Theogony,* 306–309.

[3] Geryon's son, Geryoneo, also has three bodies. Spenser invents Geryoneo, who, in his oppression of Belge, is usually read as a figure for Philip II and the Spanish dynasty.

[4] Another name for Hercules.

Which having got, he gan forth from that howre
To stirre up strife, and many a Tragicke stowre,
Giving her dearest children one by one
Unto a dreadfull Monster to devoure,
And setting up an Idole of his owne,
The image of his monstrous parent *Geryone*.[1]

14   So tyrannizing, and oppressing all,
     The woefull widow had no meanes now left,
     But unto gratious great *Mercilla* call
     For ayde, against that cruell Tyrants theft,
     Ere all her children he from her had reft.
     Therefore these two, her eldest sonnes she sent,
     To seeke for succour of this Ladies gieft:[2]
     To whom their sute they humbly did present,
     In th'hearing of full many Knights and Ladies gent.[3]

15   Amongst the which then fortuned to bee
     The noble Briton Prince, with his brave Peare;[4]
     Who when he none of all those knights did see
     Hastily bent, that enterprise to heare,
     Nor undertake the same, for cowheard feare,
     He stepped forth with courage bold and great,
     Admyr'd of all the rest in presence there,
     And humbly gan that mightie Queene entreat,
     To graunt him that adventure for his former feat.[5]

16   She gladly graunted it: then he straight way
     Himselfe unto his journey gan prepare,
     And all his armours readie dight[6] that day,
     That nought the morrow next mote stay his fare.[7]
     The morrow next appear'd, with purple hayre
     Yet dropping fresh out of the *Indian* fount,[8]

---

[1] Geryoneo's oppressive rule, his rituals, and his monster allegorize the Spanish Inquisition in the Netherlands.

[2] **gieft:** gift.

[3] **gent:** gentle, high born.

[4] **Peare:** peer—i.e., Artegall.

[5] Arthur seeks an adventure as reward for his defeat of the Souldan.

[6] **dight:** assembled.

[7] **fare:** going.

[8] I.e., the east.

And bringing light into the heavens fayre,
    When he was readie to his steede to mount;
Unto his way, which now was all his care and count.

17   Then taking humble leave of that great Queene,
        Who gave him roiall giftes and riches rare,[1]
        As tokens of her thankefull mind beseene,[2]
        And leaving *Artegall* to his owne care;
        Upon his voyage forth he gan to fare,
        With those two gentle youthes, which him did guide,
        And all his way before him still prepare.
        Ne after him did *Artigall* abide,
    But on his first adventure forward forth did ride.

18   It was not long, till that the Prince arrived
        Within the land, where dwelt that Ladie[3] sad,
        Whereof that Tyrant had her now deprived,
        And into moores and marshes banisht had,
        Out of the pleasant soyle, and citties glad,
        In which she wont to harbour happily:
        But now his cruelty so sore she drad,[4]
        That to those fennes for fastnesse[5] she did fly,
    And there her selfe did hyde from his hard tyranny.

19   There he her found in sorrow and dismay,
        All solitarie without living wight;
        For all her other children, through affray,[6]
        Had hid themselves, or taken further flight:
        And eke her selfe through sudden strange affright,
        When one in armes she saw, began to fly;
        But when her owne two sonnes she had in sight,
        She gan take hart, and looke up joyfully:
    For well she wist this knight came, succour to supply.

20   And running unto them with greedy joyes,
        Fell straight about their neckes, as they did kneele,
        And bursting forth in teares; "Ah my sweet boyes,"

---

[1] In fact Leicester complained of being seriously underfunded, according to Gough.

[2] **beseene:** to be seen, probably modifying tokens.

[3] I.e., Belge.

[4] **drad:** dreaded.

[5] **fastnesse:** safety.

[6] **affray:** terror.

(Sayd she) "yet now I gin new life to feele,
And feeble spirits, that gan faint and reele,
Now rise againe, at this your joyous sight.
Alreadie seemes that fortunes headlong wheele
Begins to turne, and sunne to shine more bright,
Then it was wont, through comfort of this noble knight."

21   Then turning unto him; "And you Sir knight"
(Said she) "that taken have this toylesome paine
For wretched woman, miserable wight,
May you in heaven immortall guerdon[1] gaine
For so great travell,[2] as you doe sustaine:
For other meede may hope for none of mee,
To whom nought else, but bare life doth remaine,
And that so wretched one, as ye do see
Is liker lingring death, then loathed life to bee."

22   Much was he moved with her piteous plight,
And low dismounting from his loftie steede,
Gan to recomfort her all that he might,
Seeking to drive away deepe rooted dreede,
With hope of helpe in that her greatest neede.
So thence he wished her with him to wend,
Unto some place, where they mote rest and feede,
And she take comfort, which God now did send:
Good hart in evils doth the evils much amend.

23   "Ay me" (sayd she) "and whether[3] shall I goe?
Are not all places full of forraine powres?
My pallaces possessed of my foe,
My cities sackt, and their sky-threating towres
Raced, and made smooth fields now full of flowres?
Onely these marishes, and myrie bogs,
In which the fearefull ewftes[4] do build their bowres,
Yeeld me an hostry[5] mongst the croking frogs,
And harbour here in safety from those ravenous dogs."

---

[1] **guerdon**: reward.
[2] **travell**: travail, hardship.
[3] **whether**: whither.

[4] **ewftes**: newts.
[5] **hostry**: lodging.

24   "Nathlesse" (said he) "deare Ladie with me goe,
        Some place shall us receive, and harbour yield;
        If not, we will it force, maugre your foe,
        And purchase it to us with speare and shield:
        And if all fayle, yet farewell open field:
        The earth to all her creatures lodging lends."
        With such his chearefull speaches he doth wield[1]
        Her mind so well, that to his will she bends
And bynding up her locks and weeds, forth with him wends.

25   They came unto a Citie[2] farre up land,
        The which whylome that Ladies owne had bene;
        But now by force extort out of her hand,
        By her strong foe, who had defaced cleene
        Her stately towres, and buildings sunny sheene;
        Shut up her haven,[3] mard her marchants trade,
        Robbed her people, that full rich had beene,
        And in her necke a Castle huge had made,[4]
The which did her commaund, without needing perswade.

26   That Castle was the strength of all that state,
        Untill that state by strength was pulled downe,
        And that same citie, so now ruinate,
        Had bene the keye of all that kingdomes crowne;
        Both goodly Castle, and both goodly Towne,
        Till that th'offended heavens list to lowre[5]
        Upon their blisse, and balefull fortune frowne.
        When those gainst states and kingdomes do conjure,[6]
Who then can thinke their hedlong ruine to recure.[7]

27   But he[8] had brought it now in servile bond,
        And made it beare the yoke of inquisition,
        Stryving long time in vaine it to withstond;

---

[1] **wield:** govern.

[2] Antwerp, which was sacked by the Spanish in 1585. According to Gough, "in stanzas 25–27 Spenser nearly forgets the mythical Geryoneo and Belge, and tells almost literally the story of Spanish oppression in the Netherlands."

[3] **haven:** harbor—the Spanish laid siege to Antwerp, closing off the river Scheldt.

[4] I.e., in the neck or center of Antwerp's territory—also signifying the city's total subjection.

[5] **lowre:** scowl.

[6] **conjure:** conspire.

[7] **recure:** repair, heal.

[8] I.e., Geryoneo.

Yet glad at last to make most base submission,
And life enjoy for any composition.[1]
So now he hath new lawes and orders new
Imposd on it, with many a hard condition,
And forced it, the honour that is dew
To God, to doe unto his Idole most untrew.

28   To him he hath, before this Castle greene,
        Built a faire Chappell, and an Altar framed
        Of costly Ivory, full rich beseene,
        On which that cursed Idole farre proclamed,
        He hath set up, and him his God hath named,
        Offring to him in sinfull sacrifice
        The flesh of men,[2] to Gods owne likenesse framed,
        And powring forth their bloud in brutishe wize,
    That any yron eyes, to see it would agrize.[3]

29   And for more horror and more crueltie,
        Under that cursed Idols altar stone;
        An hideous monster doth in darknesse lie,
        Whose dreadfull shape was never seene of none
        That lives on earth; but unto those alone
        The which unto him sacrificed bee.
        Those he devoures, they say, both flesh and bone:
        What else they have, is all the Tyrants fee;[4]
    So that no whit of them remayning one may see.

30   There eke he placed a strong garrisone,
        And set a Seneschall[5] of dreaded might,
        That by his powre oppressed every one,
        And vanquished all ventrous knights in fight;
        To whom he wont shew all the shame he might,
        After that them in battell he had wonne.
        To which when now they gan approch in sight,
        The Ladie counseld him the place to shonne,
    Whereas so many knights had fouly bene fordonne.[6]

[1] **composition:** terms of surrender. Most of the states signed the 1577 Union of Brussels, which upheld the authority of Philip II and the Catholic religion.

[2] Gough associates the "Idole" with the Catholic host, and the human sacrifice with the auto de fé of the Inquisition.

[3] **agrize:** tremble in horror.

[4] **fee:** property.

[5] **Seneschall:** governor, judicial officer.

[6] **fordonne:** destroyed.

31   Her fearefull speaches nought he did regard,
        But ryding streight under the Castle wall,
        Called aloud unto the watchfull ward,[1]
        Which there did wayte, willing them forth to call
        Into the field their Tyrants Seneschall.
        To whom when tydings thereof came, he streight
        Cals for his armes, and arming him withall,
        Eftsoones forth pricked proudly in his might,
And gan with courage fierce addresse him to the fight.

32   They both encounter in the middle plaine,
        And their sharpe speares doe both together smite
        Amid their shields, with so huge might and maine,
        That seem'd their soules they wold have ryven[2] quight
        Out of their breasts, with furious despight.
        Yet could the Seneschals[3] no entrance find
        Into the Princes shield, where it empight;[4]
        So pure the mettall was, and well refynd,
But shivered[5] all about, and scattered in the wynd.

33   Not so the Princes, but with restlesse force,
        Into his shield it readie passage found,
        Both through his haberieon,[6] and eke his corse:
        Which tombling downe upon the senselesse ground,
        Gave leave unto his ghost from thraldome bound,
        To wander in the griesly shades of night.
        There did the Prince him leave in deadly swound,
        And thence unto the castle marched right,
To see if entrance there as yet obtaine he might.

34   But as he nigher drew, three knights he spyde,
        All arm'd to point, issuing forth a pace,
        Which towards him with all their powre did ryde,
        And meeting him right in the middle race,[7]
        Did all their speares attonce on him enchace.[8]

---

[1] **ward:** guard.

[2] **ryven:** torn.

[3] I.e., the Seneschal's spear.

[4] **where it empight:** where it could im-
plant itself. Arthur's shield is described in
Book One as "Hewen out of Adamant

rocke," a mythical substance as hard as dia-
mond (I.vii.33).

[5] **shivered:** shattered.

[6] **haberieon:** coat of mail.

[7] **middle race:** the middle of the field.

[8] **enchace:** enclose.

As three great Culverings[1] for battrie bent,
And leveld all against one certaine place,
Doe all attonce their thunders rage forth rent,
That makes the wals to stagger with astonishment.

35   So all attonce they on the Prince did thonder;
    Who from his saddle swarved nought asyde,
    Ne to their force gave way, that was great wonder,
    But like a bulwarke, firmely did abyde,
    Rebutting him, which in the midst did ryde,
    With so huge rigour, that his mortall speare
    Past through his shield, and pierst through either syde,[2]
    That downe he fell uppon his mother deare,
And powred forth his wretched life in deadly dreare.

36   Whom when his other fellowes saw, they fled
    As fast as feete could carry them away;
    And after them the Prince as swiftly sped,
    To be aveng'd of their unknightly play.
    There whilest they entring, th'one did th'other stay,
    The hindmost in the gate he overhent,[3]
    And as he pressed in, him there did slay:
    His carkasse tumbling on the threshold, sent
His groning soule unto her place of punishment.

37   The other which was entred, laboured fast
    To sperre[4] the gate; but that same lumpe of clay,
    Whose grudging ghost was thereout fled and past;
    Right in the middest of the threshold lay,
    That it the Posterne[5] did from closing stay:
    The whiles the Prince hard preased in betweene,
    And entraunce wonne. Streight th'other fled away,
    And ran into the Hall, where he did weene
Him selfe to save: but he there slew him at the skreene.[6]

---

[1] **Culverings:** large cannons.

[2] Arthur's spear goes through the knight's shield and his body, piercing both his sides.

[3] **overhent:** overtook.

[4] **sperre:** bolt.

[5] **Posterne:** back or side door.

[6] Screens were commonly used as partitions in great halls.

38   Then all the rest which in that Castle were,
        Seeing that sad ensample them before,
        Durst not abide, but fled away for feare,
        And them convayd out at a Posterne dore.
        Long sought the Prince, but when he found no more
        T'oppose against his powre, he forth issued
        Unto that Lady, where he her had lore,[1]
        And her gan cheare, with what she there had vewed,
   And what she had not seene, within unto her shewed.

39   Who with right humble thankes him goodly greeting,
        For so great prowesse, as he there had proved,
        Much greater then was ever in her weeting,[2]
        With great admiraunce inwardly was moved,
        And honourd him, with all that her behoved.
        Thenceforth into that Castle he her led,
        With her two sonnes, right deare of her beloved,
        Where all that night them selves they cherished,
   And from her balefull minde all care he banished.

---

[1] **lore:** left.   [2] **weeting:** knowledge.

Canto Eleven

Prince Arthure overcomes the great
Gerioneo in fight:
Doth slay the Monster, and restore
Belge unto her right.

1   It often fals in course of common life,
     That right long time is overborne of wrong,
     Through avarice, or powre, or guile, or strife,
     That weakens her, and makes her party[1] strong:
     But Justice, though her dome[2] she doe prolong,
     Yet at the last she will her owne cause right.
     As by sad *Belge* seemes, whose wrongs though long
     She suffred, yet at length she did requight,
And sent redresse thereof by this brave Briton Knight.

2   Whereof when newes was to that Tyrant brought,
     How that the Lady *Belge* now had found
     A Champion, that had with his Champion fought,
     And laid his Seneschall low on the ground,
     And eke him selfe did threaten to confound,
     He gan to burne in rage, and friese in feare,
     Doubting sad end of principle[3] unsound:
     Yet sith he heard but one, that did appeare,
He did him selfe encourage, and take better cheare.

3   Nathelesse him selfe he armed all in hast,
     And forth he far'd with all his many[4] bad,
     Ne stayed step, till that he came at last
     Unto the Castle, which they conquerd had.
     There with huge terrour, to be more ydrad,
     He sternely marcht before the Castle gate,

---

[1] **her party:** the opposition party.
[2] **dome:** doom, judgment.

[3] **doubting:** fearing; **principle:** beginning, initial state.
[4] **many:** company.

And with bold vaunts, and ydle threatning bad[1]
    Deliver him his owne, ere yet too late,
To which they had no right, nor any wrongfull state.[2]

4   The Prince staid not his aunswere to devize,
           But opening streight the Sparre,[3] forth to him came,
       Full nobly mounted in right warlike wize;
       And asked him, if that he were the same,
       Who all that wrong unto that wofull Dame
       So long had done, and from her native land
       Exiled her, that all the world spake shame.
       He boldly aunswerd him, he there did stand
That would his doings justifie with his owne hand.

5   With that so furiously at him he flew,
           As if he would have overrun him streight,
       And with his huge great yron axe gan hew
       So hideously uppon his armour bright,
       As he to peeces would have chopt it quight:
       That the bold Prince was forced foote to give[4]
       To his first rage, and yeeld to his despight;
       The whilest at him so dreadfully he drive,
That seem'd a marble rocke asunder could have rive.

6   Thereto a great advauntage eke he has
           Through his three double hands thrise multiplyde,
       Besides the double strength, which in them was:
       For stil when fit occasion did betyde,
       He could his weapon shift from side to syde,
       From hand to hand, and with such nimblesse[5] sly
       Could wield about, that ere it were espide,
       The wicked stroke did wound his enemy,
Behinde, beside, before, as he it list apply.

7   Which uncouth[6] use when as the Prince perceived,
           He gan to watch the wielding of his hand,
           Least by such slight he were unwares deceived;

---

[1] **bad:** bade.

[2] **nor any wrongfull state:** nor any (but a) wrongful claim.

[3] **Sparre:** the bolt of the gate.

[4] I.e., to give ground.

[5] **nimblesse:** nimbleness.

[6] **uncouth:** unfamiliar, marvelous.

And ever ere he saw the stroke to land,
He would it meete, and warily withstand.
One time, when he his weapon faynd[1] to shift,
As he was wont, and chang'd from hand to hand,
He met him with a counterstroke so swift,
That quite smit off his arme, as he it up did lift.

8   Therewith, all fraught with fury and disdaine,
He brayd aloud for very fell despight,
And sodainely t'avenge him selfe againe,
Gan into one assemble all the might
Of all his hands, and heaved them on hight,
Thinking to pay him with that one for all:
But the sad steele seizd not, where it was hight,[2]
Uppon the childe,[3] but somewhat short did fall,
And lighting on his horses head, him quite did mall.[4]

9   Downe streight to ground fell his astonisht steed,
And eke to th'earth his burden with him bare:
But he him selfe full lightly from him freed,
And gan him selfe to fight on foote prepare.
Whereof when as the Gyant was aware,
He wox right blyth, as he had got thereby,[5]
And laught so loud, that all his teeth wide bare
One might have seene enraung'd disorderly,
Like to a rancke of piles,[6] that pitched are awry.

10   Eftsoones againe his axe he raught[7] on hie,
Ere he were throughly buckled to his geare,[8]
And can[9] let drive at him so dreadfullie,
That had he chaunced not his shield to reare,
Ere that huge stroke arrived on him neare,
He had him surely cloven quite in twaine.

---

[1] **faynd:** contrived, sought.

[2] **sad:** heavy; **hight:** directed.

[3] I.e., Arthur, as in viii.32.1.

[4] **mall:** maul, batter.

[5] He grew merry, as though he had won.

[6] **rancke of piles:** row of stakes.

[7] **raught:** raised.

[8] I.e., before Arthur had thoroughly prepared.

[9] **can:** began to.

But th'Adamantine shield, which he did beare,
   So well was tempred, that for all his maine,[1]
It would no passage yeeld unto his purpose vaine.

11   Yet was the stroke so forcibly applide,
       That made him stagger with uncertaine sway,
       As if he would have tottered to one side.
       Wherewith full wroth, he fiercely gan assay,[2]
       That curt'sie with like kindnesse to repay;
       And smote at him with so importune[3] might,
       That two more of his armes did fall away,
       Like fruitlesse braunches, which the hatchets slight[4]
Hath pruned from the native tree, and cropped quight.

12   With that all mad and furious he grew,
       Like a fell mastiffe through enraging heat,
       And curst, and band,[5] and blasphemies forth threw,
       Against his Gods, and fire to them did threat,
       And hell unto him selfe with horrour great.
       Thenceforth he car'd no more, which way he strooke,
       Nor where it light, but gan to chaufe[6] and sweat,
       And gnasht his teeth, and his head at him shooke,
And sternely him beheld with grim and ghastly looke.

13   Nought fear'd the childe his lookes, ne yet his threats,
       But onely wexed[7] now the more aware,
       To save him selfe from those his furious heats,
       And watch advauntage, how to worke his care:[8]
       The which good Fortune to him offred faire.
       For as he in his rage him overstrooke,[9]
       He ere he could his weapon backe repaire,
       His side all bare and naked overtooke,[10]
And with his mortal steel quite throgh the body strooke.

---

[1] **maine:** strength.

[2] **assay:** attempt.

[3] **importune:** heavy, grievous.

[4] **slight:** dexterity.

[5] **band:** swore.

[6] **chaufe:** chafe.

[7] **wexed:** grew.

[8] **care:** trouble, suffering.

[9] **overstrooke:** overswung.

[10] Arthur catches Geryoneo's exposed side.

14   Through all three bodies he him strooke attonce;
       That all the three attonce fell on the plaine:
       Else should he thrise have needed, for the nonce[1]
       Them to have stricken, and thrise to have slaine.
       So now all three one sencelesse lumpe remaine,
       Enwallow'd in his owne blacke bloudy gore,
       And byting th'earth for very deaths disdaine;
       Who with a cloud of night him covering, bore
Downe to the house of dole,[2] his daies there to deplore.

15   Which when the Lady from the Castle saw,
       Where she with her two sonnes did looking stand,
       She towards him in hast her selfe did draw,
       To greet[3] him the good fortune of his hand:
       And all the people both of towne and land,
       Which there stood gazing from the Cities wall
       Uppon these warriours, greedy[4] t'understand,
       To whether[5] should victory befall,
Now when they saw it falne, they eke him greeted all.

16   But *Belge* with her sonnes prostrated low
       Before his feete, in all that peoples sight;
       Mongst joyes mixing some tears, mongst wele,[6] some wo,
       Him thus bespake; "O most redoubted Knight,
       The which hast me, of all most wretched wight,
       That earst was dead, restor'd to life againe,
       And these weake impes[7] replanted by thy might;
       What guerdon[8] can I give thee for thy paine,
But even that which thou savedst, thine still to remaine?"[9]

17   He tooke her up forby[10] the lilly hand,
       And her recomforted the best he might,
       Saying; "Deare Lady, deedes ought not be scand[11]

---

[1] **for the nonce:** for the purpose.

[2] **dole:** suffering.

[3] **greet:** congratulate.

[4] **greedy:** desirous.

[5] **whether:** which.

[6] **wele:** happiness.

[7] **impes:** young shoot of a plant, off-spring—i.e., the two sons.

[8] **guerdon:** reward.

[9] Belge offers Arthur sovereignty over her land.

[10] **forby:** by.

[11] **scand:** judged.

By th'authors manhood, nor the doers might,
But by their trueth and by the causes right:
That same is it, which fought for you this day.[1]
What other meed then need me to requight,
But that which yeeldeth vertues meed alway?
That is the vertue selfe, which her reward doth pay."[2]

18   She humbly thankt him for that wondrous grace,
     And further sayd; "Ah Sir, but mote ye please,
     Sith ye thus farre have tendred my poore case,
     As from my chiefest foe me to release,
     That your victorious arme will not yet cease,
     Till ye have rooted all the relickes[3] out
     Of that vilde race, and stablished my peace."
     "What is there else" (sayd he) "left of their rout?
Declare it boldly Dame, and doe not stand in dout."

19   "Then wote you, Sir, that in this Church hereby,
     There stands an Idole of great note and name,
     The which this Gyant reared first on hie,
     And of his owne vaine fancies thought did frame:
     To whom for endlesse horrour of his shame,
     He offred up for daily sacrifize
     My children and my people, burnt in flame;[4]
     With all the tortures, that he could devize,
The more t'aggrate his God with such his bloudy guize.[5]

20   And underneath this Idoll there doth lie
     An hideous monster, that doth it defend,
     And feedes on all the carkasses, that die
     In sacrifize unto that cursed feend:
     Whose ugly shape none ever saw, nor kend,[6]
     That ever scap'd: for of a man they say

---

[1] I.e., truth and right, more than Arthur's physical heroism, should get credit for fighting.

[2] Arthur turns down Belge's offer of sovereignty, unlike Leicester, who in 1586 angered Elizabeth by accepting the title of Governor-General.

[3] "Relic" is a charged word, given its association with Catholic worship.

[4] Resembles Molech (2 Kings 23.10; Ps. 106.37–38).

[5] **t'aggrate:** to gratify; **guize:** custom.

[6] **kend:** knew.

It has the voice, that speaches forth doth send,
Even blasphemous words, which she doth bray
Out of her poysnous entrails, fraught with dire decay."[1]

21 Which when the Prince heard tell, his heart gan earne[2]
For great desire, that Monster to assay,
And prayd the place of her abode to learne.
Which being shew'd, he gan him selfe streight way
Thereto addresse, and his bright shield display.
So to the Church he came, where it was told,
The Monster underneath the Altar lay;
There he that Idoll saw of massy gold
Most richly made, but there no Monster did behold.

22 Upon the Image with his naked blade
Three times, as in defiance, there he strooke;
And the third time out of an hidden shade,
There forth issewd, from under th'Altars smooke,
A dreadfull feend, with fowle deformed looke,
That stretcht it selfe, as it had long lyen still;
And her long taile and fethers strongly shooke,
That all the Temple did with terrour fill;
Yet him nought terrifide, that feared nothing ill.

23 An huge great Beast it was, when it in length
Was stretched forth, that nigh fild all the place,
And seem'd to be of infinite great strength;
Horrible, hideous, and of hellish race,
Borne of the brooding of *Echidna*[3] base,
Or other like infernall furies kinde:
For of a Mayd she had the outward face,
To hide the horrour, which did lurke behinde,
The better to beguile, whom she so fond[4] did finde.

---

[1] In Spenser's previous mention, Geryoneo's monster is male (x.29).

[2] **earne:** yearn.

[3] The monsters Echidna and Typhon gave birth to the Sphinx, whom Geryoneo's monster resembles. See Apollodorus 3.5.8–9. In x.10, Geryoneo is linked to Orthrus, another of Echidna's offspring.

[4] **fond:** foolish.

24   Thereto the body of a dog she had,
          Full of fell ravin[1] and fierce greedinesse;
          A Lions clawes, with powre and rigour clad,
          To rend and teare, what so she can oppresse;
          A Dragons taile, whose sting without redresse
          Full deadly wounds, where so it is empight;[2]
          And Eagles wings, for scope and speedinesse,
          That nothing may escape her reaching might,
    Whereto she ever list to make her hardy flight.

25   Much like in foulnesse and deformity
          Unto that Monster, whom the Theban Knight,[3]
          The father of that fatall progeny,
          Made kill her selfe for very hearts despight,
          That he had red her Riddle, which no wight
          Could ever loose, but suffred deadly doole.[4]
          So also did this Monster use like slight
          To many a one, which came unto her schoole,[5]
    Whom she did put to death, deceived like a foole.

26   She comming forth, when as she first beheld
          The armed Prince, with shield so blazing bright,
          Her ready to assaile, was greatly queld,
          And much dismayd with that dismayfull sight,
          That backe she would have turnd for great affright.
          But he gan her with courage fierce assay,
          That forst her turne againe in her despight,
          To save her selfe, least that he did her slay:
    And sure he had her slaine, had she not turnd her way.

27   Tho when she saw, that she was forst to fight,
          She flew at him, like to an hellish feend,
          And on his shield tooke hold with all her might,
          As if that it she would in peeces rend,

---

[1] **ravin:** the act of preying upon, gluttony.

[2] **empight:** implanted. This is one of many similarities with the figure of Errour from Book One (I.i.13–26).

[3] Oedipus, who solved the Sphinx's riddle, causing her to kill herself. Oedipus's children, his "fatall progeny," inherited the curse against his house.

[4] **loose:** solve; **deadly doole:** sorrow of death. The Sphinx killed anyone who could not solve the riddle.

[5] Hamilton suggests that "schoole" refers to inquisitors who punished a false answer with death.

Or reave out of the hand, that did it hend.[1]
Strongly he strove out of her greedy gripe
To loose his shield, and long while did contend:
But when he could not quite it, with one stripe[2]
Her Lions clawes he from her feete away did wipe.

28   With that aloude she gan to bray and yell,
     And fowle blasphemous speaches forth did cast,
     And bitter curses, horrible to tell,
     That even the Temple, wherein she was plast,
     Did quake to heare, and nigh asunder brast.[3]
     Tho with her huge long taile she at him strooke,
     That made him stagger, and stand halfe agast
     With trembling joynts, as he for terrour shooke;
Who nought was terrifide, but greater courage tooke.

29   As when the Mast of some well timbred hulke[4]
     Is with the blast of some outragious storme
     Blowne downe, it shakes the bottome of the bulke,[5]
     And makes her ribs to cracke, as they were torne,
     Whilest still she stands as stonisht and forlorne:
     So was he stound[6] with stroke of her huge taile.
     But ere that it she backe againe had borne,
     He with his sword it strooke, that without faile
He joynted[7] it, and mard the swinging of her flaile.

30   Then gan she cry much louder then afore,
     That all the people there without it heard,
     And *Belge* selfe was therewith stonied[8] sore,
     As if the onely sound thereof she feard.
     But then the feend her selfe more fiercely reard
     Uppon her wide great wings, and strongly flew
     With all her body at his head and beard,
     That had he not foreseene with heedfull vew,
And thrown his shield atween, she had him done to rew.

---

[1] **reave:** snatch; **hend:** hold.
[2] **quite:** quit, free; **stripe:** swipe.
[3] **brast:** burst.
[4] **hulke:** a large ship.

[5] **bulke:** hull.
[6] **stound:** stunned.
[7] **joynted:** disjointed, cut off.
[8] **stonied:** astonished.

31   But as she prest on him with heavy sway,[1]
         Under her wombe his fatall sword he thrust,
         And for her entrailes made an open way,
         To issue forth; the which once being brust,
         Like to a great Mill damb forth fiercely gusht,
         And powred out of her infernall sinke[2]
         Most ugly filth, and poyson therewith rusht,
         That him nigh choked with the deadly stinke:
    Such loathly matter were small lust[3] to speake, or thinke.

32   Then downe to ground fell that deformed Masse,[4]
         Breathing out clouds of sulphure fowle and blacke,
         In which a puddle of contagion was,
         More loathd then *Lerna*,[5] or then *Stygian* lake,
         That any man would nigh awhaped[6] make.
         Whom when he saw on ground, he was full glad,
         And streight went forth his gladnesse to partake
         With *Belge*, who watcht all this while full sad,
    Wayting what end would be of that same daunger drad.

33   Whom when she saw so joyously come forth,
         She gan rejoyce, and shew triumphant chere,
         Lauding and praysing his renowmed worth,
         By all the names that honorable were.
         Then in he brought her, and her shewed there
         The present of his paines, that Monsters spoyle,[7]
         And eke that Idoll deem'd so costly dere;
         Whom he did all to peeces breake and foyle[8]
    In filthy durt, and left so in the loathely soyle.

34   Then all the people, which beheld that day,
         Gan shout aloud, that unto heaven it rong;
         And all the damzels of that towne in ray,[9]
         Came dauncing forth, and joyous carrols song:
         So him they led through all their streetes along,

---

[1] **sway:** force.

[2] **sinke:** organs of digestion and excretion.

[3] **lust:** pleasure.

[4] Punning on the Catholic Mass.

[5] A swamp where Hercules killed the Hydra.

[6] **awhaped:** stupefied.

[7] **present:** visible result; **spoyle:** remains.

[8] **foyle:** defile. Arthur's iconoclasm reflects an important Protestant response to Catholic practice.

[9] **ray:** array.

Crowned with girlonds of immortall baies,[1]
And all the vulgar did about them throng,
To see the man, whose everlasting praise
They all were bound to all posterities to raise.

35   There he with *Belgae* did a while remaine,
      Making great feast and joyous merriment,
      Untill he had her settled in her raine,
      With safe assuraunce and establishment.
      Then to his first emprize[2] his mind he lent,
      Full loath to *Belgae,* and to all the rest:
      Of whom yet taking leave, thenceforth he went
      And to his former journey him addrest,
On which long way he rode, ne ever day did rest.

36   But turne we now to noble *Artegall;*
      Who having left *Mercilla,* streight way went
      On his first quest, the which him forth did call,
      To weet to worke *Irenaes* franchisement,[3]
      And eke *Grantortoes* worthy punishment.
      So forth he fared as his manner was,
      With onely *Talus* wayting[4] diligent,
      Through many perils and much way did pas,
Till nigh unto the place at length approcht he has.

37   There as he traveld by the way, he met
      An aged wight, wayfaring all alone,
      Who through his yeares long since aside had set
      The use of armes, and battell quite forgone:
      To whom as he approcht, he knew anone,
      That it was he which whilome did attend
      On faire *Irene* in her affliction,
      When first to Faery court he saw her wend,
Unto his soveraine Queene her suite for to commend.

---

[1] Garlands of bay leaves signify victory.

[2] **emprize:** quest. Arthur returns to his search for Gloriana, and will be seen next in Book Six.

[3] **franchisement:** liberation.

[4] **wayting:** attending.

38   Whom by his name saluting, thus he gan;
    "Haile good Sir *Sergis*,[1] truest Knight alive,
    Well tride in all thy Ladies troubles than,[2]
    When her that Tyrant did of Crowne deprive;
    What new ocasion doth thee hither drive,
    Whiles she alone is left, and thou here found?
    Or is she thrall, or doth she not survive?"
    To whom he thus; "She liveth sure and sound;
But by that Tyrant is in wretched thraldome bound.

39   "For she presuming on th'appointed tyde,[3]
    In which ye promist, as ye were a Knight,
    To meete her at the salvage[4] Ilands syde,
    And then and there for triall of her right
    With her unrigteous enemy to fight,
    Did thither come, where she afrayd of nought,
    By guilefull treason and by subtill slight
    Surprized was, and to *Grantorto* brought,
Who her imprisond hath, and her life often sought.

40   "And now he hath to her prefixt a day,
    By which if that no champion doe appeare,
    Which will her cause in battailous array
    Against him justifie, and prove her cleare
    Of all those crimes, that he gainst her doth reare
    She death shall by."[5] Those tidings sad
    Did much abash Sir *Artegall* to heare,
    And grieved sore, that through his fault she had
Fallen into that Tyrants hand and usage bad.

41   Then thus replide; "Now sure and by my life,
    Too much am I too blame for that faire Maide,
    That have her drawne to all this troublous strife,
    Through promise to afford her timely aide,

---

[1] Suggests "sergeant," a knight in atten-
dance to a ruler, and an officer who sum-
mons persons to court. Gough argues that
Sergis allegorizes Sir Henry Sidney, father
of Sir Philip, who was Lord Deputy of Ire-
land before Grey (302–303).

[2] **than:** then.

[3] **tyde:** point in time.

[4] **salvage:** savage. A key reference to Ire-
land. See Introduction, 3.

[5] **by:** buy—i.e., suffer.

Which by default I have not yet defraide.[1]
But witnesse unto me, ye heavens, that know
How cleare I am from blame of this upbraide:
For ye into like thraldome me did throw,
And kept from complishing the faith, which I did owe.[2]

42   "But now aread,[3] Sir *Sergis,* how long space,
      Hath he her lent, a Champion to provide."
      "Ten daies" (quoth he) "he graunted hath of grace,
      For that he weeneth well, before that tide
      None can have tidings to assist her side.
      For all the shores, which to the sea accoste,[4]
      He day and night doth ward both far and wide,
      That none can there arrive without an hoste:[5]
So her he deemes already but a damned ghoste."

43   "Now turne againe" (Sir *Artegall* then sayd)
      "For if I live till those ten daies have end,
      Assure your selfe, Sir Knight, she shall have ayd,
      Though I this dearest life for her doe spend";
      So backeward he attone[6] with him did wend.
      Tho as they rode together on their way,
      A rout of people they before them kend,[7]
      Flocking together in confusde array,
As if that there were some tumultuous affray.[8]

44   To which as they approcht, the cause to know,
      They saw a Knight in daungerous distresse
      Of a rude rout him chasing to and fro,
      That sought with lawlesse powre him to oppresse,
      And bring in bondage of their brutishnesse:
      And farre away, amid their rakehell[9] bands,

---

[1] **defraide:** paid—i.e., met the obligation of the promise.

[2] Artegall flatly contradicts himself in this stanza, first taking blame and then deflecting it onto the heavens. Cf. iv.28. This may reflect Artegall's ambivalent guilt about his encounter with Radigund, which delayed him, as well as Spenser's ambivalence toward the vacillations of English policy in Ireland.

[3] **aread:** declare.

[4] **accoste:** border.

[5] **hoste:** army.

[6] **attone:** together.

[7] **kend:** saw.

[8] **affray:** disturbance. This begins the episode of Burbon, which Spenser probably first intended for Canto Twelve—it is mistakenly included in the argument there.

[9] **rakehell:** rascal.

They spide a Lady left all succourlesse,
    Crying, and holding up her wretched hands
To him for aide, who long in vaine their rage withstands.

45   Yet still he strives, ne any perill spares,
        To reskue her from their rude violence,
        And like a Lion wood[1] amongst them fares,
        Dealing his dreadfull blowes with large dispence,
        Gainst which the pallid death findes no defence.
        But all in vaine, their numbers are so great,
        That naught may boot to banishe them from thence:
        For soone as he their outrage backe doth beat,
    They turne afresh, and oft renew their former threat.

46   And now they doe so sharpely him assay,
        That they his shield in peeces battred have,
        And forced him to throw it quite away,
        Fro dangers dread his doubtfull life to save;
        Albe that it most safety to him gave,
        And much did magnifie his noble name.
        For from the day that he thus did it leave,
        Amongst all Knights he blotted was with blame,
    And counted but a recreant Knight, with endles shame.

47   Whom when they thus distressed did behold,
        They drew unto his aide; but that rude rout
        Them also gan assaile with outrage bold,
        And forced them, how ever strong and stout
        They were, as well approv'd in many a doubt,[2]
        Backe to recule;[3] untill that yron man
        With his huge flaile began to lay about,
        From whose sterne presence they diffused ran,
    Like scattred chaffe, the which the wind away doth fan.[4]

48   So when that Knight from perill cleare was freed,
        He drawing neare, began to greete them faire,
        And yeeld great thanks for their so goodly deed,
        In saving him from daungerous despaire

---

[1] **wood:** raging.

[2] **doubt:** danger.

[3] **recule:** recoil.

[4] See Isa. 41.15–16.

Of those, which sought his life for to empaire.
Of whom Sir *Artegall* gan then enquire
The whole occasion of his late misfare,[1]
And who he was, and what those villaines were,
The which with mortall malice him pursu'd so nere.

49 To whom he thus; "My name is *Burbon*[2] hight,
  Well knowne, and far renowmed heretofore,
  Untill late mischiefe did uppon me light,
  That all my former praise hath blemisht sore;
  And that faire Lady, which in that uprore
  Ye with those caytives saw, *Flourdelis*[3] hight,
  Is mine owne love, though me she have forlore,[4]
  Whether withheld from me by wrongfull might,
Or with her owne good will, I cannot read aright.

50 "But sure to me her faith she first did plight,
  To be my love, and take me for her Lord,
  Till that a Tyrant, which *Grandtorto* hight,
  With golden giftes and many a guilefull word
  Entyced her, to him for to accord.
  O who may not with gifts and words be tempted?
  Sith which she hath me ever since abhord,
  And to my foe hath guilefully consented:
Ay me, that ever guyle in wemen was invented.[5]

51 "And now he hath this troupe of villains sent,
  By open force to fetch her quite away:
  Gainst whom my selfe I long in vaine have bent,[6]
  To rescue her, and daily meanes assay,
  Yet rescue her thence by no meanes I may:
  For they doe me with multitude oppresse,
  And with unequall might doe overlay,[7]
  That oft I driven am to great distresse,
And forced to forgoe th'attempt remedilesse."[8]

---

[1] **misfare:** misfortune.

[2] The name alludes to Henri de Burbon, King of Navarre, later Henri IV of France. See Introduction, 9.

[3] As the heraldic device of the French monarchy, suggests France or Paris.

[4] **forlore:** forsaken.

[5] **invented:** discovered.

[6] **bent:** contended.

[7] **overlay:** overwhelm.

[8] **remedilesse:** without hope.

52   "But why have ye" (said *Artegall*) "forborne
        Your owne good shield in daungerous dismay?
        That is the greatest shame and foulest scorne,
        Which unto any knight behappen may
        To loose the badge, that should his deedes display."[1]
        To whom Sir *Burbon*, blushing halfe for shame,
        "That shall I unto you" (quoth he) "bewray;
        Least ye therefore mote happily[2] me blame,
And deeme it doen of will, that through inforcement came.

53   "True is, that I at first was dubbed knight
        By a good knight, the knight of the *Redcrosse;*[3]
        Who when he gave me armes, in field to fight,
        Gave me a shield, in which he did endosse[4]
        His deare Redeemers badge upon the bosse:[5]
        The same longwhile I bore, and therewithall
        Fought many battels without wound or losse;
        Therewith *Grandtorto* selfe I did appall,
And made him oftentimes in field before me fall.

54   "But for that[6] many did that shield envie,
        And cruell enemies increased more;
        To stint all strife and troublous enmitie,
        That bloudie scutchin[7] being battered sore,
        I layd aside, and have of late forbore,
        Hoping thereby to have my love obtayned:
        Yet can I not my love have nathemore;
        For she by force is still fro me detayned,
And with corruptfull brybes is to untruth mis-trayned."[8]

---

[1] Burbon abandons his shield in stanza 46. In giving up his shield, he parallels Henry IV, who in 1593 renounced the Protestant faith for political purposes. For the shield, see Eph. 6.16. However, cf. Artegall's fight against Grantorto (xii.22).

[2] **happily:** by chance.

[3] The Knight of Holiness, the hero of Book One. His conferring knighthood on Burbon alludes to the Protestant baptism and education of Henry IV.

[4] **endosse:** inscribe.

[5] **bosse:** the center of the shield. Redcrosse has given him a shield emblazoned with a cross.

[6] **for that:** since.

[7] **scutchin:** a shield with a coat of arms.

[8] **mis-trayned:** misled.

55 To whom thus *Artegall;* "Certes Sir knight,
    Hard is the case, the which ye doe complaine;
    Yet not so hard (for nought so hard may light,[1]
    That it to such a streight mote you constraine)
    As to abandon, that which doth containe
    Your honours stile,[2] that is your warlike shield.
    All perill ought be lesse, and lesse all paine
    Then losse of fame in disaventrous field;[3]
Dye rather, then doe ought, that mote dishonour yield."

56 "Not so;" (quoth he) "for yet when time doth serve,
    My former shield I may resume againe:
    To temporize is not from truth to swerve,
    Ne for advantage terme to entertaine,
    When as necessitie doth it constraine."[4]
    "Fie on such forgerie" (said *Artegall*)
    "Under one hood to shadow faces twaine.
    Knights ought be true, and truth is one in all:
Of all things to dissemble fouly may befall."[5]

57 "Yet let me you of courtesie request,"
    (Said *Burbon*) "to assist me now at need
    Against these pesants, which have me opprest,
    And forced me to so infamous deed,
    That yet my love may from their hands be freed."
    Sir *Artegall,* albe he earst did wyte[6]
    His wavering mind, yet to his aide agreed,
    And buckling him eftsoones unto the fight,
Did set upon those troupes with all his powre and might.

58 Who flocking round about them, as a swarme
    Of flyes upon a birchen bough doth cluster,
    Did them assault with terrible allarme,

---

[1] **light:** happen.

[2] **stile:** title, inscription, style.

[3] **disaventrous field:** disastrous fight.

[4] Burbon argues against the charge that he is a time-server and that he has temporized —i.e., that he shapes his faith to the demands of the moment. From a puritan perspective, policies of compromise and expediency in matters of faith were horrifying.

[5] I.e., above all sins may misfortune befall dissembling.

[6] **earst did wyte:** lately blamed (Burbon's wavering mind).

And over all the fields themselves did muster,
With bils and glayves making a dreadfull luster;[1]
That forst at first those knights backe to retyre:
As when the wrathfull *Boreas*[2] doth bluster,
Nought may abide the tempest of his yre,
Both man and beast doe fly, and succour doe inquyre.[3]

59   But when as overblowen was that brunt,
Those knights began a fresh them to assayle,
And all about the fields like Squirrels hunt;
But chiefly *Talus* with his yron flayle,
Gainst which no flight nor rescue mote avayle,
Made cruell havocke of the baser crew,
And chaced them both over hill and dale:
The raskall manie soone they[4] overthrew,
But the two knights[5] themselves their captains did subdew.

60   At last they came whereas that Ladie bode,[6]
Whom now her keepers had forsaken quight,
To save themselves, and scattered were abrode:
Her halfe dismayd they found in doubtfull plight,
As neither glad nor sorie for their sight;
Yet wondrous faire she was, and richly clad
In roiall robes, and many Jewels dight,[7]
But that those villens through their usage bad
Them fouly rent, and shamefully defaced had.

61   But *Burbon* streight dismounting from his steed,
Unto her ran with greedie great desyre,
And catching her fast by her ragged weed,
Would have embraced her with hart entyre.
But she backstarting with disdainefull yre,
Bad him avaunt,[8] ne would unto his lore

---

[1] **bils and glayves:** spearlike weapons; **luster:** shining, magnificence.

[2] *Boreas:* the north wind.

[3] **inquyre:** seek.

[4] Possibly should be read as "he," implying Talus alone.

[5] I.e., Artegall and Burbon.

[6] **bode:** abode, dwelt.

[7] **dight:** dressed.

[8] **avaunt:** be off, depart.

Allured be, for prayer nor for meed.[1]
Whom when those knights so forward and forlore[2]
Beheld, they her rebuked and upbrayded sore.

62 Sayd *Artegall;* "what foule disgrace is this,
    To so faire Ladie, as ye seeme in sight,
    To blot your beautie, that unblemisht is,
    With so foule blame, as breach of faith once plight,
    Or change of love for any worlds delight?
    Is ought on earth so pretious or deare,
    As prayse and honour? Or is ought so bright
    And beautifull, as glories beames appeare,
Whose goodly light then *Phebus* lampe doth shine more cleare?[3]

63 "Why then will ye, fond[4] Dame, attempted bee
    Unto a strangers love, so lightly placed,
    For guiftes of gold, or any worldly glee,[5]
    To leave the love, that ye before embraced,
    And let your fame with falshood be defaced.
    Fie on the pelfe,[6] for which good name is sold,
    And honour with indignitie debased:
    Dearer is love then life, and fame then gold;
But dearer then them both, your faith once plighted hold."

64 Much was the Ladie in her gentle mind
    Abasht at his rebuke, that bit her neare,
    Ne ought to answere thereunto did find;
    But hanging downe her head with heavie cheare,
    Stood long amaz'd, as she amated[7] weare.
    Which *Burbon* seeing, her againe assayd,
    And clasping twixt his armes, her up did reare
    Upon his steede, whiles she no whit gainesayd,
So bore her quite away, nor well nor ill apayd.[8]

---

[1] A departure from the rhyme scheme: as the *b* rhyme, this should rhyme with "yre." "Hyre" has been proposed.

[2] **forlore:** morally lost.

[3] I.e., glory, whose light shines more clearly than Phoebus'.

[4] **fond:** foolish.

[5] **glee:** entertainment, mirth, glitter.

[6] **pelfe:** riches.

[7] **amated:** confounded.

[8] **apayd:** pleased.

65   Nathlesse the yron man did still pursew
        That raskall many with unpittied spoyle,[1]
        Ne ceassed not, till all their scattred crew
        Into the sea he drove quite from that soyle,
        The which they troubled had with great turmoyle.
        But *Artegall* seeing his cruell deed,
        Commaunded him from slaughter to recoyle,
        And to his voyage gan againe proceed:
For that the terme[2] approching fast, required speed.

---

[1] **spoyle:** destruction.

[2] Grantorto has given a term of ten days for a champion to appear to support Irena (xi.42).

Canto Twelve

Artegall doth Sir Burbon aide,
And blames for changing shield:
He with the great Grantorto fights,
And slaieth him in field.

1   O sacred[1] hunger of ambitious mindes,
    And impotent[2] desire of men to raine,
    Whom neither dread of God, that devils bindes,
    Nor lawes of men, that common weales[3] containe,
    Nor bands of nature, that wilde beastes restraine,
    Can keepe from outrage, and from doing wrong,
    Where they may hope a kingdome to obtaine.
    No faith so firme, no trust can be so strong,
No love so lasting then, that may endure long.

2   Witnesse may *Burbon* be, whom all the bands,
    Which may a Knight assure, had surely bound,
    Untill the love of Lordship and of lands
    Made him become most faithlesse and unsound:
    And witnesse be *Gerioneo* found,
    Who for like cause faire *Belge* did oppresse,
    And right and wrong most cruelly confound:
    And so be now *Grantorto,* who no lesse
Then all the rest burst out to all outragiousnesse.

3   Gainst whom Sir *Artegall,* long having since
    Taken in hand th'exploit, being theretoo
    Appointed by that mightie Faerie Prince,[4]
    Great *Gloriane,* that Tyrant to fordoo,[5]
    Through other great adventures hethertoo
    Had it forslackt. But now time drawing ny,

---

[1] **sacred:** accursed.

[2] **impotent:** ungovernable.

[3] **common weales:** commonwealths.

[4] Gloriana, like Elizabeth, is sometimes called prince.

[5] **fordoo:** do in.

To him assynd, her high beheast to doo,
To the sea shore he gan his way apply,
To weete if shipping readie he mote there descry.

4   Tho when they came to the sea coast, they found
     A ship all readie (as good fortune fell)
     To put to sea, with whom they did compound,[1]
     To passe them over, where them list to tell:
     The winde and weather served them so well,
     That in one day they with the coast did fall;[2]
     Whereas they readie found them to repell,
     Great hostes of men in order martiall,
Which them forbad to land, and footing did forstall.

5   But nathemore would they from land refraine,
     But when as nigh unto the shore they drew,
     That foot of man might sound the bottome plaine,[3]
     Talus into the sea did forth issew,
     Though darts from shore and stones they at him threw;
     And wading through the waves with stedfast sway,
     Maugre the might of all those troupes in vew,
     Did win the shore, whence he them chast away,
And made to fly, like doves, whom the Eagle doth affray.

6   The whyles Sir *Artegall,* with that old knight[4]
     Did forth descend, there being none them neare,
     And forward marched to a towne in sight.
     By this[5] came tydings to the Tyrants eare,
     By those, which earst did fly away for feare
     Of their arrivall: wherewith troubled sore,
     He all his forces streight to him did reare,
     And forth issuing with his scouts afore,
Meant them to have incountred, ere thy left the shore.

---

[1] **compound:** contract, strike a deal.

[2] Just as the voyage from England to Ireland could last one day. Gough associates Artegall's landing with Lord Grey's arrival as Lord Deputy of Ireland (316).

[3] I.e., near enough to shore that a man might stand.

[4] I.e., Sir Sergis.

[5] **By this:** by this time.

7   But ere he marched farre, he with them met,
        And fiercely charged them with all his force;
        But *Talus* sternely did upon them set,
        And brusht,[1] and battred them without remorse,
        That on the ground he left full many a corse;
        Ne any able was him to withstand,
        But he them overthrew both man and horse,
        That they lay scattred over all the land,
As thicke as doth the seede after the sowers hand.

8   Till *Artegall* him seeing so to rage,
        Willd him to stay, and signe of truce did make:
        To which all harkning, did a while asswage
        Their forces furie, and their terror slake;
        Till he an Herauld cald, and to him spake,
        Willing him wend unto the Tyrant streight,
        And tell him that not for such slaughters sake
        He thether came, but for to trie the right
Of fayre *Irenaes* cause with him in single fight.[2]

9   And willed him for to reclayme with speed
        His scattred people, ere they all were slaine,
        And time and place convenient to areed,[3]
        In which they two the combat might darraine.[4]
        Which message when *Grantorto* heard, full fayne[5]
        And glad he was the slaughter so to stay,
        And pointed for the combat twixt them twayne
        The morrow next, ne gave him longer day.
So sounded the retraite, and drew his folke away.

10   That night Sir *Artegall* did cause his tent
        There to be pitched on the open plaine;
        For he[6] had given streight commaundement,
        That none should dare him once to entertaine:[7]
        Which none durst breake, though many would right faine

---

[1] Recalls that Talus attacks with a flail—he goes on in this stanza to thresh and plant his enemies.

[2] Cf. i.25.

[3] **areed:** appoint.

[4] **darraine:** settle.

[5] **fayne:** desirous.

[6] I.e., Grantorto.

[7] Perhaps Artegall has learned from his mistake with Radigund when he accepted her offer of entertainment (iv.51).

For fayre *Irena,* whom they loved deare.
But yet old *Sergis* did so well him paine,
That from close[1] friends, that dar'd not to appeare,
He all things did purvay, which for them needfull weare.

11   The morrow next, that was the dismall day,
        Appointed for *Irenas* death before,
        So soone as it did to the world display
        His chearefull face, and light to men restore,
        The heavy[2] Mayd, to whom none tydings bore
        Of *Artegals* arryvall, her to free,
        Lookt up with eyes full sad and hart full sore;
        Weening[3] her lifes last howre then neare to bee,
Sith no redemption nigh she did nor heare nor see.

12   Then up she rose, and on her selfe did dight[4]
        Most squalid garments, fit for such a day,
        And with dull countenance, and with doleful spright,
        She forth was brought in sorrowfull dismay,
        For to receive the doome of her decay.[5]
        But comming to the place, and finding there
        Sir *Artegall,* in battailous array
        Wayting his foe, it did her dead hart cheare,
And new life to her lent, in midst of deadly feare.

13   Like as a tender Rose in open plaine,
        That with untimely drought nigh withered was,
        And hung the head, soone as few drops of raine
        Thereon distill,[6] and deaw her daintie face,
        Gins to looke up, and with fresh wonted grace
        Dispreds the glorie of her leaves gay;
        Such was *Irenas* countenance, such her case,
        When *Artegall* she saw in that array,
There wayting for the Tyrant, till it was farre day.[7]

---

[1] **close:** secret.
[2] I.e., heavy with sorrow.
[3] **Weening:** judging.
[4] **dight:** place.

[5] **the doome of her decay:** her death sentence.
[6] **distill:** trickle down, infuse.
[7] **farre day:** late in the day.

14   Who came at length, with proud presumpteous gate,
    Into the field, as if he fearelesse were,
    All armed in a cote of yron plate,
    Of great defence to ward the deadly feare,
    And on his head a steele cap he did weare
    Of colour rustie browne, but sure and strong;
    And in his hand an huge Polaxe did beare,
    Whose steale[1] was yron studded, but not long,
With which he wont to fight, to justifie his wrong.[2]

15   Of stature huge and hideous he was,
    Like to a Giant for his monstrous hight,
    And did in strength most sorts of men surpas,
    Ne ever any found his match in might;
    Thereto he had great skill in single fight:
    His face was ugly, and his countenance sterne,
    That could have frayd one with the very sight,
    And gaped like a gulfe, when he did gerne,[3]
That whether man or monster one could scarce discerne.

16   Soone as he did within the listes[4] appeare,
    With dreadfull looke he *Artegall* beheld,
    As if he would have daunted him with feare,
    And grinning griesly, did against him weld
    His deadly weapon, which in hand he held.
    But th'Elfin swayne, that oft had seene like sight,
    Was with his ghastly count'nance nothing queld,
    But gan him streight to buckle to the fight,
And cast his shield about, to be in readie plight.[5]

17   The trompets sound, and they together goe,
    With dreadfull terror, and with fell intent;
    And their huge strokes full daungerously bestow,
    To doe most dammage, where as most they ment.
    But with such force and furie violent,
    The tyrant thundred his thicke blowes so fast,

---

[1] **steale:** handle.

[2] Grantorto's armor resembles that of the Galloglass, the Irish foot soldier, as Spenser describes him in *A View* (74).

[3] **gerne:** snarl.

[4] **listes:** barriers enclosing the tournament field.

[5] **plight:** position.

That through the yron walles their way they rent,
And even to the vitall parts they past,
Ne ought could them endure, but all they cleft or brast.[1]

18   Which cruell outrage when as *Artegall*
        Did well avize,[2] thenceforth with warie heed
        He shund his strokes, where ever they did fall,
        And way did give unto their gracelesse speed:
        As when a skilfull Marriner doth reed
        A storme approching, that doth perill threat,
        He will not bide the daunger of such dread,
        But strikes his sayles, and vereth[3] his mainsheat,
And lends unto it leave the emptie ayre to beat.

19   So did the Faerie knight himselfe abeare,[4]
        And stouped oft his head from shame to shield;
        No shame to stoupe, ones head more high to reare,
        And much to gaine, a litle for to yield;
        So stoutest knights doen oftentimes in field.
        But still the tyrant sternely at him layd,
        And did his yron axe so nimbly wield,
        That many wounds into his flesh it made,
And with his burdenous blowes him sore did overlade.[5]

20   Yet when as fit advantage he did spy,
        The whiles the cursed felon high did reare
        His cruell hand, to smite him mortally,
        Under his stroke he to him stepping neare,
        Right in the flanke him strooke with deadly dreare,[6]
        That the gore bloud thence gushing grievously,
        Did underneath him like a pond appeare,
        And all his armour did with purple dye;
Thereat he brayed loud, and yelled dreadfully.

21   Yet the huge stroke, which he before intended,
        Kept on his course, as he did it direct,
        And with such monstrous poise[7] adowne descended,

---

[1] **brast:** burst.

[2] **avize:** observe.

[3] **vereth:** lets out.

[4] **abeare:** comport.

[5] **overlade:** overload.

[6] **with deadly dreare:** with the grimness of death.

[7] **poise:** weight.

That seemed nought could him from death protect:
But he it well did ward with wise respect,[1]
And twixt him and the blow his shield did cast,
Which thereon seizing, tooke no great effect,
But byting deepe therein did sticke so fast,
That by no meanes it backe againe he forth could wrast.

22   Long while he tug'd and strove, to get it out,
        And all his powre applyed thereunto,
        That he therewith the knight drew all about:
        Nathlesse, for all that ever he could doe,
        His axe he could not from his shield undoe.
        Which *Artegall* perceiving, strooke no more,
        But loosing soone his shield, did it forgoe,
        And whiles he combred was therewith so sore,
He gan at him let drive more fiercely then afore.[2]

23   So well he him pursew'd, that at the last,
        He stroke him with *Chrysaor*[3] on the hed,
        That with the souse[4] thereof full sore aghast,
        He staggered to and fro in doubtfull sted.
        Againe whiles he him saw so ill bested,
        He did him smite with all his might and maine,
        That falling on his mother earth he fed:[5]
        Whom when he saw prostrated on the plaine,
He lightly reft[6] his head, to ease him of his paine.

24   Which when the people round about him saw,
        They shouted all for joy of his successe,
        Glad to be quit from that proud Tyrants awe,
        Which with strong powre did them long time oppresse;
        And running all with greedie joyfulnesse
        To faire *Irena,* at her feet did fall,

---

[1] **respect:** care, alert reaction.

[2] Artegall's act of letting go his shield can be compared with Burbon's (xi.46).

[3] Artegall's sword from Astraea (i.9). It was supposedly broken by Radigund, however (v.21).

[4] **souse:** thump.

[5] I.e., he fed upon the earth, or bit the dust.

[6] **reft:** severed.

And her adored with due humblenesse,
    As their true Liege and Princesse naturall;[1]
And eke her champions glorie sounded over all.

25   Who streight her leading with meete majestie
        Unto the pallace, where their kings did rayne,
        Did her therein establish peaceablie,
        And to her kingdomes seat restore agayne;
        And all such persons, as did late maintayne
        That Tyrants part, with close or open ayde,
        He sorely punished with heavie payne;
        That in short space, whiles there with her he stayd,
    Not one was left, that durst her once have disobayd.[2]

26   During which time, that he did there remaine,
        His studie was true Justice how to deale,
        And day and night employ'd his busie paine[3]
        How to reforme that ragged common-weale:
        And that same yron man which could reveale
        All hidden crimes, through all that realme he sent,
        To search out those, that usd to rob and steale,
        Or did rebell gainst lawfull government;
    On whom he did inflict most grievous punishment.

27   But ere he could reforme it thoroughly,
        He through occasion called was away,
        To Faerie Court, that of necessity
        His course of Justice he was forst to stay,
        And *Talus* to revoke from the right way,
        In which he was that Realme for to redresse.[4]
        But envies cloud still dimmeth vertues ray.[5]
        So having freed *Irena* from distresse,
    He tooke his leave of her, there left in heavinesse.

---

[1] I.e., by the law of nature and so by divine right.

[2] In this and the following stanzas, Spenser most clearly allegorizes English efforts in Ireland and Grey's tenure as Lord Deputy of Ireland. See Introduction, 3.

[3] **paine:** efforts.

[4] I.e., Artegall recalls Talus from the path he was in, which aimed at the reordering of the realm.

[5] Lord Grey was called back from Ireland by Elizabeth, amid complaints that his rule had been too violent. See *A View,* 103.

28   Tho as he backe returned from that land,
     And there arriv'd againe, whence forth he set,
     He had not passed farre upon the strand,[1]
     When as two old ill favour'd Hags he met,
     By the way side being together set,
     Two griesly creatures; and, to that[2] their faces
     Most foule and filthie were, their garments yet
     Being all rag'd and tatter'd, their disgraces
  Did much the more augment, and made most ugly cases.

29   The one of them, that elder did appeare,
     With her dull eyes did seeme to looke askew,
     That her mis-shape much helpt;[3] and her foule heare
     Hung loose and loathsomely: Thereto her hew
     Was wan and leane, that all her teeth arew,[4]
     And all her bones might through her cheekes be red;
     Her lips were like raw lether, pale and blew,
     And as she spake, therewith she slavered;
  Yet spake she seldom, but thought more, the lesse she sed.

30   Her hands were foule and durtie, never washt
     In all her life, with long nayles over raught,
     Like puttocks[5] clawes: with th'one of which she scracht
     Her cursed head, although it itched naught;
     The other held a snake with venime fraught,
     On which she fed, and gnawed hungrily,
     As if that long she had not eaten ought;
     That round about her jawes one might descry
  The bloudie gore and poyson dropping lothsomely.

31   Her name was *Envie,* knowen well thereby;[6]
     Whose nature is to grieve, and grudge at all,
     That ever she sees doen prays-worthily,
     Whose sight to her is greatest crosse, may fall,
     And vexeth so, that makes her eat her gall.
     For when she wanteth other thing to eat,

---

[1] **strand:** shore.

[2] **to that:** to that end.

[3] **helpt:** augmented.

[4] **arew:** in a row.

[5] **puttocks:** a kite's or buzzard's.

[6] This portrait resembles Envy in the pageant of Deadly Sins, although there Envy is male (I.iv.30–32).

She feedes on her owne maw[1] unnaturall,
And of her owne foule entrayles makes her meat;
Meat fit for such a monsters monsterous dyeat.

32   And if she hapt of any good to heare,
That had to any happily betid,[2]
Then would she inly fret, and grieve, and teare
Her flesh for felnesse,[3] which she inward hid:
But if she heard of ill, that any did,
Or harme, that any had, then would she make
Great cheare, like one unto a banquet bid;
And in anothers losse great pleasure take,
As she had got thereby, and gayned a great stake.

33   The other nothing better was, then shee;
Agreeing in bad will and cancred kynd,[4]
But in bad maner they did disagree:
For what so *Envie* good or bad did fynd,
She did conceale, and murder[5] her owne mynd;
But this, what ever evill she conceived,
Did spred abroad, and throw in th'open wynd.
Yet this in all her words might be perceived,
That all she sought, was mens good name to have bereaved.

34   For what soever good by any sayd,
Or doen she heard, she would streightwayes invent,
How to deprave,[6] or slaunderously upbrayd,
Or to misconstrue of a mans intent,
And turne to ill the thing, that well was ment.
Therefore she used often to resort,
To common haunts, and companies frequent,
To hearke what any one did good report,
To blot the same with blame, or wrest[7] in wicked sort.

35   And if that any ill she heard of any,
She would it eeke,[8] and make much worse by telling,
And take great joy to publish it to many,

---

[1] **maw:** jaws, throat, belly, or womb.
[2] **happily betid:** by chance happened.
[3] **felnesse:** malignity.
[4] **cancred kynd:** corrupted nature.
[5] **murder:** torment.
[6] **deprave:** defame.
[7] **wrest:** twist.
[8] **eeke:** increase.

That every matter worse was for her melling.[1]
Her name was hight *Detraction,* and her dwelling
Was neare to *Envie,* even her neighbour next;
A wicked hag, and *Envy* selfe excelling
In mischiefe: for her selfe she onely vext;[2]
But this same both her selfe, and others eke perplext.

36   Her face was ugly, and her mouth distort,
      Foming with poyson round about her gils,[3]
      In which her cursed tongue full sharpe and short
      Appear'd like Aspis sting, that closely[4] kils,
      Or cruelly does wound, whom so she wils:
      A distaffe in her other hand she had,[5]
      Upon the which she litle spinnes, but spils,[6]
      And faynes to weave false tales and leasings[7] bad,
   To throw amongst the good, which others had disprad.

37   These two now had themselves combynd in one,
      And linckt together gainst Sir *Artegall,*
      For whom they wayted as his mortall fone,
      How they might make him into mischiefe fall,
      For freeing from their snares *Irena* thrall,[8]
      Besides unto themselves they gotten had
      A monster, which the *Blatant beast*[9] men call,
      A dreadfull feend of gods and men ydrad,[10]
   Whom they by slights allur'd, and to their purpose lad.

38   Such were these Hags, and so unhandsome drest:
      Who when they nigh approching, had espyde
      Sir *Artegall* return'd from his late quest,
      They both arose, and at him loudly cryde,

[1] **melling:** meddling.

[2] I.e., Envie vexes only herself.

[3] **gils:** cheeks.

[4] **closely:** secretly. See Ps. 140.3.

[5] Recalls Artegall's distaff (v.23).

[6] **spils:** spoils.

[7] **leasings:** lies.

[8] Gough points out that this is the only passage to imply that Irena fell into Grantorto's power by means of Envie and Detraction.

[9] Spenser appears to have coined the word blatant, based on "bleat" and the Latin word for "to babble." The Blatant Beast is a figure for scandal and uncivil rumor, and in Book Six it will be hunted by Sir Calidore, the knight of Courtesie. See Introduction, 10. In *A View,* Spenser writes of how "Envy list to blatter against" Lord Grey (28).

[10] **ydrad:** feared.

As it had bene two shepheards curres, had scryde[1]
A ravenous Wolfe amongst the scattered flockes.
And *Envie* first, as she that first him eyde,
Towardes him runs, and with rude flaring lockes
About her eares, does beat her brest, and forhead knockes.

39   Then from her mouth the gobbet[2] she does take,
        The which whyleare she was so greedily
        Devouring, even that halfe-gnawen snake,
        And at him throwes it most despightfully.
        The cursed Serpent, though she hungrily
        Earst chawd thereon, yet was not all so dead,
        But that some life remayned secretly,
        And as he past afore withouten dread,
Bit him behind, that long the marke was to be read.[3]

40   Then th'other comming neare, gan him revile,
        And fouly rayle, with all she could invent;
        Saying, that he had with unmanly guile,
        And foule abusion[4] both his honour blent,
        And that bright sword, the sword of Justice lent
        Had stayned with reprochfull crueltie,
        In guiltlesse blood of many an innocent:
        As for *Grandtorto*, him with treacherie
And traynes having surpriz'd, he fouly did to die.[5]

41   Thereto the Blatant beast by them set on
        At him began aloud to barke and bay,
        With bitter rage and fell contention,
        That all the woods and rockes nigh to that way,
        Began to quake and tremble with dismay;
        And all the aire rebellowed againe.
        So dreadfully his hundred tongues did bray,
        And evermore those hags them selves did paine,
To sharpen[6] him, and their owne cursed tongs did straine.

---

[1] **scryde:** descried.

[2] **gobbet:** piece of raw meat.

[3] The snake bites Artegall, enacting the phrase "back-biting."

[4] **abusion:** deception, abusive behavior.

[5] Gough connects these accusations to the massacre Grey ordered at Smerwick (319). For Smerwick, see Introduction, 3. In *A View,* Spenser writes of Grey that "complaint was made against him, that he was a bloodie man" (103).

[6] **sharpen:** goad.

42 And still among[1] most bitter wordes they spake,
    Most shamefull, most unrighteous, most untrew,
    That they the mildest man alive would make
    Forget his patience, and yeeld vengeaunce dew
    To her, that so false sclaunders[2] at him threw.
    And more to make them pierce and wound more deepe,
    She with the sting, which in her vile tongue grew,
    Did sharpen them, and in fresh poyson steepe:
Yet he past on, and seem'd of them to take no keepe.

43 But *Talus* hearing her so lewdly raile,
    And speake so ill of him, that well deserved,
    Would her have chastiz'd with his yron flaile,
    If her Sir *Artegall* had not preserved,
    And him forbidden, who his heast[3] observed.
    So much the more at him still did she scold,
    And stones did cast, yet he for nought would swerve
    From his right course, but still the way did hold
To Faery Court, where what him fell shall else be told.

---

[1] **among:** during that time.

[2] **sclaunders:** slanders.

[3] **heast:** command.

THE LETTER TO RALEIGH

A
Letter of the Authors expounding his
whole intention in the course of this worke: which for that it giueth great light to the Reader, for the better vnderstanding is hereunto annexed.

To the Right noble, and Valorous, Sir Walter Raleigh knight, Lo. Wardein of the Stanneryes, and her Maiesties liefetenaunt of the County of Cornewayll.[1]

Sir knowing how doubtfully all Allegories may be construed, and this booke of mine, which I have entituled the Faery Queene, being a continued Allegory, or darke conceit, I have thought good aswell for avoyding of gealous opinions and misconstructions, as also for your better light in reading thereof, (being so by you commanded,) to discover unto you the general intention and meaning, which in the whole course thereof I have fashioned, without expressing of any particular purposes or by accidents therein occasioned. The generall end therefore of all the booke is to fashion a gentleman or noble person in vertuous and gentle discipline:[2] Which for that I conceived shoulde be most plausible[3] and pleasing, being coloured with an historicall fiction, the which the most part of men delight to read, rather for variety of matter, then for profite of the ensample: I chose the historye of king Arthure, as most fitte for the excellency of his person, being made famous by many mens former workes, and also furthest from the daunger of envy, and suspition of present time. In which I have followed all the antique Poets historicall, first Homere, who in the Persons of Agamemnon and Ulysses hath ensampled a good governour and a vertuous man, the one in his Ilias, the other in his Odysseis: then Virgil, whose like intention was to doe in the person of Aeneas: after him Ariosto comprised them

[1] Appended to the 1590 edition of *The Faerie Queene,* Spenser's "Letter to Raleigh," also called "A Letter of the Authors," has been read as a preface, detailing both the larger plot and the poetics underlying the poem. It was not included in the 1596 edition, and so only discusses the first three books directly.

[2] **discipline:** learning, training, orderly conduct, the system by which a church exercises control over its members.

[3] **plausible:** deserving applause, acceptable.

both in his Orlando:[1] *and lately Tasso dissevered them againe, and formed both parts in two persons, namely that part which they in Philosophy call Ethice, or vertues of a private man, coloured in his Rinaldo: The other named Politice in his Godfredo.*[2] *By ensample of which excellente Poets, I labour to pourtraict in Arthure, before he was king, the image of a brave knight, perfected in the twelve private morall vertues, as Aristotle hath devised,*[3] *the which is the purpose of these first twelve bookes: which if I finde to be well accepted, I may be perhaps encoraged, to frame the other part of polliticke vertues in his person, after that hee came to be king.*[4] *To some I know this Methode will seeme displeasaunt, which had rather have good discipline delivered plainly in way of precepts, or sermoned at large, as they use, then thus clowdily enwrapped in Allegoricall devises. But such, me seeme, should be satisfide with the use of these dayes seeing all things accounted by their showes, and nothing esteemed of, that is not delightfull and pleasing to commune sence. For this cause is Xenophon preferred before Plato, for that the one in the exquisite depth of his judgement, formed a Commune welth such as it should be, but the other in the person of Cyrus and the Persians fashioned a government such as might best be: So much more profitable and gratious is doctrine by ensample, then by rule.*[5] *So have I laboured to doe in the person of Arthure: whome I conceive after his long education by Timon, to whom he was by Merlin delivered to be brought up, so soone as he was borne of the Lady Igrayne, to have seene in a dream or vision the Faery Queen, with whose excellent beauty ravished, he awaking resolved to seeke her out, and so being by Merlin armed, and by Timon throughly instructed, he went to seeke her forth in Faerye land. In that Faery Queene I meane glory in my generall intention, but in my particular I conceive the most excellent and glorious person of our soveraine the Queene, and her kingdome in Faery land. And yet in some places els, I doe otherwise shadow her. For considering she beareth two persons, the one of a most royall Queene or Empresse, the other of a most vertuous and beautifull Lady, this latter part in some places I doe expresse in Belphoebe, fashioning her name according to your owne excellent conceipt of Cynthia, (Phoebe and Cynthia being both names of Diana).*[6] *So in the person of*

---

[1] Lodovico Ariosto, Italian author of *Orlando Furioso* (1532).

[2] Torquato Tasso, Italian author of *Rinaldo* (1562) and *Gerusalemme Liberata* (1581), in which the hero Godfredo embodies public or political virtues.

[3] Aristotle does not name twelve particular moral virtues in the *Nicomachaean Ethics*. There are, however, several Medieval and Renaissance commentaries on Aristotle from which twelve could be construed.

[4] Spenser indicates that he planned twelve books for *The Faerie Queene* and would

willingly write twenty-four, the former matching Virgil, the latter Homer.

[5] Spenser says that Xenophon's *Cyropaedia*, celebrated for teaching by example, is commonly preferred to Plato's *Republic*, which taught by precepts.

[6] Belphoebe appears in Books Two, Three, and Four. Cynthia refers to Raleigh's poem of that name, which also celebrated Elizabeth. Spenser suggests that Gloriana, the Faerie Queen, represents Elizabeth's public role as monarch, while Belphoebe personifies her private, virginal life.

Prince Arthure I sette forth magnificence in particular, which vertue for that (according to Aristotle and the rest) it is the perfection of all the rest, and conteineth in it them all, therefore in the whole course I mention the deedes of Arthure applyable to that vertue, which I write of in that booke. But of the xii. other vertues, I make xii. other knights the patrones, for the more variety of the history: Of which these three bookes contayn three. The first of the knight of the Redcrosse, in whome I expresse Holynes: The seconde of Sir Guyon, in whome I sette forth Temperaunce: The third of Britomartis a Lady knight, in whome I picture Chastity. But because the beginning of the whole worke seemeth abrupte and as depending upon other antecedents, it needs that ye know the occasion of these three knights severall adventures. For the Methode of a Poet historical is not such, as of an Historiographer. For an Historiographer discourseth of affayres orderly as they were donne, accounting as well the times as the actions, but a Poet thrusteth into the middest,[1] even where it most concerneth him, and there recoursing to the thinges forepaste, and divining of thinges to come, maketh a pleasing Analysis of all. The beginning therefore of my history, if it were to be told by an Historiographer should be the twelfth booke, which is the last, where I devise that the Faery Queene kept her Annuall feaste xii. dayes, uppon which xii. severall dayes, the occasions of the xii. severall adventures hapned, which being undertaken by xii. severall knights, are in these xii books severally handled and discoursed. The first was this. In the beginning of the feast, there presented him selfe a tall clownishe[2] younge man, who falling before the Queen of Faries desired a boone (as the manner then was) which during that feast she might not refuse: which was that hee might have the atchievement of any adventure, which during that feaste should happen, that being graunted, he rested him on the floore, unfitte through his rusticity for a better place. Soone after entred a faire Ladye in mourning weedes, riding on a white Asse, with a dwarfe behind her leading a warlike steed, that bore the Armes of a knight, and his speare in the dwarfes hand. Shee falling before the Queene of Faeries, complayned that her father and mother an ancient King and Queene, had bene by an huge dragon many years shut up in a brasen[3] Castle, who thence suffred them not to yssew: and therefore besought the Faery Queene to assygne her some one of her knights to take on him that exployt. Presently that clownish person upstarting, desired that adventure: whereat the Queene much wondering, and the Lady much gainesaying, yet he earnestly importuned his desire. In the end the Lady told him that unlesse that armour which she brought, would serve him (that is the armour of a Christian man specified by Saint Paul v. Ephes.[4]) that he could not succeed in that enterprise, which being forthwith put upon him with dewe furnitures[5] thereunto, he seemed the goodliest man in al that company, and was well liked of the Lady. And

---

[1] See Horace, *Ars Poetica*, 146–52.

[2] **clownishe:** rustic.

[3] **brasen:** strong like brass.

[4] See Eph. 6.11–17.

[5] **dewe furnitures:** proper equipment.

eftesoones[1] *taking on him knighthood, and mounting on that straunge Courser, he went forth with her on that adventure: where beginneth the first booke, vz.*

A gentle knight was pricking on the playne. &c.

The second day ther came in a Palmer bearing an Infant with bloody hands, whose Parents he complained to have bene slayn by an Enchaunteresse called Acrasia: and therfore craved of the Faery Queene, to appoint him some knight, to performe that adventure, which being assigned to Sir Guyon, he presently went forth with that same Palmer: which is the beginning of the second booke and the whole subject thereof.[2] *The third day there came in, a Groome who complained before the Faery Queene, that a vile Enchaunter called Busirane had in hand a most faire Lady called Amoretta, whom he kept in most grievous torment, because she would not yield him the pleasure of her body. Whereupon Sir Scudamour the lover of that Lady presently tooke on him that adventure. But being unable to performe it by reason of the hard Enchauntments, after long sorrow, in the end met with Britomartis, who succoured him, and reskewed his love.*

But by occasion hereof, many other adventures are intermedled, but rather as Accidents, then intendments.[3] *As the love of Britomart, the overthrow of Marinell, the misery of Florimell, the vertuousnes of Belphoebe, the lasciviousnes of Hellenora, and many the like.*[4]

Thus much Sir, I have briefly overronne to direct your understanding to the welhead of the History, that from thence gathering the whole intention of the conceit, ye may as in a handfull gripe al the discourse, which otherwise may happily[5] *seeme tedious and confused. So humbly craving the continuaunce of your honorable favour towards me, and th'eternall establishment of your happines, I humbly take leave.*

23. January. 1589.[6]

Yours most humbly affectionate.
Ed. Spenser.

---

[1] **eftesoones:** immediately.

[2] This description is at variance with the beginning of Book Two at several points— e.g., the Palmer is already with Guyon when they encounter the bloody baby in Canto One.

[3] **intendments:** matters of central import.

[4] This description seems to make Scudamour the hero, rather than Britomartis.

[5] **happily:** by chance.

[6] In the new calendar, 1590.

The Life of Edmund Spenser

Spenser (c. 1552–1599) was from a merchant family, possibly involved in the cloth trade and probably living in London. Although he may have been related to the noble family of Spencers, Spenser was not a gentleman. He was fortunate to attend the Merchant Taylors' School, an academy founded by the tailors' guild, and was registered there as a "poor scholar." The school, however, was excellent; in his eight years there, Spenser received a humanist education that was rich in classical scholarship and languages. In 1569 he entered Pembroke Hall, Cambridge. Again he was a scholarship student, called a sizar, earning room and board by performing servants' duties. In the same year that he arrived at Cambridge, Spenser was first published: several of his translations from Italian and French appeared in the Protestant miscellany *A Theatre for Worldlings*. Spenser completed a Bachelor of Arts degree in 1573, and then, in 1576, a Master of Arts (finishing 66th out of a class of 70). Spenser then began a career as secretary to high-ranking men, a position of some importance involving a broad array of duties that included much traveling and writing. Intermittent records show him serving as an emissary for the earl of Leicester, and in 1578 he was secretary to John Young, Bishop of Rochester. In 1579 he married Maccabaeus Chylde; we know little about the couple's family life other than the fact that they had two children. In 1580 he was appointed secretary to Lord Grey de Wilton, the new Lord Deputy of Ireland, and traveled there with him. Spenser's career as a secretary and subsequent work as a civil servant in Ireland no doubt took up much of his time. But he was simultaneously establishing a second career as a poet. Probably while working for Leicester, Spenser met Philip Sidney and entered into his sophisticated literary circle. In 1579 Spenser published *The Shepheardes Calendar*, his innovative and enormously influential collection of pastorals. It revealed Spenser as not only one of England's most skilled poets, but as a deeply interested and progressive Protestant thinker. He also cultivated his university friendship with the humanist scholar Gabriel Harvey, which in 1580 led to the publication of several of their letters. The Harvey letters mention several lost works, and suggest that by 1580 Spenser had begun working on *The Faerie Queene*.

Meanwhile, in Ireland with Lord Grey, Spenser participated in the complicated and exceedingly violent project of English colonialism. Grey was sent to govern a country that was struggling broadly against English domination, and he adopted a strategy of overwhelming force, including the notorious slaughter of 600 military prisoners at Smerwick, and policies aimed at subduing the population through famine. To what extent Spenser participated in Grey's governance, and to what extent he merely accompanied him and performed secretarial duties, is unclear. But it is clear that Spenser profited personally from empire building. Although Grey was recalled to England in 1582, Spenser made Ireland his permanent home, first in the New Abbey estate, and in 1589 in the three thousand acres of the Kilcolman estate. Throughout the 1580s, Spenser received a number of governmental appointments and established himself in Ireland as a well-off planter and gentleman. His complex relationship to Ireland is largely understood through *A View of the Present State of Ireland,* a prose dialogue that forthrightly defends Grey's violent tactics and advocates deeply repressive measures against the Irish. It has called forth both defenses of the poet and declarations of his complicity in the outrages of colonialism. The subtleties of *A View* cast a similarly complicated light on *The Faerie Queene,* which was written in Ireland, and reflects its beautiful and pitifully war-torn landscape.

In Ireland Spenser became friends with the explorer, author, and courtier, Sir Walter Raleigh, who in 1589 traveled with him to England. Probably with the sponsorship of Raleigh, Spenser presented the first three books of *The Faerie Queene* to Elizabeth, who, by Spenser's report, was well pleased. Spenser secured the printer William Ponsonby in London, and Books One through Three of *The Faerie Queene* were published in 1590. The poem was a clear effort to win court favor, with a dedication to Elizabeth and as many as seventeen dedicatory sonnets to the major figures in court. As a reward, Spenser was granted a pension of £50 a year for life. Such a position in the patronage system of the day was not unusual, as poetry was commonly used as a means of preferment in court—for noblemen such as Sidney and Raleigh, it was one more personal accomplishment; for those like Spenser who were not noble, it was a way to win social and economic advantages. Spenser, however, maintained skepticism toward court life. In his pastoral "Colin Clouts Come Home Again," which tells of his and Raleigh's journey to court, Colin declares that

> it is no sort of life,
> For shepheard fit to lead in that same place,
> Where each one seeks with malice and with strife, .
> To thrust downe other into foule disgrace,
> Himselfe to raise.   (688–92)

Spenser returned to Ireland, where he lived, worked, and wrote throughout the 1590s. He published several important poems under the title of *Complaints* in 1591. In 1594 he married Elizabeth Boyle, resulting in at least one child, and in the following year he published *Amoretti* and *Epithalamion,* which celebrate their love and marriage. Throughout these years he continued work on *The Faerie Queene,* and in 1596 published the second edition. This extended the poem to six books; its final form was reached in the posthumous 1609 edition, with the inclusion of the fragment of a seventh book, *The Mutabilitie Cantos.* In 1596 he also published *Fowre Hymnes* and *Prothalamion.*

Spenser may have traveled to London to oversee the second printing of *The Faerie Queene.* If so, he returned to an Ireland wracked by rebellion. In 1598 the Tyrone Rebellion reached Munster, and Spenser and his family fled Kilcolman just before the estate was sacked and burned. Spenser carried letters from the President of Munster to the Privy Council in England, describing the military crisis. On January 13, 1599, while still in England, Spenser died. His life ended under the shadow cast by the destruction of his home and the scattering of his interests in Ireland, which Ben Jonson described, possibly hyperbolically, as dying "for lack of bread." Spenser's hearse was reportedly attended by poets, who threw their verses and pens into his tomb as he was buried in Poets' Corner at Westminster Abbey.

Textual Notes

This text is based upon the 1596 edition of *The Faerie Queene,* from microfilm of the volume in the Huntington Library (STC 23082). It has been checked against the 1609 edition, from microfilm of the volume in the Harvard University Library (STC 23083). Spelling and punctuation follow the 1596 edition. Quotation marks have been added; *i, j, s, u,* and *v* have been modernized; and abbreviations, ampersands, and diphthongs have been spelled out. Departures from the 1596 edition have been made with the aim of clarifying the text for modern readers. The table below lists substantive variants.

Proem 11.2 place] 1596; stead, 1609.

i.16.2 why?] 1609; why, 1596.

i.25.1 Now] 1609; now, 1596.

ii.2.7 As] 1609; And, 1596.

ii.4.1 hee] 1609; she, 1596.

ii.32.4 earth] 1609; eare, 1596.

ii.37.7 be?] 1609; be., 1596.

ii.46.9 way.] 1596; lay., 1609.

ii.50.5 make] 1609; makes, 1596.

iii.40.6 we] 1609; were, 1596.

iv.36.8 halfe] 1596; arm'd, 1609.

iv.39.3 doale] 1609; doile, 1596.

vi.4.7 from] 1596; for, 1609.

vi.17.5 Heard] 1609; Here, 1596.

vi.24.1 their] 1596; her, 1609.

vi.34.7 their] 1596; that, 1609.

vii.21.4 could'st] 1609; coulst, 1596.

vii.38.5 bad] 1596; sad, 1609.

viii.16.1 them] 1609; then, 1596.

viii.43.3 love] 1609; loves, 1596.

viii.49.1 mad] 1596; bad, 1609.

ix.18.4 hard]1609; hart, 1596.

ix.33.8 rebellions] 1596; rebellious, 1609.

ix.44.1 appose] 1596; oppose, 1609.

x.37.6 hard] 1596; had, 1609.

xi.60.2 had] 1596; have, 1609.

xii.16.6 sight] 1609; fight, 1596.

xii.17.5 such] 1596; sure, 1609.

Glossary

albe: Although, despite.

Assay: Attempt, attack, proof.

beheast: Command, promise.

bewray: Reveal.

carle: Churl, villain.

doome: Judgment, fate.

earst: Earlier, lately.

eftsoones: Soon after, immediately.

eke: (Adverb) and; (verb) increase.

fone: Foes.

hew: Appearance.

hight: Called.

lore: Wisdom, learning.

maugre: Despite.

meed(e): Reward, bribe.

mickle: Much.

Paynim: Pagan.

pight: Placed, pitched.

preasse, preace: Press, crowd.

prove: Try, test.

read, reed: (Verb) read, determine, judge; (noun) judgment, subject.

rout: Crowd, mob.

sleight, slight: Trick, trap.

stoure, stowre: Storm, time of turmoil.

traine, trayne: Treachery, strategy, trap.

weed(s): Clothing.

weet, weete, wote: Know.

wend: Go.

whylome: In the past, once upon a time.

wight: Person, creature.

INDEX OF CHARACTERS

References to and appearances of major characters in Book Five are listed by canto and stanza. In parentheses are references and appearances in other books, listed by book, canto, and stanza. This index is indebted to Shohachi Fukuda's "The Characters of *The Faerie Queene*" in Hamilton.

WORKS CITED AND BIBLIOGRAPHY

Anderson, Judith. "'Nor Man It Is': The Knight of Justice in Book V of Spenser's *Faerie Queene." PMLA* 85 (1970): 65–77.

Aptekar, Jane. *Icons of Justice: Iconography and Thematic Imagery in Book V of* The Faerie Queene. New York: Columbia University Press, 1969.

Ariosto, Ludovico. *Orlando Furioso.* Translated by Guido Waldman. Oxford: Oxford University Press, 1998.

Aristotle. *The Nicomachean Ethics.* Translated by H. Rackham. Cambridge: Harvard University Press, 1982.

Bellamy, Elizabeth. "The Vocative and the Vocational: The Unreadability of Elizabeth in *The Faerie Queene." ELH* 54 (1987): 1–30.

Bieman, Elizabeth. "Britomart in Book V of *The Faerie Queene." University of Toronto Quarterly* 37 (1968): 156–74.

Borris, Kenneth. *Spenser's Poetics of Prophecy in* The Faerie Queene V. Victoria, Canada: English Literary Studies, University of Victoria, 1991.

Bowman, Mary. "'She there as Princess rained': Spenser's Figure of Elizabeth." *Renaissance Quarterly* 43 (1990): 509–28.

Bradshaw, Brendan, Andrew Hadfield, and Willy Maley, eds. *Representing Ireland: Literature and the Origins of Conflict, 1534–1660.* Cambridge: Cambridge University Press, 1993.

Brady, Ciarán. "Spenser's Irish Crisis: Humanism and Experience in the 1590s." *Past and Present* 111 (1986): 17–49.

Coleridge, Samuel Taylor. *Lectures 1808–1819: On Literature.* Edited by R. A. Foakes. Princeton, NJ: Princeton University Press, 1987.

Coughlan, Patricia, ed. *Spenser and Ireland: An Interdisciplinary Perspective.* Cork: Cork University Press, 1989.

Dunseath, T. K. *Spenser's Allegory of Justice in Book Five of* The Faerie Queene. Westport, CT: Greenwood Press, 1979.

Eggert, Katherine. *Showing Like a Queen: Female Authority and Literary Experiment in Spenser, Shakespeare, and Milton.* Philadelphia: University of Pennsylvania Press, 2000.

Fletcher, Angus. *Allegory: The Theory of a Symbolic Mode.* Ithaca, NY: Cornell University Press, 1964.

———. *The Prophetic Moment: An Essay on Spenser.* Chicago: University of Chicago Press, 1971.

Fowler, Alastair. *Spenser and the Numbers of Time.* New York: Barnes & Noble, 1964.

Fowler, Elizabeth. "The Failure of Moral Philosophy in the Work of Edmund Spenser." *Representations* 51 (1995): 47–76.

Gallagher, Lowell. *Medusa's Gaze: Casuistry and Conscience in the Renaissance.* Stanford, CA: Stanford University Press, 1991.

Goldberg, Jonathan. *James I and the Politics of Literature: Jonson, Shakespeare, Donne and Their Contemporaries.* Baltimore: Johns Hopkins University Press, 1983.

Graziani, René. "Elizabeth at Isis Church." *PMLA* 79 (1964): 376–89.

Greenblatt, Stephen. "Murdering Peasants: Status, Genre, and the Representation of Rebellion." *Representations* 1 (1983): 1–29.

———. *Renaissance Self-Fashioning: From More to Shakespeare.* Chicago: The University of Chicago Press, 1984.

Greenlaw, Edwin, et al. *The Works of Edmund Spenser: A Variorum Edition.* Baltimore: The Johns Hopkins Press, 1932–57.

Gregory, Tobias. "Shadowing Intervention: On the Politics of *The Faerie Queene*, Book 5, Cantos 10–12." *ELH* 67 (2000): 365–97.

Gross, Kenneth. *Spenserian Poetics: Idolatry, Iconoclasm, and Magic.* Ithaca, NY: Cornell University Press, 1985.

Hadfield, Andrew. *Edmund Spenser's Irish Experience: Wilde Fruit and Salvage Soyl.* Oxford: Clarendon Press, 1997.

———, ed. *The Cambridge Companion to Spenser.* Cambridge: Cambridge University Press, 2001.

Hamilton, A. C., et al., eds. *The Spenser Encyclopedia.* Toronto: University of Toronto Press, 1990; rev. 1992.

Harrington, John. *Orlando Furioso: In English Heroical Verse.* London, 1591.

Heale, Elizabeth. The Faerie Queene: *A Reader's Guide.* Second edition. Cambridge: Cambridge University Press, 2000.

Hesiod, *The Theogony.* Translated by Hugh G. Evelyn-White. Cambridge: Harvard University Press, 1982.

King, John. *Spenser's Poetry and the Reformation Tradition.* Princeton: Princeton University Press, 1990.

Lewis, C. S. *The Allegory of Love: A Study in Medieval Tradition.* Oxford: Oxford University Press, 1936.

———. *Studies in Medieval and Renaissance Literature.* Cambridge: Cambridge University Press, 1966.

———. *Spenser's Images of Life.* Edited by Alastair Fowler. Cambridge: Cambridge University Press, 1967.

Lotspeich, Henry Gibbons. *Classical Mythology in the Poetry of Edmund Spenser.* New York: Gordian Press, 1965.

Maley, Willy. *A Spenser Chronology.* Lanham, MD: Barnes & Noble Books, 1994.

———. *Salvaging Spenser: Colonialism, Culture and Identity.* New York: St. Martin's Press, 1997.

Mallette, Richard. *Spenser and the Discourses of Reformation England.* Lincoln: University of Nebraska Press, 1997.

Marcus, Leah S., Janel Mueller, and Mary Beth Rose. *Elizabeth I: Collected Works.* Chicago: University of Chicago Press, 2000.

McCabe, Richard A. "The Masks of Duessa: Spenser, Mary, Queen of Scots, and James VI." *English Literary Renaissance* 17 (1987): 224–42.

McCaffrey, Isabel G. *Spenser's Allegory: The Anatomy of Imagination.* Princeton, NJ: Princeton University Press, 1976.

Meyer, Russell J. The Faerie Queene: *Educating the Reader.* Boston: Twayne Publishers, 1991.

Miller, David Lee, and Alexander Dunlop, eds. *Approaches to Teaching Spenser's* Faerie Queene. New York: The Modern Language Association of America, 1994.

Ovid. *Metamorphoses.* Translated by Frank Justus Miller. Cambridge: Harvard University Press, 1994.

Patterson, Annabel. "The Egalitarian Giant: Representations of Justice in History/Literature." *The Journal of British Studies* 31.2 (1992): 97–132.

Phillips, James E., Jr. "Renaissance Concepts of Justice and the Structure of *The Faerie Queene,* Book V." *Huntington Library Quarterly* 33 (1970): 103–20.

Prescott, Anne Lake. "Foreign Policy in Fairyland: Henri IV and Spenser's Burbon." *Spenser Studies* 14 (2000): 189–214.

Quilligan, Maureen. *The Language of Allegory: Defining the Genre.* Ithaca, NY: Cornell University Press, 1979.

———. "The Comedy of Female Authority in *The Faerie Queene." English Literary Renaissance* 17 (1987): 156–71.

Radcliffe, David Hill. *Edmund Spenser: A Reception History.* Columbia, SC: Camden House, 1996.

Roche, Thomas P. *The Kindly Flame: A Study of the Third and Fourth Books of Spenser's* Faerie Queene. Princeton, NJ: Princeton University Press, 1964.

Spenser, Edmund. *The Faerie Queene, Book V.* Edited by Alfred B. Gough. Oxford: Clarendon Press, 1918.

———. *The Faerie Queene.* Edited by A. C. Hamilton. London: Longman, 2001.

———. *A View of the State of Ireland.* Edited by Andrew Hadfield and Willy Maley. Oxford: Blackwell Publishers, 1997.

Stump, Donald. "Isis versus Mercilla: The Allegorical Shrines in Spenser's Legend of Justice." *Spenser Studies* 3 (1982): 87–98.

———. "Fashioning Gender: Cross-Dressing in Spenser's Legend of Britomart and Artegall." *Spenser Studies* 15 (2001): 95–119.

Teskey, Gordon. *Allegory and Violence.* Ithaca, NY: Cornell University Press, 1996.

Treip, Mindele Anne. *Allegorical Poetics and the Epic: The Renaissance Tradition to Paradise Lost*. Lexington: University of Kentucky Press, 1994.

Tuve, Rosemond. *Allegorical Imagery: Some Mediaeval Books and Their Posterity*. Princeton, NJ: Princeton University Press, 1966.

Wagner, Geoffrey. "Talus." *ELH* 17 (1950): 79–86.

Walker, Julia M. "Spenser's Elizabeth Portrait and the Fiction of Dynastic Epic." *Modern Philology* 90 (1992): 172–99.

Waters, D. Douglas. "Spenser and the 'Mas' at the Temple of Isis." *Studies in English Literature, 1500–1900* 19:1 (1979): 43–53.

Wells, Robin Headlam. *Spenser's* Faerie Queene *and the Cult of Elizabeth*. Totowa, NJ: Barnes & Noble Books, 1983.

Woods, Susanne. "Spenser and the Problem of Women's Rule." *Huntington Library Quarterly* 48 (1985): 141–58.

Yates, Frances. *Astraea: The Imperial Theme in the Sixteenth Century*. London: Routledge & Kegan Paul, 1975.